W9-BMH-681

"Usually, you have to go to different sections of the bookstore to find good books on biblical theology, systematic theology, ministry, the church, and the Christian life. At the very least, the relationship between theory and practice seems strained. However, this book brings these concerns together. Michael Lawrence believes that good shepherds are theologians and good theologians are shepherds. For anyone who believes that theology needs the church and the church needs theology, this will be a welcome resource. For anyone playing with the idea, it will be a compelling one."

MICHAEL HORTON, J. Gresham Machen Professor of Systematic Theology and Apologetics, Westminster Seminary California

"I am grateful that this book has been written. It's an ambitious book—broad in scope and simultaneously rich in insight. Its biblical, systematic and pastoral theology are presented in a lucid and accessible way, its case studies are pastorally helpful, and its polemics are thought-provoking and penetrating.

Michael has done us a great favor by grounding his subject material in the cut and thrust of ordinary pastoral ministry while at the same time stimulating us intellectually. His unshakable commitment to propositional revelation, the centrality of the Bible in church ministry, and his unflinching belief that God works by his Word are a great foil to much theology in vogue in the church today.

This book is a bell ringing in the fog of American Christianity—with its extremes of prosperity, market-driven, and emergent theology—that we at the ends of the earth in South Africa have sadly not escaped. It calls us back to the old fashioned, tried and tested practices of exegesis, hermeneutics, and preaching that have fed the Christian church for centuries. May God use it to nourish his church, which often seems undernourished both in sub-Saharan Africa and elsewhere."

GRANT J. RETIEF, Rector, Christ Church, Umhlanga, Durban, South Africa

"According to the apostle Paul, one of the central works of pastoral ministry is rightly dividing the Word of truth (2 Timothy 2:15), and it takes diligent study to be able to do it. According to Michael Lawrence, it is also vital to rightly apply the Word of truth to the life of a congregation, and to be certain that the application is faithful to the united story of the entire Scripture. In his book *Biblical Theology in the Life of the Church*, Lawrence skillfully guides his readers in constructing a biblical theology, "the whole story of the whole Bible," and teaches them how to derive lessons from that story. But Lawrence's heartbeat is the right application of the story and those lessons to the daily life scenarios every minister faces. This work is a succinct, readable manual on the right application of the storyline of the whole Bible to the common issues of daily life which pastors will inevitably face as they minister in the twenty-first century. It is a valuable addition to the library of any pastor who yearns to see God's Word bear fruit for eternity."

ANDREW DAVIS, Senior Pastor, First Baptist Church, Durham, North Carolina

"With biblical illiteracy in the church at an all-time high, faithless and banal preaching the seeming norm, and Christian leaders impressed more by stories of success in the marketplace than the biblical story of redemption, *Biblical Theology in the Life of the Church* comes as a much needed correction. Michael Lawrence is surely right: One must understand the grand story of Scripture to rightly interpret its constituent parts. When the story is misunderstood or ignored, then Christian preaching and ministry will inevitably suffer. Through definition, explanation, and example, Lawrence has produced a thorough and practical guide to correct biblical interpretation, Spirit-empowered exposition, and faithful ministry."

TODD L. MILES, Assistant Professor of Theology, Western Seminary, Portland, Oregon

"Every thoughtful preacher or teacher of the Bible sooner or later faces questions of the nature of biblical theology, its relationship to doctrine (systematic theology), and the practical application of both to the ministry that edifies the church. Following in the footsteps of Geerhardus Vos and Edmund Clowney, Michael Lawrence has provided us with a masterly study that relates biblical theology to systematics, and then applies both to the ministry of the church. This skillfully executed integrative approach breaks new ground in the practical application of biblical theology. Its thoroughness without being over-technical makes it accessible to anyone who wants to be a better preacher or teacher of the Bible."

GRAEME GOLDSWORTHY, Visiting Lecturer in Hermeneutics, Moore Theological College, Sydney, Australia.

"Studies on the relationship of theology to ministry seem to be quite rare. In fact, some books designed as 'guides for ministry' often portray suspicion of and hostility toward the theological enterprise. On the other hand, some theologians think that such guides are not worthy of serious attention. What is desperately needed is a work that recognizes the significance of the work of theology for ministry, while simultaneously recognizing the importance of doing theology for the church. Michael Lawrence has brilliantly met this need in this clearly written and compelling volume, which envisions afresh the work of pastor-theologians. I believe that *Biblical Theology in the Life of the Church* will certainly be one of the most important books for pastors and theologians to read this year."

DAVID S. DOCKERY, President, Union University

"Biblical theology is the missing tool for so many pastors—and yet is such an essential tool for rightly handling the Word of God. Michael Lawrence leads us step by step from theological foundations all the way through to real life applications of biblical theology. In other words, he shows us how to read and use the Bible rightly on its own terms. He skillfully blends scholarly insight with down-to-earth pastoral awareness and covers a huge amount of ground in the process. This is a great example of theological thinking for the work of ministry. You may not agree with every conclusion he draws but you cannot fail to benefit from interacting with his thinking."

GRAHAM BEYNON, Minister, Avenue Community Church, Leicester, UK

"I am deeply thankful for this important book and pray it will be widely read and greatly influential! There is no greater need in the church than biblically grounded theological discernment that informs everyday life. The perspective and methods of "doing theology" that Michael Lawrence provides are crucial for developing this distinctively Christian view of life. Ministry methods and foci today are so often determined by pragmatism, consumerism, trends, and the latest opinion polls rather the an holistic understanding of the Bible. *Biblical Theology in the Life of the Church* points the way out of this man-centered approach and helps equip leaders for God-honoring, gospel-advancing ministry. Lawrence writes with the depth of a careful theologian and the heart and experience of a loving pastor. Here he models what he is wanting to produce with this book—pastor-theologians who understand the whole counsel of God's Word, and are able to translate it into the lives of God's people for the glory of God."

ERIK THOENNES, Associate Professor of Biblical Studies and Theology, Biola University; Pastor, Grace Evangelical Free Church, La Mirada, California

Biblical Theology
in the Life of the Church

Other 9Marks Books:

The Church and the Surprising Offense of God's Love
Jonathan Leeman

What Is a Healthy Church?
Mark Dever

What Is a Healthy Church Member?
Thabiti M. Anyabwile

The Gospel and Personal Evangelism
Mark Dever

What Does God Want of Us Anyway?
Mark Dever

What Is the Gospel?
Greg Gilbert

It Is Well
Mark Dever and Michael Lawrence

Church Planting Is for Wimps
Mike McKinley

Michael Lawrence

FOREWORD BY
Thomas R. Schreiner

:: CROSSWAY

WHEATON, ILLINOIS

Biblical Theology in the Life of the Church: A Guide for Ministry

Copyright © 2010 by Michael Lawrence

Published by Crossway
    1300 Crescent Street
    Wheaton, Illinois 60187

All rights reserved. No part of this publication may be reproduced, stored in a retrieval system, or transmitted in any form by any means, electronic, mechanical, photocopy, recording, or otherwise, without the prior permission of the publisher, except as provided for by USA copyright law.

Cover design: Tobias Outerwear for Books

First printing 2010

Printed in the United States of America

Unless otherwise indicated, scripture references are from *The Holy Bible: New International Version*®. Copyright © 1973, 1978, 1984 Biblica. Used by permission of Zondervan. All rights reserved. The "NIV" and "New International Version" trademarks are registered in the United States Patent and Trademark Office by Biblica. Use of either trademark requires the permission of Biblica.

Scripture quotations marked ESV are from the ESV® Bible (*The Holy Bible, English Standard Version*®), copyright © 2001 by Crossway. Used by permission. All rights reserved.

Scripture quotations marked HCSB have been taken from *The Holman Christian Standard Bible.*® Copyright © 1999, 2000, 2002, 2003 by Holman Bible Publishers. Used by permission.

All emphases in Scripture quotations have been added by the author.

Trade paperback ISBN: 978-1-4335-1508-8

PDF ISBN: 978-1-4335-1509-5

Mobipocket ISBN: 978-1-4335-1510-1

ePub ISBN: 978-1-4335-2463-9

Library of Congress Cataloging-in-Publication Data

Lawrence, Michael, 1966–
    Biblical theology in the life of the church : a guide for ministry / Michael Lawrence.
        p. cm.
    ISBN: 978-1-4335-1508-8 (tpb)
    I. Bible—Theology. 2. Theology—Methodology. 3. Pastoral theology. I. Title.
BS543.W38   2010
230'.041—dc22   2009036659

Crossway is a publishing ministry of Good News Publishers.

VP		20	19	18	17	16	15	14	13	12	11	10
15	14	13	12	11	10	9	8	7	6	5	4	3	2

In memory of
MEREDITH KLINE
(1922–2007)

And dedicated to
SCOTT HAFEMANN, GORDON HUGENBERGER,
RICK LINTS, and DAVID WELLS
my professors,
who taught me not only to love theology,
but to love the church as well.

Contents

Foreword

Idon't know anything about how to fix cars. A couple of times when I was younger and financially pressed, I tried to fix my car on my own. I solicited some advice and went to work. Not surprisingly the results were disastrous. Something unanticipated always went wrong, and I would get stuck. The problem was my limited knowledge of cars. I lacked the broader perspective necessary to fix them.

Too often as pastors we may encounter the same problem I did in attempting to repair my car. We desire to help people with their problems, but we lack the broader framework we need to truly assist them. Our ministry could end up doing more harm than good if we fail to understand the Scriptures. Our fundamental calling as pastors is to shepherd those under our care, but how can we fulfill our calling if we lack a map of the whole Bible, if we don't know how to put the Bible together? How can we give wise spiritual advice if we are ignorant of the whole counsel of God (Acts 20:27)?

In 1 Corinthians 1–4 we discover that the Corinthian church was divided over Paul, Apollos, Peter, and even Christ. Apparently, they measured the effectiveness of Paul and Apollos by their speaking abilities. Some exalted Apollos over Paul because they believed he was rhetorically more effective. Perhaps they argued that the Holy Spirit was working more powerfully in Apollos. What would you say to the Corinthians if you were their pastor? I suspect many of us would simply say, "Stop being divisive. Show your love as Christians and become united in the gospel. How foolish it is to create divisions over which speaker is rhetorically more effective." When Paul confronts the problem, however, he probes deeper and reflects on the matter theologically. He argues that their divisions reflect a fundamental misunderstanding of the cross of Christ. If they truly grasped the message of Christ crucified, they would not fall prey to such a secular worldview. By being entranced with the speaking ability of Paul and Apollos and by boasting in them, they were denying the fundamental truth of the cross, namely, that God saves sinners. Their boast in Paul and Apollos was a mask for their own pride. We could continue to reflect on Paul's response to the Corinthians. My point in bringing up this matter is simply this: how many of us when confronted with such an issue would think theologically and see a failure to understand the cross?

All of us need instruction on how to think theologically. What a joy, therefore, to read this book by Michael Lawrence. Dr. Lawrence is a veteran pastor, and his pastoral wisdom shines through these pages. The best theology in the history of the church has always been written by pastors. We think of Augustine, Luther, Calvin, Edwards, Spurgeon, and Lloyd-Jones. Pastor Lawrence provides a wonderfully clear and helpful entrée into biblical theology, so that we see the importance of covenants and canon, prophecy and typology, continuity and discontinuity. Furthermore, we are treated to an illuminating sketch of biblical theology from creation to consummation, where some of the main arteries of the storyline of the Scriptures are explicated. This book is not long, but it is packed with wisdom, and it always has its eye on the usefulness of biblical theology for the church and for pastoral ministry. The last two chapters on biblical theology and preaching and teaching, and biblical theology and the local church are alone worth the price of the book. I was instructed and encouraged in reading this book. I am reminded of the words Augustine heard when he was in the garden before his conversion, "Take up and read!"

Thomas R. Schreiner
James Buchanan Harrison Professor of
    New Testament Interpretation,
The Southern Baptist Theological Seminary;
Preaching Pastor,
Clifton Baptist Church

Preface

This is a book for people who are passionate about ministry in the local church. It's not a book for theologians and academics (though I hope both will read it and like it). It's a book for pastors and church leaders who can't even remember the last time they had a discussion using words like "compatibilism" or "theodicy" but who every week must help someone understand why we even bother to pray if God already knows everything, or why God hasn't allowed them to conceive a child or find a job. In other words, it's a book for people like me.

It's for people like a fellow elder of mine who was recently having lunch at a burger joint with a friend. This man had lost his job in the latest economic downturn and his car had broken down just a few days before. And now he was looking at a savings account that was dwindling toward nothing.

However, he'd been listening to preachers on television. And they had promised that God would provide material blessings today, if only he would have faith today. The friend quipped, "You know, like in Deuteronomy, where God says that he will bless us in our homes and in our fields if we only follow him."

How should my fellow elder have responded? Does Deuteronomy promise Christians that God will bless us in the city, bless us in the country, bless us when we are coming in, and bless us when we are going out? If you have a Bible nearby, look at the first few verses of Deuteronomy chapter 28. You'll see that it certainly promises such blessings to the Israelites. And the talk of blessings there doesn't mean warm spiritual fuzzies. The blessings God promises mean full barns and fruitful wombs, the praise of nations and the respect of enemies. It means their best life today!

Yet are those promises true for Christians? Can the unemployed Christian expect that God will quickly provide a job if only the Christian can muster up enough faith? What about the barren couple who longs for children? Should we say to them, "You just need to *believe*, and God will give you the child you long for"? Or do the blessings God promised Israel merely foreshadow the gospel-believing Christians' promised inheritance in eternity?

The answer to these questions directly affects how my fellow elder should have ministered to his unemployed friend. It affects how you and I should minister to people around us.

I'm not going to tell you what my fellow elder said to his friend (we'll come back to this story at the end of the book). Yet, this story illustrates the premise of this book: our theology determines the shape and character of our ministry. Theology is how we move from the text of Scripture to how we should live our lives today.

The Critical Importance of Biblical Theology

This is a book about theology. But it's really a book about ministry, because I'm convinced that if we want our ministry to have a lasting impact and our churches to be healthy we must first do our theology well. In this book we are going to talk about how to do theology that will in turn help us do something practical, namely, pastoral ministry. Not only that, I hope to talk about doing theology in a practical way, so that you will know how to *do* it yourself!

You may have noticed that this book belongs to the 9Marks series. 9Marks is a ministry dedicated to equipping local churches and pastors, and it takes its name from Mark Dever's book *Nine Marks of a Healthy Church*. The second mark of a healthy church, Dever says, is biblical theology.[1] But what Dever means by "biblical theology" is theology that's biblical, or theology that's *sound*.

The word "sound," Dever points out, means reliable, accurate, and faithful.[2] And it's the word "sound" that Paul uses over and over with his disciples Timothy and Titus to describe their doctrine and their teaching. Sound doctrine opposes ungodliness and sin (1 Tim. 1:10–11). Sound instruction opposes false doctrine (1 Tim. 6:3). Sound teaching is the pattern Timothy has seen in Paul (2 Tim. 1:13). Sound doctrine will be rejected by the churches who would rather hear what their itching ears want to hear (2 Tim. 4:3). And, again, sound doctrine will encourage those who hold firmly to the trustworthy message and refute those who oppose it (Titus 1:9). Over and over, Paul tells these two men to "teach what is in accord with sound doctrine" (Titus 2:1). Sound doctrine, or theology that is *biblical*, is a big part of what I want to talk about in this book. Chapters 4 and 5 are largely devoted to the topic, and the remainder of the book tries to work it out in practice.

But sound theology is not all I want to talk about. I also want to talk

---

[1] Mark Dever, *Nine Marks of a Healthy Church*, new exp. ed. (Wheaton, IL: Crossway, 2004), ch. 2.
[2] Mark Dever, *What is a Healthy Church?* (Wheaton, IL: Crossway, 2007), 70.

about biblical theology in a narrower sense. In this sense, biblical theology is about reading the Bible, not as if it's sixty-six separate books, but a single book with a single plot—God's glory displayed through Jesus Christ. Biblical theology is therefore about discovering the unity of the Bible in the midst of its diversity. It's about understanding what we might call the Bible's metanarrative. In this sense, biblical theology as a discipline has been around for a couple of centuries in one form or another. Lately, it's become especially popular among evangelicals. I'll describe how we do this in chapters 2 and 3, and then define it more carefully in chapter 4.

But here at the start, I want to make the point that the most practical thing we can do, the most important tool we need in ministry, is biblical theology. And I mean that in both senses of the phrase. Learning how to *do* biblical theology is no mere academic exercise. No, it's vital to your work as a pastor or church leader. It shapes your preaching, your counseling, your evangelizing, your ability to engage wisely with culture, and more. You will not be a very good theologian, which means you will not be a very good pastor, if you do not learn how to do biblical theology.

Reading the Bible means learning how to use the tools of biblical theology, in the narrow sense of the word. Applying the Bible means learning how to use the tools of systematic theology. Strangely, the two disciplines of biblical theology and systematic theology are often pitted against one another. But the church and the pastor need both. And so here we will consider how to do biblical theology, so that we might be better systematic theologians, so that we might become better pastors.

What all this means is that you are holding in your hands a "how-to" book. Learning how to *do* biblical theology will help you learn how to pastor well. Or, if you're not a pastor, it will help you learn how to better teach, disciple, and counsel other Christians. And that's the work of every Christian. Through the course of this book we will think together about how to read and apply the Bible for ministry in the church. This book will follow that basic outline—from biblical theology, to systematic theology, to pastoral ministry. In my mind, that progression translates into really useful theology.

I realize that saying theology is useful, even necessary, for ministry is a bold assertion. I make it for two reasons.

Ministry Is Theology in Action

First, if you are a pastor or are involved in ministry, you should be a theologian. This doesn't mean you need to write books of theology (though reading them can be helpful). This doesn't even mean you need to know the inside and outside of every theological controversy on the radar screen (though you should know how to detect a false teacher when you see one).

Rather, your role as a theologian means:

- You have taught the church about God's goodness and sovereignty, so that when a child is diagnosed with cancer, the parents will be grief-stricken but not completely undone.
- You have equipped the eighteen-year-olds heading off to college with the necessary tools for facing the radical relativism of their professors.
- You know how to help the man in your church who is struggling with whether or not God knows the future because his brother-in-law from another church gave him a bad book.
- You have helped a young wife and mother who struggles with perfectionism and people-pleasing to find her justification and worth in the gospel.
- You have prepared the engaged couple for the challenges of marriage through premarital counseling that focuses on God's plan for our holiness and not just instantaneous happiness.

Now, I said that every pastor *should* be a theologian. It would probably be more accurate to say that every pastor *is* a theologian, whether he is conscious of that fact or not. We'll talk more about this in chapter 5, but every pastor (and every human, really) relies upon some set of theological assumptions when addressing situations like these. The question is, are your assumptions sound? Are they biblical?

Biblical theology, then, is the discipline that helps us to be better theologians and, therefore, better ministers. It's how you get from texts like Deuteronomy 28 to the theology of the gospel. It's how you travel from the words of this ancient text all the way to how to encourage an unemployed Christian friend.

A Word-Centered Model of Ministry

The second reason theology is useful, even necessary for ministry is this: God's Word has real power to change lives. Therefore, as people in ministry, we have a vested interest in knowing how to understand and apply the Word correctly.

God has spoken through his written Word. In his Word, he has revealed who he is, who we are, and how he calls humanity generally and his people specifically to live. Non-Christians are saved and Christians grow in grace through the preaching, teaching, counseling, and speaking of God's Word, applied by God's Spirit. Our goal as pastors and Christians in ministry is to present this Word to others, so that the Word might do its work. We hold it up and say, "Here it is. This is what God says. Please, hear and heed." We're called to read it, yes, and we're called to "give the sense" of it for our hearers (Neh. 8:8, esv).

Not everyone agrees with this emphasis on the Word of God. I recently had the opportunity to contribute to a "five-views" book on worship in which different writers contributed one of five perspectives on corporate worship in the church. Then each of us had the opportunity to respond to the other writers in order to point out places of agreement and disagreement. In the chapter I co-wrote with Mark Dever, we emphasized the centrality of the Word of God in the church's weekly gatherings. Everything that we say, sing, pray, and practice in our church gatherings, Mark and I argued, should come from the Bible.

In response to our chapter, one of the other authors felt that we overemphasized the role of God's Word. In fact, he said that he does not believe "the classic 'preaching the Word' is the only (or even primary) way that people come to faith and are built up in their faith." Growth does not primarily occur through the ears, he said, but through the eyes—"watching others live out their faith in daily action is the primary vehicle of transformation." The idea that people are transformed through hearing the Word spoken or preached, he says, turns preaching the Word into something "magical."[3]

Now, I trust that this brother values God's Word and uses it in his ministry, and I certainly affirm the importance of the church's faithful witness for backing up the church's words. Yet I fear that he has missed what the Bible says about itself. God tells us that his word will "accomplish" his desire and "achieve" his purpose (Isa. 55:11). His Word both "calls things that are not as though they were" (Rom. 4:17), and then it "sustains all things" (Heb. 1:3). Michael Horton has summarized this very well: God's Word does not merely impart information; it actually creates life. It's not only descriptive; it's effective, too. God speaking *is* God acting.[4]

Evangelicals have defended the propositional nature of God's Word against modernists and liberals who would undermine its truthfulness. But what about the pragmatism in our own evangelical backyard that would undermine its sufficiency? To this emphasis on Word *as proposition* we must add Word *as powerful and effectual*, because God's Word is carried along by God's Spirit in order to perform exactly what he intends for it. All

---

[3]Dan Wilt, "Responses to Michael Lawrence and Mark Dever," in *Perspectives on Christian Worship: 5 Views*, J. Matthew Pinson, ed. (Nashville: B&H, 2009), 278.
[4]Michael S. Horton, *People and Place: A Covenant Ecclesiology* (Louisville, KY: Westminster John Knox Press, 2008), 40.

creation "was formed at God's command" (Heb. 11:3; Ps. 33:6), and we become new creations by that same command (Rom. 10:17; 2 Cor. 4:6). We have been "born again . . . through the living and enduring word of God" (1 Pet. 1:23). That's why, speaking to the churches, the apostles refer to the Word "planted in you, which can save you" (James 1:21); the Word that "abides in you" (1 John 2:14); and the Word which should "dwell in you richly" (Col. 3:16).[5]

In short, the model of ministry I'm relying upon in this book begins with a Trinitarian understanding of God's Word. In creation and new creation, we see the Father speaking through the Son by the power of the Spirit. In ministry, then, our primary task is to point to the Son with the Son's Word, trusting the Spirit to either harden or soften as he pleases (Mark 4:1–20). The local church, therefore, is the place where God's Word "dwells" or, more literally, makes a house (Col. 3:16). So we plant and water the Word, plant and water the Word, always trusting God to make it grow when and how he pleases (1 Cor. 3:6).

What does all of this have to do with biblical theology? Biblical theology is how we go about the task of reading the Word and ensuring that it's God's Word rather than our words that are shaping people's lives. Biblical theology is how we bring people into the life-changing story of God's redemptive plan.

The Plan for This Book

The Introduction gets the ball rolling by asking what the biblical text is. The Bible is a different sort of text than any other, and we'll consider how and why.

Chapter 1 presents some of the basic tools of exegesis, tools that may already be familiar to you.

Chapters 2 and 3 introduce you to the basic tools of biblical theology. The large question to be answered here is how we put the Bible together.

Chapters 4 and 5 turn to comparing biblical theology and systematic theology, as well as a discussion of what systematic theology is and how to think theologically.

Then in chapters 6 to 10, I will trace out five different biblical-theological themes in order to consider what they teach us for systematic theology of pastoral relevance.

Chapters 11 and 12 are the most practical of all. Chapter 11 will

---

[5]Ibid., 39–40.

present several preaching "case studies." I'll start with a text and then look at how one might preach it in light of everything we've learned about biblical and systematic theology. Then in chapter 12, I'll conclude by considering the relevance of biblical theology for other areas of ministry, including counseling, missions, and more.

How should you go about reading this book? Some of you are going to find the early chapters daunting. We're going to deal with some technical issues of theological method. If that sounds like more than you bargained for, I'd encourage you to treat this book like the instruction manuals you get with a new computer. There's the thick manual that tells you everything you'd ever want to know, and then some. And then there's the single page Quick Start guide for those that just want to turn the computer on and get going.

If what you're looking for is the Quick Start guide, turn straight to chapter 6 and start reading there. That's where the computer gets turned on and everything comes to life because that's where you see me actually do the things the first five chapters are talking about. Later, when you're ready to figure out how to do it yourself, go back and look at the earlier chapters.

One thing this book will *not* do is tell the storyline of the whole Bible in the way that most basic biblical theology texts do. Nor will it give a full-blown systematic theology. For that reason, this book would be well accompanied by two others: one that lays out the storyline itself, and another that covers systematics. For a systematic theology, you can't do much better than Wayne Grudem's *Systematic Theology*.[6] For the Bible's storyline, let me recommend three. Graeme Goldsworthy's *Gospel and Kingdom* (which can now be found in *The Goldsworthy Trilogy*[7]) is a great introductory text that tells the story of the Bible as the story of God's people, in God's place, under God's rule. A slightly simpler version of this book, which admits its debt to Goldsworthy from the very beginning, is Vaughan Robert's excellent *God's Big Picture*.[8] Finally, if you're up for a book that's just a little more academic, I trust you will benefit immensely from Stephen Dempster's *Dominion and Dynasty*.[9] It's well worth the extra time you will spend getting through it.

---

[6]Wayne Grudem, *Systematic Theology* (Grand Rapids, MI: Zondervan, 1994).
[7]Graeme Goldsworthy, *The Goldsworthy Trilogy* (Exeter: Paternoster Press, 2000).
[8]Vaughan Roberts, *God's Big Picture: Tracing the Story-line of the Bible* (Downers Grove, IL: InterVarsity Press, 2002).
[9]Stephen Dempster, *Dominion and Dynasty: A Biblical Theology of the Hebrew Bible* (Downers Grove, IL: InterVarsity Press, 2006).

Acknowledgments

This book would never have been written had my friend and colleague, Mark Dever, not had the vision to develop a whole community of writers to address each of the nine "marks" of a healthy church. I am grateful to him for his encouragement to take the mark of biblical theology, make it my own, and then do something useful with it for the church.

The first step was a series of sermons preached at Capitol Hill Baptist Church during the summer of 2006. The encouragement and feedback I received from the congregation, especially the service review guys, convinced me of the usefulness of the material, and served to make it better. Special thanks go to John Ingold and Lisa Law for transcribing those sermons.

Twice, in the fall of 2007 and again in 2008, I was able to work through some of this material on the mission field. I'm grateful to the leadership of the IMB's Central Asia region for giving me the opportunity and privilege to work with their people. While this book has been written with a North American audience in mind, it was that experience that convinced me of how practical, and how cross-cultural, biblical theology really is.

Those sermons, trotted out all over the world, now form section 2 of this book, though in greatly modified form.

But if it weren't for Jonathan Leeman, those useful sermons would still be languishing in my files. It's because of Jonathan that this *particular* book has been written. His vision and partnership, first in helping me expand my vision from those initial sermons to the book you are holding, and then in creating a class at CHBC that would give me the chance to write the manuscript, and finally in editing the completed product, have been invaluable.

Steve Wellum also read the manuscript and provided insightful critiques that saved me from more than one blunder.

Josh Manley, Matt Merker, Ryan Bishop, and Mark Stam, some of the CHBC Spring 2009 interns, helped cheerfully with formatting and research. Geoff Chang helped with graphs.

I'm also grateful to Allan Fisher and the editors at Crossway. They have been a pleasure to work with from the first stage of this book until the last.

Finally, I owe a great debt to my wife, Adrienne, who managed to keep a busy household of seven running smoothly and simultaneously read and comment on the vast majority of the manuscript. We had all the same professors at seminary and have been in ministry together for nearly twenty years now. She remains my most important theological conversation partner, and the love of my life.

With all this help, this book is markedly better than it would have been. Despite all this help, the flaws that remain are wholly my own. My hope is that God will use it, flaws and all, to encourage the work of his church and to promote the glory of his gospel.

Michael Lawrence
Capitol Hill Baptist Church
Washington, DC

The Text to Be Examined

As church leaders, you and I are faced with problems and questions every day that require us to turn to the Bible for answers, guidance, and wisdom. Along with prayer, the Bible is the most important and the most fundamental tool we've been given for the work of pastoral ministry. If you've been doing ministry for any length of time, you've probably grown quite familiar with this tool. You know your way around all sixty-six books. You have favorite passages you turn to again and again—the twenty-third Psalm for hospital visits, Romans 8 for the discouraged and hard-pressed Christian, John 3 for evangelistic conversations, Nehemiah for lessons on leadership, Isaiah 6 for the young person considering a call to ministry. You wouldn't dream of walking into a church meeting or a hospital room without a Bible in hand.

But for all your familiarity with the Bible, when was the last time you thought about what this powerful tool is that you're holding in your hand? Sure, it's a collection of sixty-six inspired books. And yes, it records for us the history of ancient Israel, the ministry of Jesus Christ, and the founding of the Christian church. But, taken as a whole rather than in individual parts, how do you answer the question, "What is the Bible?"

The Importance of Definitions

The answer I'm really concerned with isn't the one you learned in seminary or Sunday school, but your working answer. I'm asking how you use the Bible day in and day out in your ministry because that will show you and me what you really think the Bible is.[1]

---

[1] In putting it this way, I am not meaning to imply that function determines meaning or authority. Postliberals (for one example, see George Lindbeck, *The Nature of Doctrine: Religion and Theology in a Postliberal Age* [Philadelphia: Westminster, 1984]) have argued that the Bible *is* Scripture because it *functions* that way in the church. But in contrast to that view, the point of this book is that precisely because the Bible *is* the inspired and inerrant record of God's redemptive activity in history, revealing his purposes and his character, it should *function* for us as both normative and sufficient Scripture. Functionality for ministry therefore arises from and is constrained by ontology, not the other way around.

For example, when I pick up a hammer, I don't think of it in the technical terms of its material construction or component parts. I think of it as something that will help me drive a nail into a wall, and use it accordingly. On the other hand, I have chopsticks scattered all over my house, but I don't always think of them as eating utensils. It turns out they are just the right size to release the locks on bedroom and bathroom doors when one of my younger children has accidently locked himself or herself in. Functionally, those chopsticks have become keys, regardless of their proper definition.

It's no different with the Bible. Regardless of the correct definition, your working definition will determine how you use it. Sometimes that means you'll use it as intended, the way I use a hammer. But sometimes that means you'll misuse it, the way I misuse chopsticks. And while no real harm comes from my misuse of chopsticks, we all know that real harm can result from the misuse—the misapplication—of a tool as powerful as the Bible.

Two Possible Answers

So what is the Bible? My own church's statement of faith provides one possible answer, one that I think many of us tend to use. In our very first article of faith, we affirm that the Bible is "a perfect treasure of heavenly instruction," that "it reveals principles by which God will judge us," and therefore is "the supreme standard by which all human conduct, creeds, and opinions should be tried."[2] I think every single one of those statements is true, but notice their emphasis. The Bible is a collection of instructions, principles, and standards. To put it in more colloquial terms, the Bible is an "answer book" for life's problems or a compendium of principles by which to live and die. But is this definition adequate for ministry?

Let's take that definition of the Bible and apply it to a question the elders of my church recently faced. A family was considering making a large capital purchase. Yet to provide the required down payment, they would have had to alter their tithe to the church for a short period. They hoped to make it up to the church later, but there was no guarantee they could. They came to us for advice.

If the Bible is fundamentally an answer book, then we'll expect to find a verse or passage that gives this family the counsel they need. But which passage do we turn to? Malachi 3:10—"Bring the whole tithe into the storehouse"—seems to provide an answer, but then what do we do with

---

[2]*The New Hampshire Confession*, Article I, "Of the Scriptures" (rev., 1853), adopted by Capitol Hill Baptist Church, Washington, DC, at its incorporation on February 28, 1878. For the full text of the confession see William L. Lumpkin, *Baptist Confessions of Faith*, rev. ed. (Valley Forge, PA: Judson Press, 1969), 361–367.

2 Corinthians 9:7? "Each man should give what he has decided in his heart to give, not reluctantly or under compulsion, for God loves a cheerful giver." Consider also the story of Ananias and Sapphira in Acts 5. Does the story mean we should have warned this family, or is it just a story about what happened to two people in Jerusalem in a unique time of the church's life with no normative implications for our lives? As you can see, the "answer book" approach to the Bible raises a host of questions before we even get to the answer we're looking for.

Another possible answer to the question, "What is the Bible?" is that it's a story, a narrative of God's interaction with the world he made. Though there are lots of people in this story, it's fundamentally about what God has done and will do to bring this world to judgment and his people to salvation. According to this working definition, the Bible reveals the plan of salvation and how God has accomplished that plan, first through Israel and finally through Jesus Christ. Is this definition more useful for ministry than the previous one?

Let's apply it to the question we just considered. If the Bible is merely, or mostly, the story of God's saving actions in history, then beyond trusting in Christ for their salvation, rather than in worldly riches, it doesn't have much to say to their question. We might refer them to Luke 16 and the story of Lazarus and the rich man, or to Hebrews 11 and the character of faith which looks forward to "a better country—a heavenly one." But at the end of the day, unless we revert to the answer book approach or to pragmatic wisdom, this definition of the Bible leaves us with very little to say to the family which wants to know if they can delay their tithe in order to purchase property. As you can see, the story of salvation approach to the Bible may be faithful to the main point, but it also seems to contradict 2 Peter 1:3, where we are promised that we have been given "everything we need for life and godliness through our knowledge of him who called us by his own glory and goodness."

A Better Definition

So what should we do? What we need is a better understanding of what the Bible is, one that doesn't reduce it to life's little answer book, but keeps the focus on God, where it belongs. But we also need an understanding that doesn't reduce it to the story of how we get saved and go to heaven, leaving the rest of life up for grabs. We need a working definition of the Bible that allows for systematic answers to almost any question that comes up, but that also provides those answers in the context of the biblical storyline itself. We don't want to rip verses out of their context, and so misapply them, but neither do we want a story that never touches down into the nitty-gritty of our lives.

Biblical theology helps us establish that better understanding of what the Bible is. When we talk about biblical theology, we mean a theology that not only tries to systematically understand what the Bible teaches, but to do so in the context of the Bible's own progressively revealed and progressively developing storyline. Faithful biblical theology attempts to demonstrate what systematic theology assumes: that the Scriptures are not an eclectic, chaotic, and seemingly contradictory collection of religious writings, but rather a single story, a unified narrative that conveys a coherent and consistent message. Thus biblical theology is concerned not just with the moral of the story, but the telling of the story, and how the very nature of its telling, its unfolding, shapes our understanding of its point.

Now, this doesn't mean that biblical theology is prior to systematic theology, or that it's more important or more faithful to the Bible than systematic theology. In fact, as we're going to see, biblical theology assumes and depends upon a number of things demonstrated by systematic theology: things like the infallibility and inerrancy of revelation as it comes to us in Scripture, the objectivity of the knowledge of God through revelation, and the trustworthiness of inspiration.

Everything that follows is intended to help you construct a faithful and sound biblical theology. Once you have that, you'll have a functional definition of the Bible that allows you to speak powerfully from God's Word into the lives of people like the couple we just considered. In the next few chapters, we'll look at the tools of biblical and systematic theology and how they work together. Then we're going to spend five chapters actually doing biblical theology—telling the whole story of the whole Bible and demonstrating how that story touches down into the details of our lives. Then we'll wrap up with two chapters that explore the use of biblical theology in the life of the church, from preaching, to counseling and discipling, to missions, to our understanding of the relationship between the church and our culture.

The Character of Divine Revelation[3]

That said, there are several features of God's revelation of his truth in the Bible that I want to discuss here. These features determine how we go about studying the Bible and constructing a biblical theology. There are four main characteristics of God's self-revelation as it is recorded in the Bible that we

---

[3]This section draws heavily from Geerhardus Vos's *Biblical Theology* (Carlisle, PA: Banner of Truth, 1975).

need to understand if we're going to understand the Bible and its teaching correctly, as opposed to misinterpreting and misapplying the text.[4] You'll notice that in this section, I'm speaking of revelation as "divine activity" in history, rather than as the inscripturated record of those divine actions, what we call the Bible.[5] God's self-revealing actions precede his self-explanatory words. This book is all about how to understand and apply those words to life. But to do that we first want to understand the character of how God has acted in history to reveal himself.

First, God's revelation is progressive. Islam understands that the Koran was revealed to Mohammed all at once, miraculously lowered down from heaven. The sacred texts of Buddhism and Confucianism are confined to the lifetime of a single man. But the Bible was not written in a moment, or even in a single lifetime. The Bible was written over two millennia, as God progressively revealed more and more of himself and his story. That's because the Bible, as we've already said, isn't the revelation of a set of principles, but the revelation of Redemption. And God's redemption, his salvation of his people, occurs both in history and over the course of history. Thousands of years separate God's act of creation from his future act of new creation. In between, humanity falls into sin and God acts to save sinners and then to explain those saving acts. We can point to the exodus and conquest of Canaan; the exile and then return of Israel; and ultimately the incarnation, crucifixion, and resurrection of Jesus Christ. The Bible is both the record of God's saving acts and the explanation of them and therefore of necessity has a progressive historical character.

Second, God's revelation is not only progressive, it is fundamentally historical in character. So, for example, the crucifixion and resurrection of Christ are objective events in history that not only reveal something about God and redemption, but actually accomplish redemption. The Bible therefore is not merely a story told by humans about God's salvation of them; it is a story enacted and then explained by God about God. There is a God-centered focus in all of this as God objectively and concretely invades human history and acts to redeem his people to his own glory. Thus, in biblical theology we speak of redemptive history.

Third, there is an organic nature to this progressive revelation of God and his redemptive plan. It doesn't simply proceed like a construction site, which moves progressively from blueprint to finished building. Rather it unfolds and develops from seed-form to full-grown tree. In seed form,

---

[4]Ibid., 5–9.
[5]Ibid., 5.

the minimum and beginning of saving revelation is given. By the end, that simple truth has revealed itself as complex and rich, multilayered and profoundly beautiful. It's this character of revelation that's going to help us understand the typological character of Scripture, the dynamic of promise and fulfillment, and the presence of both continuity and discontinuity across redemptive history.

Fourth, God's revelation in history, and therefore biblical theology, is practical. God's intent in revelation is not to stimulate us intellectually, but to lead us into a saving relationship with God. So don't think that biblical theology is just for history and literature buffs. Far from it. If revelation is the story of God's saving acts, a story that begins at the beginning and ends at the end, then it's a story that contains our lives and our age, and therefore is extremely practical.

The Character of the Bible

If this is the character of revelation that is going to shape our approach to biblical theology, what specifically does this mean for the Bible? Just what kind of text are we looking at? I want to highlight five things about the Bible that we're going to come back to again and again. These characteristics of Scripture are going to determine how we study it. They're also going to shape what we expect the outcome of our study to be.

1) Historical/Human

First, the Bible was written by humans who lived in particular times of history. Second Peter 1:19–21 says,

> And we have the word of the prophets made more certain, and you will do well to pay attention to it, as to a light shining in a dark place, until the day dawns and the morning star rises in your hearts. Above all, you must understand that no prophecy of Scripture came about by the prophet's own interpretation. For prophecy never had its origin in the will of man, but men spoke from God as they were carried along by the Holy Spirit.

Most of the time people turn to this verse to demonstrate the divine character of Scripture—and we'll do that in a minute. But, quite significantly, it also clearly speaks to the historical and human character of the Bible. It refers to prophets as men who spoke, and by implication wrote, the Bible. When men speak, they use human language. That language both creates and reflects the culture they live in. So Isaiah spoke and wrote in ancient Hebrew, and used images like "soaring on wings like eagles," not "soaring on wings like jet planes"! What's more, as we've already mentioned, the various human authors of Scripture lived in a variety of cultures over the course of dozens of centuries. They didn't all speak the same language, live in the same place under the same government, or structure their families the same way.

Practically, what this means is that the Bible is an intensely human book. And to understand it, we have to understand the languages and cultures and contexts of the various authors. We can't assume that what we mean by a word or poetic image is what they would have meant. We're going to have to engage in grammatical, literary, and even cultural study if we're going to avoid reading into the Bible our own ideas and culture. We want to do exegesis, not eisegesis. We want to read out of the text, not into the text, and so in the first chapter we're going to look more closely at the exegetical tools of biblical theology.

Don't start worrying that you need several degrees in theology to really understand your Bible. The human and historical character of the Bible doesn't merely imply distance from us as people who live in a different time and place. It also implies continuity with us, because this was written by people, not angels. Sure, they may have spoken different languages and eaten different food. But underneath the real cultural differences, they, like us, are people made in the image of God, with the same fears and hopes and problems and capacities that we have. Across the gulf of time, we can relate to the human authors as people, and they to us. What's more, what God did for them can also apply to us.

2) Divine

Not only is the Bible a human book, it is also a divine book. As 2 Peter 1:19–21 points out, behind the various human authors and prophets stood God, who through his Holy Spirit inspired the prophets to say exactly what he wanted them to say. As Paul says in 2 Timothy 3:16, "all Scripture is God-breathed."

This is the doctrine of inspiration, a doctrine that doesn't mean God blanked out the minds and personalities of the human authors and used them like a keyboard. Rather it is the Scripture's own description of itself, as the product of the Holy Spirit working sovereignly through the human author. This has several implications. To begin with, it means that what the Bible says, God says. So the Scriptures are not simply people's religious musings of what God might be like. Rather, it is God's self-revelation.

Second, it means that the Bible is infallible (trustworthy) and inerrant (without error) in all that it affirms and all that it intends to say. No doubt there are many things the Bible doesn't even speak to. No doubt the human authors were sinners just like us. But the text they produced, under the inspiration of the Holy Spirit, has the entirely trustworthy and perfect character of the divine author.

Third, it means that despite the plethora of human authors, behind the text of Scripture stands a single divine author, a single mind and will. Why does this matter? Not only does it mean that we will not find contradiction (though we may find mystery), it means that we should expect to find unity and coherence to the overarching story. The human authors may not have been able to see it at the time of their writing, but the divine author could and did see the whole story, and wrote it so that it all fits together.

Here is the basis for understanding the typological, promise-fulfillment character of Scripture, which we will discuss further in coming chapters. So, for example, it's not that New Testament writers, trying to explain Jesus, noticed certain similarities to David, and exploited them for their own purpose. It's that God created David and sovereignly ordered his life so that he would be a picture and promise of a greater King to come. This is Paul's point in 1 Corinthians 10:11: "These things happened to them [providential control of history] as examples [typology] and were written down [inspiration] as warnings for us [application], on whom the fulfillment of the ages has come [progressive redemptive history]."

Far from being an eclectic, rag-tag collection of other people's religious experience, the Bible is God's story of God's actions in history to save sinners for his own glory. It is a single, coherent story, planned and executed and recorded by a single omnipotent, omniscient God.

3) A Narrative

One of the clear implications of what I've just said is that the Bible as a whole is best understood as a narrative. This is not to say that narrative is the only genre in the Bible. Far from it. The Bible is composed not only of historical narrative, but also of various genres such as poetry, law, apocalyptic, letters, and gospels. Having said that, the Bible as a whole is in fact best understood as a single story. A story about a King, a kingdom, and the King's relationship with his subjects. Richard Gaffin put it this way: "[The Bible] is not so much divinely given *gnosis* to provide us with knowledge concerning the nature of God, man and the world as it is divinely inspired interpretation of God's activity of redeeming men so that they might worship and serve him in the world."[6]

But this narrative of God's activity is not simply a story. It's a story that starts at the beginning of history and ends at the end of history. This means it's not an ancient story from the past, but a once and future story that encompasses us today. Scholars would call it a metanarrative; a story that explains everything and so provides us with a worldview. What we need to understand is that this narrative is intended by God to envelop us and redefine us. It provides us with a way of understanding reality that is different from the narratives that our fallen culture provides. This connection of narrative with reality is important. The narrative of Scripture is not meant to be merely inspiring, so that we can cope with the difficult reality of our lives. No, the narrative of Scripture was inspired in order to let us know what reality really is. Biblical theology, as it arises from Scripture, provides a framework, a fabric of meaning for our lives; it allows us to see with new eyes, and that begins with the way we view ourselves. It's not just that we interpret the Bible. The Bible interprets us, by declaring what the main events of reality are, and then telling us to read ourselves in light of that story.

I said that this story is the story of a King and his kingdom. That means this story doesn't just interpret us, it exercises authority over us. It's not merely a descriptive account of reality. The narrative of Scripture has a normative, or authoritative, function in our lives and over our churches. Now exactly how we determine that normative function requires that we pay attention to where in the narrative we are, and how the part we occupy relates to other parts. It requires us to keep in mind the central themes of the story, and the progressive nature of that story. Yet when we do those things, we discover a story that challenges our tendencies to reduce Christianity to a limited set of doctrinal propositions and instead claims the totality of our lives under the Lordship of the King.

4) Structured by Covenants

The story of any kingdom is in part the story of the relationship between a king and his subjects. In Scripture, this relationship is defined and structured according to covenants. Covenants are not merely contracts or promises. Rather, covenants are relationships under authority, with both obligations and rewards. The terms and benefits of the relationship are

---

[6]Richard B. Gaffin, Jr., "Introduction," in *Redemptive History and Biblical Interpretation: The Shorter Writings of Geerhardus Vos*, ed. Richard B. Gaffin, Jr. (Phillipsburg, NJ: P&R, 1980), xvii.

spelled out, and so are the consequences if the relationship is broken. But what is perhaps most significant about biblical covenants is that when God enters into a covenant, he must condescend to initiate it, he sets the terms, he provides the benefits, and he executes the judgment when the covenant is broken.

In the ancient Near East, in the second millennium BC, the time of Abraham and Moses, international relations were governed by treaties between great kings and vassal, or lesser, kings. These treaties took the form of covenants, in which the great king promised his protection and blessing in return for the vassal king's loyalty and obedience. So long as the vassal obeyed, he would enjoy the great king's favor. But when the vassal broke the terms of the covenant, the great king would bring a swift and final judgment. What's more, the vassal stood as a mediator or representative for his entire people. So his obedience or disobedience did not merely affect him, but all those who stood under him as their representative.

In the providence of God, Moses was inspired to write the first five books of the Old Testament at a time when this covenantal structure was widely known and recognized. In condescension to human understanding, God used this covenantal structure to reveal his own relationship as the great King to the people he had made in his own image to rule over the earth as vice-regents, vassal kings to the great King of heaven.

We'll look more closely at the various covenants God made and how they help to structure the unfolding story of God's redemptive plan in chapters 2 and 3. Most of the covenants you may already be familiar with: the Old Covenant and the New Covenant, or the Mosaic Covenant and the Davidic covenant. There are even more, and we'll talk about them. But here I want to briefly introduce the distinction between two types of covenant in the Bible: a covenant of works and a covenant of grace.

A covenant of works is exactly what it sounds like. Blessings are offered in return for works performed. Failure to perform the works leads to the covenant curses. This was pretty much the standard covenant of the ancient Near East, and we see this type of covenant clearly displayed with Adam and with Moses. Do this, and you'll live; do that, and you'll die.

But there is another kind of covenant in the Bible. In this covenant, it's not the vassal king that must perform a work in order to receive the great King's blessing. Instead, the great King himself undertakes to secure the blessing for the vassal, and risks the penalties himself should the covenant be broken. This is called a covenant of grace, and it's beautifully pictured in the Abrahamic covenant in Genesis 15. It's also the character of the New Covenant established in Jesus Christ and proclaimed in the gospel.

As we try to interpret and apply the Scriptures, one of the basic questions we'll have to ask is, in what covenantal period—in what epoch of God's redemptive activity—is this particular text found? How does the text function in that covenant? And what is my relationship to that covenant?

5) The Center: God's Glory in Salvation through Judgment[7]

The grace of God in the gospel through the sacrificial death of Jesus Christ not only describes the climax of the covenants but the climax of God's redemptive acts in history. It also brings us, finally, to the point and center of gravity of the story. Since this story is the story of redemption, it's quite easy to fall into the habit of thinking that that the point of the story is me, or us: the people being redeemed. But that would be a misreading of the story. Though we benefit immeasurably from this story, the center and point of the story is God and his glory (Eph. 1:6, 12, 14).

This does not mean God is some sort of giant, preening, celestial peacock, impressed with himself in narcissistic obsession. In fact, the display of God's glory in Scripture is filled with irony. For though God's glory is seen in his ability to save, that salvation comes only through judgment. And that judgment is borne by himself, in the person of his own Son. It is in the cross that God's glory is seen, in the suffering and sacrifice of him who is most worthy for those who are not worthy at all.

Here is the grace of God, and the glory of God, as he walks through those animals cut in two, as he provides a ram for Abraham's son, Isaac, and as he provides a Passover lamb for the Israelites. All this that he provided for his people was but a picture and foretaste of his ultimate provision: his one and only beloved Son, Jesus, sacrificed on the cross for sinners, bearing the judgment they deserved, that God's glory might be displayed in salvation and mercy, even as he met the demands of justice himself.

Conclusion

What then are the practical "how-tos" from this chapter? Just as a carpenter needs to know what kind of wood he's working on, we have begun by considering the material that we're to use in the work of biblical theology. In the Bible we find a divinely inspired text written by human beings at

---

[7]I am indebted to Jim Hamilton for the idea of "the glory of God in salvation through judgment" as the center of gravity for biblical theology. He works this idea out in greater scope and detail than I present in this section in James Hamilton, "The Glory of God in Salvation through Judgment: The Centre of Biblical Theology?" *Tyndale Bulletin* 57 (2006): 57–84.

different points of history, which, nonetheless, sustains one overarching narrative that's structured by covenants and focuses on the glory of God.

When we come to interpret this text and consider its relevance for pastoral ministry, therefore, we want to keep these things in mind. We should ask where in the storyline any given passage falls. We should ask how it displays God's glory. We should also ask where the person to whom we are ministering falls in the storyline. Finally, we'll ask what relevance it has for him or her.

So let's come back, briefly, to the question I began this chapter with, the couple's question of whether it's okay with God to delay their tithe in order to make a large purchase. We haven't even looked at the tools we'll need to answer this question, but you should already sense that the words about tithing in Malachi 3:10 need to be understood in their Old Testament context and how that relates to our own New Testament context before we apply the verse to the lives of New Testament believers. Yet I hope you can also see that we should expect the Bible to have something to say to believers and their stewardship of the resources that God has given them. We don't have a straightforward answer book. But neither are we left to our own devices, or the worldly advice of a financial planner. God's grand drama of redemption includes the humble stories of our lives as aliens and strangers following Christ to a better country.

SECTION ONE

The Tools
That Are Needed

Exegetical Tools:
Grammatical-Historical Method

I began this book by promising a "how-to" guide for ministry, one that would result in really useful theology. But so far, what I've mainly given you is definition and foundation. We've said that biblical theology is not merely theology that finds its source in the Bible, but a theology that attempts to make sense of the Bible as a whole. We've also said that the Bible is not just a collection of inspired religious books written by various prophets and apostles, but that it's a single story, a coherent narrative of the redemptive acts of God. This single story has God as its author, its primary actor, and its center, and the climax of this story is the glory of God in salvation through judgment. And yet, it is an emphatically practical story, since it encompasses the humble realities that define each of our lives.

But with this chapter, I mean to begin to make good on my promise of practical help. After all, as soon as we define the Bible as we have, we are confronted with a problem. How can we be sure that we're reading and understanding the story correctly? For that matter, how can we be sure that we're reading and understanding the various *parts* of the story correctly? Let's set aside for a moment the incredible idea that we could understand the mind and purposes and, therefore, the Word of God. How can we be confident that we can accurately understand the words of a Hebrew prophet living and writing three thousand years ago? Aren't words, human words, much less divine words, incredibly slippery and malleable? Isn't the meaning of a text an incredibly subjective idea? I mean, unless an author is present to tell us what he meant, who's to say that one interpretation of a text is better or more accurate or more faithful or more meaningful than another?

I'm going to consider below some of the technical aspects of this problem, but let me start by illustrating this in a context where many of us operate every week: youth ministry. Every Wednesday morning, I lead the sixth grade boys' devotions at my children's school. We're slowly working our way through the Gospel of Mark. To keep them engaged, as well as to teach them how to study the Bible on their own, I don't teach a lesson. Instead I ask them to read the passage out loud, and then I ask them questions about the text they just read. Almost all of my questions can be answered from the text itself, or the immediate context. They are not always easy questions, but they are always questions that arise from the passage we read.

The boys are bright, motivated, talkative, and happy to be there. They go through similar exercises in their literature class, so they're familiar with the process. But every Wednesday morning, several boys will quickly blurt out answers without even really looking at the text. These quick answers invariably fall into one of several categories. There's the Sunday school answer—whatever the question, the answer must be Jesus, the cross, sin, or some combination of them all. There's the "I heard my pastor/parent/Sunday school teacher say . . ." answer. This really isn't an answer at all, but an appeal to authority so they don't have to personally think about it. But the most common answer by far always begins, "I think it means . . ." When I respond to this answer by asking them to show where their idea came from in the text, as often as not I get a blank stare or a confused mumble, as if I've just asked them something crazy, like which sixth grade girl they like best! By sixth grade, many of them have decidedly, if unconsciously, adopted the attitude that the meaning of religious texts is a profoundly private affair that needs no further justification than their own sincerely held belief. If this is the case in sixth grade morning devotions, it is even more the case in the small group Bible studies populated by the adults of your church and mine.

The Problem of Meaning

If you're at all familiar with current discussions of theories of interpretation, what scholars call "hermeneutics," you'll know that, these days, many are quite skeptical about our ability to know with any precision what an author meant when he wrote something, unless we have direct access to that author. Distance and discontinuity between author and reader in language and culture, historical context and even personal experiences, it is said, effectively cut the reader off from knowing objectively and certainly what the author meant. For some, that's caused a real crisis. For others, it's been cause for celebration. For them, the loss of what we call the "author's original intent" means that finally we can be honest in our reading and acknowledge that we use texts for our own purposes, to mean what we want them to mean.

Meaning now no longer needs to be cleverly and dishonestly attached to the author's mind, but can simply be the meaning that the reading community finds there. What meaning do they find? They find the meaning that they need, the meaning that they want, the meaning that seems reasonable in light of their own context. In effect, this modern approach to interpretation, based on the supposed inaccessibility of the author's intent, means that there is no such thing as an authoritative text or interpretation, only an authoritative community. For thousands of years, societies have served texts, both sacred and political, usually to the benefit of those in power and to the detriment of minorities and the oppressed. Now, with what is known as the hermeneutical turn, there has been a great liberation. We don't serve texts anymore. The text serves us.[1]

Now, of course, there are some areas where this idea has not caught on. Most parties to written contracts want to insist that the contract has a stable and accessible meaning. But in other areas of law, especially constitutional law, as well as politics more generally, ethics and religion, and especially modern pop culture, this way of thinking, known as postmodernism, has taken hold with a vengeance and breathed a new and dangerous life into old fashioned relativism.

All of this brings me back to the question I posed earlier. If the Bible is a story with God as its author, but a story whose component parts are texts written by people in different languages, cultures, and historical periods, how can we be sure that we're reading the story correctly? Is there even such a thing as a correct reading?

In fact, there is such a thing as a correct meaning of a text, precisely because God, who created this world, our brains, and thus our ability to use language, is himself a speaking God. It was God who created rationality and language so that language could accurately convey meaning from one mind to another mind. And he himself proved this not only by acting in history, but also by condescending to use human language to authoritatively explain and interpret his own actions. We see this again and again on the pages of Scripture—God not only sends the ten plagues against Egypt, he speaks to Moses and Aaron explaining what he is doing. God not only parts

---

[1] I was first introduced to this idea as an undergraduate studying English literature in the 1980s. While the post-structuralism and anti-foundationalism of Derrida, Foucault, Fish, and others have gone through considerable critique and development since then, the inaccessibility of the author's original intent and its irrelevance as an authoritative source of meaning continues to be a fundamental characteristic of the postmodern experience of interpretation. For an excellent, brief introduction and survey of this movement, see D. A. Carson, *The Gagging of God* (Grand Rapids, MI: Zondervan), 57–92.

the Red Sea, he speaks and explains what he's about to do and why. God not only makes Israel into a nation, he speaks audibly to the whole nation from Mount Sinai, telling them so.

I could continue to multiply examples, but perhaps most telling is the incarnation of Christ himself. When God decided to definitively reveal himself once and for all, he didn't send angels or miraculous signs and wonders in the sky. He became a man and spoke to us in a language that people could understand. As the author to the Hebrews put it, "In the past God spoke to our forefathers through the prophets at many times and in various ways, but in these last days he has spoken to us by his Son" (Heb. 1:1–2). And to make absolutely clear that we should listen to his Son, not once but twice God spoke from heaven, first at Jesus' baptism, and then again at his transfiguration. This is the conclusion Peter drew:

> We did not follow cleverly invented stories when we told you about the power and coming of our Lord Jesus Christ, but we were eyewitnesses of his majesty. For he received honor and glory from God the Father when the voice came to him from the Majestic Glory, saying, "This is my Son, whom I love; with him I am well pleased." We ourselves heard this voice that came from heaven when we were with him on the sacred mountain. And we have the word of the prophets made more certain, and you will do well to pay attention to it, as to a light shining in a dark place, until the day dawns and the morning star rises in your hearts. (2 Peter 1:16–19)

What this means is that words, when placed in sentences and paragraphs, convey meaning. And not just any meaning. They convey the meaning of the author who constructed the sentence and the paragraph, as a reflection of his authorial intent. As readers of words, and particularly as readers of God's Word, our obligation—and privilege—is to read in such a way as to recover and understand the meaning the author wanted to communicate.

Now of course, you read this way all the time, every day of your life. When you pick up a newspaper or magazine article, your goal is not to read your own ideas into the story. You're trying to understand what the person is saying. You may go on to reject it or be inspired by it. You may think it was well-written or poorly written. You might think of all sorts of application for your newfound knowledge that the author hadn't considered at all. But regardless of what you do with what you've read, the first thing you do, quite naturally, is look for the author's original intent. And when you do that, you are engaged in the process of exegesis.

Exegesis is the disciplined attempt to lead out of a text the author's original intent, rather than my own preference or experience or opinion.

Jerome, who knew Greek and Hebrew long after most people had forgotten both and could only read Latin, put it this way in the late fourth century: "The office of a commentator is to set forth not what he himself would prefer, but what his author says."[2]

So all of you, every day, are exegetes of the texts you read, from recipes to instruction manuals, from *Sports Illustrated* to your favorite blog. You're also exegetes of Scripture. Yet while exegeting the newspaper is nearly automatic, since it's written in our own language and culture, exegeting Scripture requires a more conscious approach. It's written in other languages and at other times, and so we must take even greater care not to misread it. What we're going to do in the rest of this chapter, first, is to look at the method of exegesis known as the grammatical-historical method. Second, we'll provide a brief overview of the various literary forms or genres that make up the Bible. And third, we'll examine how we apply our method to those various genres.

Grammatical-Historical Method

The basic method of exegesis that we use to determine an author's original intent has come to be known as the grammatical-historical method. John Owen described it this way:

> There is no other sense in it [Scripture] than what is contained in the words whereof materially it doth consist . . . In the interpretation of the mind of anyone, it is necessary that the words he speaks or writes be rightly understood; and this we cannot do immediately unless we understand the language wherein he speaks . . . the [idiom] of that language, with the common use of and intention of its . . . expressions.[3]

rules # principles # govern sentence *strike*

Discerning the meaning of the text in this way immediately plunges us into an exploration and study of the grammar, syntax, and literary and historical context of the words we're reading—thus the phrase: grammatical-historical method.

Now in discovering the author's original intent, we need to avoid what is known as the "intentional fallacy." That's the idea that through the text, we can somehow get beyond the text into the thought world, feelings, and unexpressed intentions of the author. In fact, we don't have access to the author's psyche or motives, unless he explicitly expresses those things through his words. The mind, and therefore the meaning, that we have

---

[2] Jerome, *Letters*, "To Pammachius" 17.
[3] John Owen, *Works*, IV, 215, quoted in J. I. Packer, *A Quest for Godliness: The Puritan Vision of the Christian Life* (Wheaton, IL: Crossway, 1990), 101.

access to is the expressed mind, the mind that has revealed itself through the words on the page.[4]

However, in focusing on words, we have to recognize that words, by themselves, don't mean anything in particular. We may know that the word "ball" has a range of possible meanings, but until I put the word "ball" into a sentence, and then that sentence into a paragraph, you can't be certain what I mean by the word. For example, think about at what point the meaning of the word "ball" becomes unambiguous in the following paragraph:

> We had a ball. Everyone came in their fanciest clothes and danced the night away. But since Cinderella didn't attend, we were disappointed.

In fact, it's not until the final word of the last sentence that the precise meaning of "ball" becomes clear. Up until that point, it could have meant a "sphere you bounce" or "a really good time." But with the word "disappointed" you know for certain that ball meant "fancy party." So the basic unit of meaning is not the word, but the sentence. And the unit that determines what sentences mean, and therefore the words in them, is the paragraph.

This means that the primary question that the historical-grammatical method is seeking to answer is not, "What does that word mean?" but "What does that sentence mean?" In answering that question, we quickly realize that context is king.[5] So the first step of exegesis is to read the text, the whole text, over and over again. Interpretation actually begins with the whole, not the part. Then, in the context of the whole, we work backwards through the parts, back to sentences, back all the way down to individual words. What we learn and discover there then takes us back to the whole with a more accurate and perhaps nuanced understanding of meaning.

Grammatical

All of this begins with a basic grammatical and structural analysis of the text.

- First, how does the larger text break up into units? This is a function of genre: for epistles, it's the paragraph; for poetry, it's the stanza; for narrative history, it's the event or story.

---

[4]For a fuller discussion of many common fallacies, see D.A. Carson, *Exegetical Fallacies* (Grand Rapids, MI: Baker, 1984).
[5]Many have made this point, but I'm grateful to Scott Hafemann, who first drilled this concept into my brain many years ago as a first-year student at Gordon-Conwell Theological Seminary.

- What's the general flow of argument in the text you're looking at? Is there an assertion, supported by subordinate clauses? Is a contrast being drawn, a principle being illustrated, a pattern being established, a response being encouraged?
- Looking at a particular sentence, what's the subject, the verb, and the object, and how do they relate? (If you ever diagrammed sentences in school, it comes in handy here!)
- How are the sentences connected? Paying attention to the connections allows you to establish the detailed flow of thought. The goal here is discourse analysis, an attempt to make explicit the logical flow in order to identify the author's main point, and the various ways he supports that point.

Feeling overwhelmed? Be encouraged. For each of these steps, all that's really needed is patient reading and a basic understanding of grammar and logic. No commentaries are required at this point!

Historical

Next, how do the various larger contexts inform your understanding of the meaning of the text?

- How does your text fit within the larger argument of the book or section of Scripture you're reading?
- Does the historical context (author, date, audience, and provenance), if known, throw light on your understanding of words or arguments?
- Is there a cultural context that you need to be aware of? For example, what are Pharisees? What rights did women have in the Roman world? Or, what's the difference between a concubine and a wife in ancient Israel?
- Are there issues of geography, politics, or history that throw light on the meaning? For example, where is Tarshish in relation to Nineveh? What's so special about Caesarea Philippi that Jesus would elicit Peter's confession there?

Now unless you're a full-time Bible scholar, most of these sorts of issues won't be in your category of general knowledge. Here's where commentaries, Bible dictionaries, encyclopedias, and atlases are extremely helpful.

Biblical

Finally, perhaps the most important contextual question is how this text relates to the rest of Scripture. I'm going to spend more time on this in a later chapter, but suffice it to say that if the text quotes, alludes to, or resembles another part of the Bible, that's significant for our understanding of what the author was intending to communicate.

Importance of Literary Forms

I mentioned earlier that the basic unit of thought would vary depending on the genre, or literary form, that we're dealing with. Yet I didn't stop to explain what I meant by genre.

Genre is simply a word that literary types use to describe the different recognized forms of writing that exist. This is important for us in understanding the Bible for several reasons. First, distinct genres tend to have distinct rules or patterns of communicating. We intuitively recognize this. On the whole, poetry doesn't even look like a newspaper article. That's because poetry and narrative are different genres, with their own unique set of internal rules. These rules and patterns have a real bearing on the meaning of the words and sentences an author writes. What's more, certain word patterns are so closely associated with a genre that their use almost immediately defines what we're looking at and how we interpret it. "Once upon a time . . ." signals fairy tale, not history, while "Dear Joe . . . love, Sally" signals epistle, not a legal brief. If we're going to read a text literally—that is, according to the sense of the words and the author's original intent—we need to identify the text's genre.

The second reason it's important to understand genre is because it doesn't take long to realize that the Bible consists of multiple genres. The entire Bible is true, and it all needs to be read literally, but reading the legal statutes of Exodus literally is going to look different than reading the poetry of Psalm 17 literally. Otherwise, we run the risk of having to say that David in Psalm 17 contradicted the second commandment by describing God as having wings like a mother hen under which he could hide.

Third, it's important to understand genre because it helps us with books or passages that feel culturally foreign and difficult to grasp. Two obvious examples of this are genealogies and apocalyptic literature. Neither are types of text you come across in your daily reading, yet the Bible has quite a few examples of both. Do we just apply the rules of genre from narrative or epistle? That's what some have done, and it produces rather boring genealogies and rather fantastical apocalyptic. But in fact, both of these genres have specific rules and conventions, and if we're going to read them correctly we need to understand those rules.

Interpreting the Diverse Genres of Scripture

So what are the genres of Scripture? There are more than we have time to deal with in one chapter, but let me conclude by laying out the seven major forms, and demonstrate with each how we go about exegeting them using the grammatical-historical method.

1) Narrative

Narrative makes up the largest portion of the Bible—40 percent of the Old Testament and 60 percent of the New Testament. Not only that, narrative provides the overall framework within which we understand all the other genres. How do we exegete narrative?

- First, we pay attention to the story and its details. The main point is in the plot and its development. And biblical narrative, like every other, is going to use all the devices you're used to:
  - chronological development
  - plot and rhetorical devices, such as dialogue, shifting points of view, and climax
  - character development
  - literary devices such as *inclusio* (using repeated words or phrases as bookends) and *chiasm* (a-b-c-b?-a? pattern)
  - scene arrangement, including things like flashbacks and cut-aways
- Second, remember that the narrator has had to be selective in what he records, so the details that are present are significant. How do they contribute to the point of the narrative? How do they connect this narrative to what came before and what comes after?
- Third, context is king. How does this narrative fit into the rest of the book, the rest of the section of Scripture, and the narrative of the Bible as a whole?
- Fourth, what's the point of the narrative in light of the author's purpose in writing the book? Story is not an end in itself, and we (personal application) are not necessarily the point either!
- Example: 1 Samuel 17—the story of David and Goliath. When we pay attention to the details and the context, we see that this is not a morality tale about courage in the face of long odds. We also avoid turning it into an allegory, in which every detail represents a spiritual truth. Rather, this is our introduction to the unlikely king who in single combat defeats the enemy and delivers God's people. In the context of 1 Samuel, this story sets up a contrast with Saul, the obvious and apparent king who turns out to be a fraud. Ultimately the story points us to Christ, who in the most unlikely way defeats the enemies of God's people in single combat on the cross and delivers us to God!

2) Parable

Parable is an important and often misunderstood genre, largely found in the Gospels, but also in the Old Testament prophets. Fundamentally, a parable is a pictorial comparison between something familiar and known and a spiritual truth or reality. The picture is typically fictional, though realistic. They are not generally allegorical, even when various parts of the picture represent various spiritual truths. Many times the details just add vividness to the picture. How do we exegete parables?

- The most important question to ask about a parable is, "What's the main point or points?"
- Pay attention to repetition (which is like putting something in bold), the reversal of expectations, or changes in voice from first to third person. These are all clues to the main emphasis.
- The conclusion or main point is typically at the end, and usually centers on the nature of the kingdom or the King.
- Context is still king, so interpret parables in light of the context of the larger surrounding narrative. Don't rip them out of the context in which the author has placed them, as if they were a random collection of Aesop's Fables.
- Example: Mark 4:30–32—The parable of the mustard seed. The point of this parable is found in the conclusion, and in light of the context. Jesus is illustrating the surprising and unexpected growth of the kingdom from tiny to huge. The application therefore is not to despise it, or grow discouraged by the kingdom's present obscurity. We aren't meant to allegorize the birds in its branches, or be thrown off by the fact that there are smaller seeds and larger garden plants.

3) Poetry

One third of the Old Testament (which is more than the whole New Testament) is poetry! It exists by itself (the Psalms), but is also found throughout other genres such as Wisdom and Prophecy. The key to exegeting Hebrew poetry is to realize that, like English poetry, Hebrew poetry presents extremely compressed and image-rich language. Poetry in any language is intended not only to communicate truth but also to evoke emotion. On the other hand, unlike English poetry, Hebrew poetry does not have rhyme and meter that we would recognize. Instead, it uses other devices to provide structure. How do we exegete poetry?

- The most common feature of Hebrew poetic structure is parallelism in three different forms—synonymous (an idea is repeated for emphasis), synthetic (one idea builds upon another), and antithetical (one idea is contrasted with another).

- Other features include word play, alliteration and alphabetic acrostic, repetition, hyperbole, contrast, metonymy (substitution), and synecdoche (the whole stands for the part or vice versa).
- Like English poetry, it uses metaphor and simile, figurative images, irony, and euphemism.
- Perhaps the most important key to interpreting poetry is to remember that it's a poem. A literal reading of a poem will look different than a literal reading of narrative.
- Example: Psalm 19:7–11. These verses are an extended example of synonymous parallelism. David is not talking about six different things, but one thing—the Word of God. He's treating it like a cut diamond held up to the light. In each phrase he turns the single diamond slightly in order to examine a different facet. The point of the poetic meditation is both to engender in us a high view and value of God's Word and to convince us of his conclusion in verse 11.

4) Wisdom

For many, the wisdom literature of Scripture is both much loved and highly problematic. It's loved because it seems so practical. It's problematic because it is least like the genres we interact with in the modern world. It also seems strangely disconnected from the main point of Scripture, which is redemption in Christ Jesus.

In fact, wisdom literature is very practical precisely because it's so closely connected with the main point of Scripture. Wisdom literature is about living well in God's world and in light of God's character. Wisdom is the fruit of the fear of the Lord, which means being correctly oriented toward God and the creation he's made, including other people. It speaks of what is generally true, but it also addresses what appear to be the exceptions to that general truth. How do we exegete wisdom literature?

- We need to recognize that wisdom literature comes to us in multiple forms, or sub-genres.
  - Drama (Job, Song of Solomon)
  - Sayings (Proverbs 9–31)
  - Autobiographical confession and admonition (Ecclesiastes, Proverbs 1–8).
- Whatever the form, the key in interpretation is to read it in context and according to its stated purpose.
  - Job intends to address the problem of unjust suffering.
  - Ecclesiastes intends to realistically address the point of life.
  - The Proverbs intend to engender the fear of God and then show how that fear (or lack of it) demonstrates itself in all sorts of contexts. It is emphatically not law code.

- Song of Solomon is a celebration of human love in marriage that points beyond itself to God's love for his people.
- Example: Proverbs 12:21—"No harm befalls the righteous, but the wicked have their fill of trouble." A quick reader will make one of two mistakes. He will assume that this is always true, and therefore take suffering as a divine judgment against wickedness. Alternatively, he will simply point to Job, or to Jesus, and say the proverb is clearly false. But this proverb is neither making an absolute promise, nor is it a contradiction of Job. Rather, like all proverbs, it is proverbial, or generally true. In the moral universe that God has created, wickedness usually brings trouble on itself, and righteousness usually brings blessing. Beyond the proverbial character of the statement, the proverb also points to the ultimate blessing and judgment that comes from God. Even though there are exceptions in this life, God will ultimately keep this proverb at the final judgment.

5) Prophecy

The prophetic books contain both narrative and poetry, but what sets them apart as their own genre is the presence of the prophetic oracle—"Thus says the Lord"—and the function these oracles play in Scripture. The prophets arrive on the biblical scene as attorneys for the prosecution, arguing God's case in a covenant lawsuit against Israel for breaking the covenant. But not only do they make the case, they prophetically warn of the judgment to come (calling for repentance) and prophetically proclaim the salvation to come (calling for faith). How do we exegete prophecy?

- The basic feature—and problem—of interpretation is the promise-fulfillment dynamic. This is what divides interpreters. When, where, and how a prophecy is fulfilled helps us understand its meaning.
- One important aspect of prophecy is the prophetic foreshortening of events. The prophets see the mountains on the distant horizon as a single, two-dimensional line. Once we actually get there in history and travel into those mountains, we discover that there are multiple ranges broad distances apart. This means that most, if not all, prophecies have multiple horizons of fulfillment.
  - For example, in the flow of Isaiah's narrative, the "sign of Immanuel" in Isaiah 7 is fulfilled in Isaiah 8 with Isaiah's own son. But that's just the first range of mountains. Behind and towering over that range is the text's ultimate fulfillment in the birth of Jesus Christ.
  - Another example is found in the apocalyptic prophecy of judgment in Isaiah 24–27. This prophecy is fulfilled first by the Babylonian invasion of Palestine. A second mountain range of fulfillment perhaps arrives with Rome's destruction of Jerusalem in 70 AD. Ultimately, in light of Revelation, we

recognize that this prophecy is fulfilled at the end of the world on the last day.

- A common feature of prophecy is to use the language and images of the past in order to describe the future. Creation, garden of Eden imagery, the flood, Sodom and Gomorrah, and the exodus are all used to describe future events. These provide a theological understanding of what's happening, not necessarily a literal understanding.

- Not all prophecies are unconditional. The most famous example of this is Jonah preaching to Nineveh. He prophesied that in three days Nineveh would be overturned, unless the people repented. The people repented, so the prophecy was not fulfilled.

- Quite a bit of prophecy is not predictive, but descriptive (typological). For example, the New Testament understands that much of King David's life anticipated the coming Messiah.

- As always, context is king. In the case of prophecy, the shape of the story of the Bible as a whole is crucial. We need to remember that revelation is progressive, and in the revelation of Jesus Christ, we've been given both the main point and the end of the story. This means that we have an advantage over Old Testament readers. We work from the story of the whole Bible back to the prophecy, not the other way around. As Peter assures us in 1 Peter 1:10–13, the gospel gives us clearer vision than even the Old Testament prophets had. Therefore the New Testament determines the ultimate meaning of Old Testament prophecy, not the other way around.

- Example: Isaiah 11—the prophecy of the reign of the Branch of Jesse. This prophecy draws on imagery from Genesis 2 (Eden), Exodus, and Joshua. It describes the future in overlapping images: a return to Eden, a second exodus, and a completion of the unfinished work of conquering the Promised Land. In piling up these images, many of which are also poetic, we need to recognize that the prophet is making a theological point, and not necessarily a literal historical prediction. All of this will be accomplished through the righteous judgment of a shoot from the stump of Jesse, who is described in terms taken from God's presence in the exodus (vv. 10–11). So the prophecy points forward ultimately to the divine Son of David, the God-man Jesus Christ, and his universal rule in the new heavens and new earth.

6) Epistles

Epistles are the most straightforward of the genres, because they are letters written to people in the exact same part of the story as we are—believers living in between the resurrection of Christ and his second coming. How do we exegete epistles?

- As always, context is extremely important. These letters are occasional documents, not abstract theological treatises intended for a library. They were written by the apostles to real live Christians facing real problems, either moral or doctrinal or both.

- Since these letters were almost always motivated by a problem(s) or conflict(s), the author is attempting to apply the truth of the gospel in order to address the issue(s) at hand. This means his basic form of speech will be logical argument. Because of this, we must pay attention to both the flow of the argument and its details.

- The apostles self-consciously understood themselves to be the recipients of and the fulfillment of the Old Testament promises in light of what Christ had done. Therefore the primary "context" of New Testament epistles is not Greco-Roman, but the Old Testament!

- Application of epistles is typically straightforward, but some cultural and redemptive-historical discontinuity remains. We need to be sensitive to those questions.

- Example: Ephesians 2:11–22. A typical application of this passage in many evangelical churches is racial reconciliation. But if we're paying attention to both the letter itself and the large biblical context, we'll realize that, first and foremost, Paul is talking about the removal of the division between Jew and Gentile. That division wasn't merely ethnic, but theological, for it defined the boundaries of God's people. The removal of that division in Christ meant that the nations were now welcome, and not to be excluded from God's salvation. Only secondarily is this passage about reconciliation across other divides.

7) Apocalyptic

Without doubt, apocalyptic is the most intriguing but also the most difficult of all the genres. Science fiction is the closest thing that we have to it! The point and purpose of apocalyptic literature is to give God's people hope in the midst of present sufferings based on God's certain victory over their enemies, both now and in the future. To do that, apocalyptic draws heavily on the images of the past, as well as other stylized imagery. The point is to review the sweep of history and show it's culmination in the victory of God's kingdom. How do we exegete apocalyptic?

- Two main examples of apocalyptic in the Bible are Daniel and Revelation. But neither is merely apocalyptic. Daniel is prophetic literature and Revelation is a prophetic epistle.

- Literary context is important. Biblical apocalyptic draws specifically on biblical images from the Old Testament (Babylon, plagues), as well as "stock" images from the wider genre (the horn, celestial bodies, etc).

- Apocalyptic provides a schematization of history, but that scheme is not necessarily chronological. For example, each series of seven plagues in Revelation (seals, trumpets, bowls) ends with the end of the world. And yet, it would be easy to read the series as sequential. So how many times does the world end? In fact, there is a pattern in these series. History is recapitulated from different perspectives, leading to the climax of the last two chapters.

- Without going into a detailed treatment of the various approaches to interpreting Revelation, we can all agree that the main point is clear. God's people can endure present suffering because of their confidence that God wins. And they know he wins, not because of prophetic revelation, but because of what Christ has already accomplished in the past, through his death and resurrection.

- Example: Revelation 5—the revelation of the Lion of Judah. John hears of the Lion of Judah, the one who will open the scroll and bring about God's purposes in history. But when he turns to see the one he has heard of, he sees the Lamb who was slain. Did he hear wrong? Are there in fact two different individuals? Not at all. To the contrary, what he sees explains what he heard about. Jesus is worthy to be the Lion, the one who accomplishes God's purposes precisely because he humbled himself as the Lamb of God on the cross. Jesus is worthy of glory and honor, and able to open God's book of judgment, not merely because of his preexistent divinity, but especially because he purchased God's people with his own blood. The cross therefore stands at the center of the revelation of the glory of God.

Conclusion

So there you have it: how to exegete every part of the Bible! Of course I'm being facetious. What I hope you see, however, is that interpreting a passage is not simply arbitrarily imposing on it the meaning that I want it to have. It is in fact nothing more or less than a close and careful reading of a text in its context, both narrow and broad. It's as basic as observation (What does it say?) and interpretation (What did this mean to the original readers?). All of us need the right tools to do this well, but with patient and frequent reading, all of us can become faithful readers of the text, reading out of it what the original divine and human authors meant, rather than reading into it our own ideas.

This is exactly what I've experienced with my group of sixth grade boys. With patience and practice, they've gradually rid themselves of some of their worst habits of interpretation. Now, on Wednesday mornings, they are increasingly eager to actually read the text of Mark's Gospel, and think about what Mark meant under the inspiration of the Holy Spirit. Just last week we studied Mark 1:40–2:12, the healing of the man with leprosy and the paralytic. I asked the boys if the point of Jesus' ministry was to make people physically well. One of them said "No," and I asked him why. It had been weeks since we'd looked at it, but he quickly turned to Mark 1:35–39 (context!) and pointed out that Jesus came to preach the gospel, not do miracles. So I asked them why he healed a leper at all. They weren't sure at first, so we thought together about the larger biblical context. After we finished discussing the details of leprosy (these are sixth grade boys, after all), some of them remembered that having leprosy meant you couldn't go to the temple or go home, that you were cut off from God and people. Then we looked at the healing of the paralytic. I asked them why Jesus healed the man, and they immediately pointed to verse 10, and said that it was to prove that Jesus could forgive sin. At that point, it was as if a light bulb went off. Leprosy was a picture of sin. Sin cuts us off from God and others. By healing lepers and lame men, Jesus wasn't just proving how powerful he was; he was showing us what he had come to do—not make our bodies well, but to make our hearts clean, and so bring us back into a relationship with God.

If sixth grade boys can learn to exegete Scripture, then so can we, and so can the members of our churches. When we take the time to do this well and to teach others to do it too, we'll find, as Peter declared, "We have the word of the prophets made more certain . . . a light shining in a dark place, until the day dawns and the morning star rises in [our] hearts" (2 Pet. 1:19).

CHAPTER TWO

Biblical Theology Tools 1: Covenants, Epochs, and Canon

Having considered the art of exegesis, are we now ready to read the text and construct a biblical theology—a theology that is both faithful and that tells the whole story of the whole Bible? Not quite. There are two other sets of tools every reader of Scripture needs if we're to put it all together faithfully. We not only need exegetical tools, we also need biblical theology and systematic theology tools. In this chapter and the next we'll consider the tools of biblical theology and how to use them. Then we'll take up the tools of systematic theology in the following chapters. Only at that point will we be ready to start building.

Introduction

I want to start with a question: why do you read the Bible? While there are lots of reasons to read the Bible, fundamentally, we read the Bible in order to know God.

In some ways, knowing God is like knowing anybody else. To know God we need to know what pleases him and what makes him angry, what's important to him and what doesn't matter so much. We need to know his character, what he's like as a person, and how he responds in different situations. Yet it's not just his personality and character that we need to know. As with any other person, we need to know something of his history. (What has he been up to before we met him?) And we need to know something of his goals. (Where is he heading and what is he committed to?) Finally, we also would want to know something about his family and friends. After all, really knowing someone means knowing who they like to be with, and who they really love.

But for all the ways that knowing God is comparable to knowing a human being, there is one very important difference. Unless God reveals the answers to all of those questions that I asked above (and more), we will never get to know him. As I said at the outset of this book, the revelation of God is necessarily self-revelation. Unless God tells us who he is and what he's doing, we're in the dark.

How different that is from our experience of getting to know another person these days. The fact is, whether I want you to or not, you could get to know quite a bit about me, if you had a mind to. You could use Google, Facebook, and a couple other websites to learn about what I do, who I know, and where I've been. You would learn what we might call the "public horizon" of Michael Lawrence's life.

But as good as that horizon is, it doesn't tell everything there is to know about me. If you wanted to get to know me better, you could move to Washington, DC and join my church. From the sermons I preach, to the way I conduct our members' meetings, to the way I interact with people in the hallways of our church, you're going to learn what kind of person I am. Am I gracious or rude? Am I patient or short-tempered? Am I cheerful, or serious, or moody? All of this you could learn by hanging out in my church for a while. We might call that the "personal horizon" of Michael Lawrence's life.

But if you really want to know me, you'll have to move from being a member of my church to one of my confidants, or even move in with my family. Here, you'll find far more than you wanted to know. You'll hear my unguarded comments and see my thoughtless actions. You'll know what I'm like before my first cup of coffee, or how I act when I'm being silly with my kids. This is the "private horizon" of Michael Lawrence's life, and only God can go deeper than that.

Is one of these horizons more "true" than the others? No. They all tell you something about me. We tend to think that the private is the most real, but if that's all you knew about me, you wouldn't know me very well. What's more, not only do all three horizons tell you something about me, each interacts with and informs the others. If you're reading this book, you now know something of my public horizon. But if you attend my church and read this book, you know that this book is a reflection of my ministry priorities and the product of many sermons. And if you live in my house, attend my church, and read this book, then you know that my ministry priorities, sermons, and now this book flow out of my study of Scripture first thing in the mornings.

We can't Google God. And ever since Genesis 3, we haven't been able to live in the same house with him. That means there's not a single horizon of God's life that we can know unless he reveals it to us. The absolutely amazing truth of Scripture is that, in the Bible, God has revealed himself.

And he has not only revealed his public face, the public horizon of his life, but he has revealed to us his Son, Jesus Christ. And it doesn't get more intimate than that with God.

When we come to the Bible, we're coming to God's self-revelation. And in a way that is analogous to the horizons of my life, every passage of Scripture we read must be understood within multiple horizons of meaning. The horizons are not public, personal, and private, but they are a series of ever-expanding contexts. And with each new context, each new horizon, we come to a fuller appreciation of the meaning and the application of the text to our own lives and ministry. The goal of this chapter is to help us read the Bible in light of each of these horizons, and so, in the end, to read the Bible biblically.

The Three Horizons of God's Self-Revelation in Scripture

The three horizons of Scripture are the textual horizon, the epochal horizon, and the canonical horizon.[1] The previous chapter was really all about the textual horizon. It sought to answer the question, How can we read and understand what a text is saying in its immediate context? We do this by patiently and carefully using the tools of exegesis. But knowing a text in its immediate context is a bit like knowing only the private horizon of my life. It's close, detailed, and particular, but what does it have to do with everything else going on? For that, we need to pull back and understand the text in the broader contexts of epoch and canon. To explain those two horizons, we need to pick up another topic from the Introduction. We need to talk about covenants.

When God condescended to reveal himself to humanity and enter into a relationship with us, he structured those relationships in what we have come to recognize as covenants. God uses covenants in an extraordinary act of condescending anthropomorphic communication. And as we'll see, there are few more important concepts to grasp if we're going to understand the whole biblical story and each of its parts.

What's a Covenant?[2]

As we considered in the Introduction, international relations in the ancient Near East were governed by treaties between great kings and vassal kings

---

[1] For an excellent introduction to and discussion of these ideas, developed from earlier work by Edmund Clowney, see Richard Lints, *The Fabric of Theology: A Prolegomenon to Evangelical Theology* (Grand Rapids, MI: Eerdmans, 1993), 293–310.

[2] This entire section, but especially the first two paragraphs, is largely taken from Meredith Kline, *Treaty of the Great King* (Grand Rapids, MI: Eerdmans, 1965). A more recent, and more accessible, treatment of this can be found in O. Palmer Robertson, *The Christ of the Covenants* (Phillipsburg, NJ: P&R, 1980), 167–170.

that took the specific form of covenants. The great king promised his protection and blessing in return for the vassal king's loyalty and obedience. Not only that, the vassal king's obedience or disobedience affected both him and all those who stood under him as their representative.

In their formal literary form, the covenants of the late second millennium took a consistent, standardized form. They began with a *preamble*, identifying the great king who authors the covenant. They next present a brief *historical prologue*, outlining what the great king has already done for the vassal king. This prologue serves as the foundation for the vassal's obedience. Then come the covenant *stipulations* (what is expected of the vassal), both summary and detailed. Following the stipulations covenants often included a *document clause*, a paragraph requiring that copies of the covenant be placed in the temples of each of the kings and that the vassal king periodically read the covenant publicly and pass it on to his sons. Next, witnesses were called—typically the gods of both kings. Finally, the covenant concluded with a list of *blessings* that would accrue if the covenant was kept, and a list of *curses* that would be invoked should the covenant be broken. After it was written, the covenant would then be ratified by an oath that involved the shedding of sacrificial blood.

As I've already said, God used this structure to reveal himself as *the* great king, and he used it to teach his people that they were his vice-regents, or vassal kings to the great King of heaven. In fact, we see half of this covenantal structure in summary form in the Ten Commandments themselves:

Exodus 20:2–17

Preamble:	[2] "I am the LORD your God,
Historical Prologue:	who brought you out of Egypt, out of the land of slavery.
Stipulations:	[3] "You shall have no other gods before me.
	[4] "You shall not make for yourself an idol . . .
	[7] "You shall not misuse the name of the LORD your God . . .
	[8] "Remember the Sabbath day by keeping it holy . . .
	[12] "Honor your father and your mother. . . .
	[13] "You shall not murder.
	[14] "You shall not commit adultery.
	[15] "You shall not steal.
	[16] "You shall not give false testimony against your neighbor.
	[17] "You shall not covet. . . . "

The stipulations are spelled out in more detail in Exodus 21–23. Then, in Exodus 24:1–11, the covenant is read publicly, with both God and the people serving as witnesses. Exodus 25:21 states that the covenant is to be placed in the ark in the Holy of Holies, which is both God's throne room and Israel's temple. Where are the blessings and curses? In fact, Israel breaks the covenant before they ever have a chance to recite them. We don't finally get them until Deuteronomy 27 and 28.

The Mosaic covenant is not the only place we see a covenantal structure. Yet I've taken the time to unpack this example so that you'll see that a covenant is not merely a "contract" or a "promise" as we understand such things. Rather, it's a bond that establishes an all-encompassing relationship. A covenant is not merely a financial obligation or a military treaty. It's a claim on someone's total loyalty and allegiance. It has an authority structure to it, with ongoing obligations, blessings, and curses. And what's more, it's generational. When Israel entered the covenant, they did so for the generations yet to come.

But not only was a covenant written out, it was also cut. The Old Testament term for making a covenant is in fact to cut a covenant. That's because a covenant almost always involved the shedding of blood, as both a sign and a seal of the covenant. In Exodus 24, Moses sacrificed young bulls, took their blood, and sprinkled the blood on both the altar and the people as "the blood of the covenant." In the ancient Near East, not only would animals be sacrificed, they would also be mutilated, torn in two, or have a leg shoved down their throat, all as a sign of what would happen to the vassal and his people should they break the covenant. As Palmer Robertson has aptly said, a covenant is not simply a bond; it's a bond in blood,[3] a commitment to loyalty and allegiance that was secured with the life of the covenant mediator, the vassal king. He didn't actually die to secure the covenant, but he was represented vicariously by the sacrificed and mutilated animals. Perhaps you can already begin to see how important this is for understanding not only Exodus 20 but Mark 14 and Hebrews 9.

Two Kinds of Covenants

If that is the basic structure of the covenant as we find it in the Bible, I need to introduce one important variation. Sometimes, out of the magnanimity of his heart, a great king would decide to enter into a covenant without stipulations. In this covenant, there were no conditions or terms that the vassal had to keep, no "obey, and I'll bless you; disobey, and I'll

[3]Robertson, *The Christ of the Covenants*, 7ff.

curse you." Instead, the great king simply staked himself, his word, and his resources as guarantor of the covenant blessings. In contrast to the standard covenant of works, this sort of covenant is what we would call a covenant of grace.

In the ancient Near East, you might encounter such a covenant of grace when a great king grants an inalienable inheritance to a valiant warrior or faithful servant. We see this kind of covenant in the Old Testament as well. Genesis 15:9–21 is perhaps the best example. There, God promises Abraham an inheritance. And to make matters certain, God seals his promise with an oath. Animals are torn in two, and one party to the covenant walks down the bloody path. But it is God, not Abraham, who takes that walk. In effect, God says, may what happened to these animals happen to me, if I fail to keep my promise to Abraham. What does Abraham have to do in return? Nothing, except continue to believe in God.

So we have two kinds of covenants: covenants of works and covenants of grace.[4] Both follow the same sort of pattern. But the crucial difference lies in who takes the oath and so undertakes to suffer the curses should the covenant be broken. As we will see, that difference is the difference between salvation and damnation, between heaven and hell. All of us deserve to suffer the consequences of a broken covenant with God. But Jesus suffered those consequences for us—if, like Abraham, we repent and believe in the promise of God.

The Covenants of Scripture

I've referred to the covenant we see in Exodus 20, and have alluded to the new covenant that Jesus made with his own blood. Yet these aren't the only covenants in Scripture. In fact, covenants are a fairly prominent feature of the entire Bible. I want to briefly lay out the seven major examples of covenants in the Bible. I've summarized some key features in the table on page 61. These covenants provide a structure for the narrative as a whole. The word covenant is not necessarily used in each case, but I'm following an old hermeneutical law: if it looks like a duck and quacks like a duck, it's probably a duck.

---

[4]In saying this, I realize that in fact the textual contexts of each and every covenant are more complex than this simple, binary classification. This complexity flows from the fact that every covenant between God and man implies a gracious condescension and prior initiative on his part. God's grace also changes and redefines us, and so places new obligations and expectations on the recipients of grace. Nevertheless, for all its limitations, the distinction helps us articulate the unilateral nature of salvation—it is God alone, in the person of the incarnate Son, who meets the terms and bears the curse of the covenant of works, thereby earning the reward of a redeemed humanity, saved wholly by grace.

Covenant of Creation

This is the initial covenant made with Adam in Genesis 2:15–17. As Romans 5 makes clear, he entered into that covenant as the representative of the entire human race. Its blessings or curses would fall on us all. The blessing was implied—the promise of eternal sinless life. The curse was death. The stipulation was to refrain from eating from the Tree of the Knowledge of Good and Evil, as well as working and guarding the garden of Eden. In Genesis 3, Adam and Eve's loyalty to God was tested. They failed the test and broke the stipulations. The curses followed immediately and have continued to work themselves out through all of history and each of our lives.

Covenant of Redemption

This is an intra-Trinitarian covenant in which the Father, Son, and Holy Spirit agree together to accomplish the redemption of a people. This covenant is implied in Genesis 3:15, and referred to in other Old and New Testament passages (cf. Isaiah 49, Psalm 2, Psalm 110, John 5, Revelation 5). What's interesting about Genesis 3:15 and what suggests that there is covenant behind these words is that in the midst of the curse on the serpent, God himself undertakes obligations and makes promises. This covenant becomes the basis for the covenant of grace in all its various administrations. Its outlines are worked out through the rest of Scripture.

Noahic Covenant

This covenant is made with Noah and all living creatures in Genesis 9:8–17. It's called a covenant of grace because of the unilateral promise on God's part. It's called a covenant of *common* grace because it applies to all people, whether they trust in God or not. The purpose of this covenant is to provide the field upon which the story of redemption will run its course. Judgment is postponed until redemption is fully accomplished. Thus, quite appropriately, the sign of this covenant is the rainbow, a symbol of God the warrior's bow, held at rest!

Abrahamic Covenant

This covenant is recorded in Genesis 15:1-21 and picks up God's original purpose with Adam—the creation of a people who will display his glory as vice-regent image-bearers on earth. However, it's made not with all humanity, but with Abraham and his seed. God does make demands upon Abraham's obedience, but this is fundamentally a covenant of grace. God promises Abraham a people and a place under God's benevolent rule, and the blessings of this covenant will eventually flow to all the earth. The sign of the covenant—circumcision—is given in Genesis 17.[5]

Mosaic Covenant

This covenant is established in Exodus 20-25 and is re-established in Deuteronomy. It builds on the Abrahamic Covenant by working out in detail what God's vice-regents should look like: a holy kingdom, in distinction from the seed of the serpent, who bless the earth by their very distinctiveness (Deut. 4:5-8; cf. Ex. 19:4-6). Unlike the Abrahamic covenant, however, this is a covenant of works. The judges, successors to Moses, are the continuing covenant mediators. Though the sign of circumcision continues, God declares in Exodus 31:12-18 that the corporate sign for this covenant is the Sabbath. The blessing of this covenant was continued possession of the Promised Land. The curse of the covenant was exile.

Davidic Covenant

This covenant is established in 2 Samuel 7 and gives the nation's responsibility to reflect God's glory particularly to the King. He now represents the whole, and so is called the son of God, just as Israel had been at the Exodus, and Adam was at the beginning. The vice-regency is once again focused in a single person. He's called to fulfill the Mosaic covenant (Deut. 17:18-20), and the covenant promises discipline if he does not (2 Sam. 7:14). Still, the covenant remains a unilateral covenant of grace since God personally guarantees Davidic inheritance of the throne of Israel. The sign of the covenant is the birth of a son.

New Covenant

This final covenant of grace is promised in both Jeremiah 31:27–34 and Ezekiel 36:24–28 (cf. Deut. 30:6–8). It is not fulfilled and established until Christ comes, who picks up and fulfills the various strands of the previous covenants. He is the perfect image (Colossians 1), the promised seed (Galatians 3), the true Son (Matthew 3), and the messianic King (Matthew 21).

The prophets explicitly contrast this covenant with the old Mosaic covenant. Unlike that one, this new covenant would not be broken. This is the covenant Jesus declares he is establishing in Matthew 26:27–30 through

---

[5]There's disagreement among scholars over whether this is a different covenant or not.

shedding his blood on the cross. In fact, Jesus mediates this covenant by standing before God as our representative substitute (Romans 5). He guarantees the covenant by taking on the curse of Genesis 3 and the Mosaic Covenant through his death on the cross (Gal. 3:13). Those who trust in Christ are therefore no longer under the old covenant's curse, but are free to enjoy the blessings of forgiveness and reconciliation with God. Accordingly, the sign of the new life of this covenant is baptism (Romans 6).

Table of Major Biblical Covenants

Name	Type	Blessing	Curse	Sign	Text
Creation	Works	Eternal sinless life	Spiritual & Physical death	The Tree of Life (?)	Gen. 2:15–17
Redemption	Works (intra-Trinitarian)	Redemption of the seed of the woman	Judgment of the seed of the serpent	Enmity between the seeds	Gen. 3:15
Noahic	Grace	Judgment postponed	None	Rainbow	Gen. 9:8–17
Abrahamic	Grace	A place and people under God's rule, blessing the nations	None	Circumcision	Genesis 15, 17
Mosaic	Works	Possession of the land	Exile	Sabbath	Exodus 20ff.
Davidic	Grace	An eternal kingdom	None	A Son	2 Samuel 7
New	Grace	Forgiveness and eternal life in the kingdom of God	None	Baptism	Jer. 31:27–34; Matt. 26:27–30

To study these covenants is to study God's revelation of how he relates to his people in history. When we recognize that, we realize right away that how these various covenants relate to each other is a matter of real importance for understanding the story of the Bible. We also realize that it's important to understand which covenant we stand under as New Testament believers, and which covenant any text of Scripture we're reading stands under. Otherwise, we run the risk of reading our covenant situation inappropriately into a passage, or conversely, applying a previous covenantal arrangement to ourselves.

Now that we've looked at covenants, we can finally return to the three horizons of God's self-revelation in Scripture, which is where we began this chapter. As I said previously, chapter 1 was a discussion of the first horizon, the textual horizon. There is a second horizon, the epochal horizon, and it is largely determined by covenants. As the Bible unfolds, we see that God changes his covenantal arrangements at key points in the history of redemption, and that he relates to his people differently as redemptive history moves from one covenantal epoch to another.

Epochs

Up until this point, we've been considering texts in their immediate context. For instance, the story of God's covenant with Abraham in Genesis 15 can be understood and interpreted solely in terms of what God is doing with Abraham. But when we back up a little, we realize that the call of Abraham and the covenant God makes with him marks a turning point in the story, and everything that follows builds on it. From Genesis 12 to Exodus 2, the entire narrative revolves around understanding how God is faithful to his promise to Abraham. But then, in Exodus 2 with the birth of Moses, a new epoch dawns. God's people are now a nation defined by the Exodus events, and their relationship with God is put on a new footing. That relationship is outlined in the Mosaic covenant. The Abrahamic covenant isn't gone or revoked, as Paul will show in Galatians 3. But something new is happening, and subsequent stages of the story now have to take this new epoch into account in God's unfolding plan.

In pointing out different epochs, defined by different covenants that have different terms, I don't mean to say, as some old-school Dispensationalists said, that God saved people in different ways at different times. Nothing could be further from the truth. God doesn't change, and neither do his promises of salvation. Everyone who is saved is saved by faith in the gracious promises of God, to whatever extent he's revealed them at that point in history. And all of those promises find their fulfillment in the death and resurrection of Jesus Christ (2 Cor. 1:20). However, I do mean to say that the way God reveals that salvation does develop, like a seed growing into a tree. And recognizing where the passage you're studying fits in that development is crucial to its interpretation.

For example, Leviticus 17 forbids offering sacrifices anywhere but at the Tent of Meeting. You couldn't offer sacrifices just anywhere. But Genesis tells us that Abraham built an altar and offered sacrifices wherever he went. So was Abraham breaking the law of Leviticus 17? And, by the way, where do you offer your sacrifices these days?

You see my point. If we want to correctly understand the restriction of Leviticus 17, the freedom of Abraham, and the even greater freedom of the Christian, we need to understand each passage in its epochal context. Abraham was an alien and a stranger in Canaan; he had not yet received the Promised Land. Every time he built an altar, he was declaring in hope: this is God's land! Israel, on the other hand, came into possession of a land filled with local altars to every god imaginable. God wanted to make clear to every Israelite that they were a single people with only one God. Moreover, that one God had revealed exactly how and when and where he would be worshiped. Public worship would henceforth be an act that assembled the people in their unity as a nation of priests, rather than fragment and disperse them to worship however they saw fit. As Christians, we no longer sacrifice animals at all, for Christ was the perfect and final sacrifice, once and for all (Hebrews 10).

Epoch matters. It matters for interpretation. It matters even more for application.

Dividing the Epochs

How do we decide where one epoch ends and another begins? As I've said, the covenants serve as markers. But we have more help than that. The biblical authors point the way. The most obvious division occurs between the Old and New Testaments. In Romans 5, Paul speaks of the division of time before and after the giving of the Mosaic law, as well as the division before and after Adam's fall. In Galatians 3, he describes the Mosaic epoch as a caretaker period: it prepared, but did not actually deliver humanity to salvation. Peter marks a major division of world history at the flood in 2 Peter 3:6–7, and then goes on to look forward to yet another world still to come. In Acts 7, Stephen divides history into the epoch of the patriarchs, the Mosaic epoch, and the monarchy. In Isaiah 63–64, Isaiah contrasts the time of Abraham and the time of Moses with the exilic period, concluding with a prayer for another Sinai event in which God rends the heavens and comes down to redeem his people.

But not only do we need to understand the divisions, we also need to pay attention to the main themes and concerns of each epoch. The patriarchal period is very much concerned with faith in the promises of God. On the other hand, while not abandoning faith, the Mosaic period more clearly sounds the note of God's people as holy and distinct from the world. It also establishes the theme of judgment. The monarchy continues those themes, but adds another one—the Messiah King, the champion and representative of the nation. He so identifies with the people that it's not an overstatement to say, as the King goes, so goes the nation.

So, to summarize what we've covered so far—if we're going to understand a text of Scripture, we need to understand the words, sentences, and paragraphs through the grammatical-historical method. Once we've done that, we then have to ask the question, what covenant(s) governs God's people at this point? Answering that question will help us understand what epoch the text is in. Only at that point will we see how the text fits into God's revelation of himself up to that point in time, and how it functioned for the faith and obedience of God's people.

Canonical

There is one other horizon that we need to consider if we are going to understand a text in its full and complete context, and that's the canonical context. From Moses to John, the conviction of all the biblical authors is that God is faithful. He makes promises in one epoch and fulfills them in another. The fulfillment may look different than people expected, but there's fundamental continuity across the breadth of the story because God fulfills his Word.

It's the task of this final horizon of interpretation, this final contextual reading, to discern how it all fits together. Let's return to Genesis 15 and the covenant with Abraham. The textual horizon asks questions like: what's going on with cutting up animals, and what did this mean for Abraham? The epochal horizon asks questions like: how was this promise fulfilled and kept in the life of Isaac, Jacob, and Joseph, and how does it relate to the patriarchal family's departure for the land for Egypt and their eventual exodus? The canonical horizon asks question like: how does this promise relate to the new covenant established in Christ's blood? In just what sense are Christians the seed of Abraham and so participants in that promise? Should we expect an inheritance in Palestine, or does later revelation suggest that the land/rest promises are fulfilled in Christ some other way?

If we want to apply the Scriptures correctly to our lives, especially the Old Testament and the Gospels, then we must consider the canonical horizon. After all, we not only live in the New Testament age, as opposed to the Old Testament age, we live on the resurrection side of the cross. Why does that last distinction make a difference? Consider Luke 17:14, for example, where Jesus says to the ten lepers he healed, "Go, show yourselves to the priests." Regardless of what we think about miraculous healing today, we can't move directly from that text to our lives for the simple reason that we don't live under the Mosaic law for lepers, while Jesus and those men did.

But what the canonical horizon also means is that there is no way we can understand Jesus and the rest of the New Testament without understanding it in light of the Old. Jesus is repeatedly presented as a second Adam (Romans 5), a second Moses (Mark 6; John 5), a second David (Matthew 12), and a second Solomon (Luke 11). The salvation he brought is described as a second Exodus (Hebrews 12) and a return from exile (Luke 4); and the church is described as a living temple (1 Peter 2) and the Israel of God (Galatians 6). How are we going to understand and apply these New Testament texts if we haven't grappled with the canonical context, the story as a whole? By the same token, unless we have this larger context, the entire Old Testament is really nothing more than a bare chronology that gets us to Jesus. It's interesting history, if you're into that sort of thing, but is otherwise largely irrelevant. However, when you read the Old Testament with a canonical view, you begin to see that Jesus leaps off every page.

REMEMBER THIS

Putting it All Together

I want to conclude with a brief demonstration of how these three horizons come together as we look at a single text of Scripture. Let's use Psalm 18 for our example.

> I love you, O LORD, my strength. [2] The LORD is my rock, my fortress and my deliverer; my God is my rock, in whom I take refuge. He is my shield and the horn of my salvation, my stronghold. [3] I call to the LORD, who is worthy of praise, and I am saved from my enemies. [4] The cords of death entangled me; the torrents of destruction overwhelmed me. [5] The cords of the grave coiled around me; the snares of death confronted me. [6] In my distress I called to the LORD; I cried to my God for help. From his temple he heard my voice; my cry came before him, into his ears. [7] The earth trembled and quaked, and the foundations of the mountains shook; they trembled because he was angry. [8] Smoke rose from his nostrils; consuming fire came from his mouth, burning coals blazed out of it. [9] He parted the heavens and came down; dark clouds were under his feet. [10] He mounted the cherubim and flew; he soared on the wings of the wind. [11] He made darkness his covering, his canopy around him—the dark rain clouds of the sky. [12] Out of the brightness of his presence clouds advanced, with hailstones and bolts of lightning. [13] The LORD thundered from heaven; the voice of the Most High resounded. [14] He shot his arrows and scattered *the enemies*, great bolts of lightning and routed them. [15] The valleys of the sea were exposed and the foundations of the earth laid bare at your rebuke, O LORD, at the blast of breath from your nostrils. [16] He reached down from on high and took hold of me; he drew me out of deep waters. [17] He rescued me from my powerful

enemy, from my foes, who were too strong for me. [18] They confronted me in the day of my disaster, but the LORD was my support. [19] He brought me out into a spacious place; he rescued me because he delighted in me. [20] The LORD has dealt with me according to my righteousness; according to the cleanness of my hands he has rewarded me. [21] For I have kept the ways of the LORD; I have not done evil by turning from my God. [22] All his laws are before me; I have not turned away from his decrees. [23] I have been blameless before him and have kept myself from sin. [24] The LORD has rewarded me according to my righteousness, according to the cleanness of my hands in his sight. [25] To the faithful you show yourself faithful, to the blameless you show yourself blameless, [26] to the pure you show yourself pure, but to the crooked you show yourself shrewd. [27] You save the humble but bring low those whose eyes are haughty. [28] You, O LORD, keep my lamp burning; my God turns my darkness into light. [29] With your help I can advance against a troop; with my God I can scale a wall. [30] As for God, his way is perfect; the word of the LORD is flawless. He is a shield for all who take refuge in him. [31] For who is God besides the LORD? And who is the Rock except our God? [32] It is God who arms me with strength and makes my way perfect. [33] He makes my feet like the feet of a deer; he enables me to stand on the heights. [34] He trains my hands for battle; my arms can bend a bow of bronze. [35] You give me your shield of victory, and your right hand sustains me; you stoop down to make me great. [36] You broaden the path beneath me, so that my ankles do not turn. [37] I pursued my enemies and overtook them; I did not turn back till they were destroyed. [38] I crushed them so that they could not rise; they fell beneath my feet. [39] You armed me with strength for battle; you made my adversaries bow at my feet. [40] You made my enemies turn their backs in flight, and I destroyed my foes. [41] They cried for help, but there was no one to save them—to the LORD, but he did not answer. [42] I beat them as fine as dust borne on the wind; I poured them out like mud in the streets. [43] You have delivered me from the attacks of the people; you have made me the head of nations; people I did not know are subject to me. [44] As soon as they hear me, they obey me; foreigners cringe before me. [45] They all lose heart; they come trembling from their strongholds. [46] The LORD lives! Praise be to my Rock! Exalted be God my Savior! [47] He is the God who avenges me, who subdues nations under me, [48] who saves me from my enemies. You exalted me above my foes; from violent men you rescued me. [49] Therefore I will praise you among the nations, O LORD; I will sing praises to your name. [50] He gives his king great victories; he shows unfailing kindness to his anointed, to David and his descendants forever.

The psalm describes David's distress and God's deliverance of him. It begins with a summary statement of this theme and then describes David's agony and God's deliverance. The remainder of the psalm then meditates on why God delivered David, what this reveals about God's character, and how God has exalted him as king, to the praise of God's covenant faithfulness.

At the textual horizon we immediately notice the vivid imagery. David has been overwhelmed, like a man caught in a flood. But God has been faithful. Verses 4 and 5 give a clear example of Hebrew parallelism, the effect of which is to emphasize the extremity of David's plight and, therefore, the magnitude of God's salvation. At this level, the psalm is a song of personal thanks for deliverance from enemies and for success in his calling as king. If we stopped reading now, the Christian might be tempted to appropriate this psalm as a personal expression of thanksgiving when God brings us through our own trials. As we'll see, while this application is not entirely inappropriate, it frankly misses the main point of the psalm and therefore its main application.

At the epochal horizon, we can't help but notice in verses 6 to 19 that David draws on the imagery of God descending on Mount Sinai and other events from Exodus and the conquest. It seems a bit grandiose and poetic in the extreme, until we remember that during the monarchy, the king represented the nation, and he spoke of his relationship with God in those terms. David is not merely speaking as a private citizen of Israel. This also helps us understand his language of covenant faithfulness in verses 20 to 29. David is not claiming that he's personally sinless, but that he has been faithful to the covenant on behalf of the people. Also, his triumph over his enemies in verses 37 to 42 is clearly patterned after the image of holy war found in Joshua. So again, what we are hearing is not personal vindictiveness, but covenant faithfulness. Finally, verses 43 and beyond point past the Mosaic context to the Davidic covenant of 2 Samuel 7. David is rejoicing in the establishment of his throne, not out of personal pride, but in praise to the faithfulness of God, who keeps his promises. So, far from being merely a personal song of thanksgiving, this psalm is a testimony to the covenant faithfulness of God, who continues to save his people, as he did at the exodus, through the vindication of his anointed one.

At the canonical horizon, we see that this psalm is ultimately fulfilled in Jesus Christ, the anointed King who experienced the cords of the grave not just figuratively, but literally. And he was faithful not just to Moses' covenant, but God's covenant with Adam. Psalm 18 finds its truest sense on the lips of Jesus, who is literally God come down to save his people, but who accomplishes that salvation ironically, by suffering the pangs of death that they deserved. Yet like David before him, whose life he fulfills even as he surpasses it, Jesus is vindicated by God through his resurrection from the dead and his triumph over all his enemies. He has been crowned as King of the nations forever, and the day is soon coming when every knee will bow, and every tongue confess "that Jesus Christ is Lord, to the glory of God the

Father" (Phil. 2:10–11). Ultimately, Psalm 18 is not just David's personal song of praise, or Israel's national psalm of thanksgiving. It is a prophetic description of God's vindication of his Son and a prophetic promise that he will reign over the nations forever and ever. It is, in other words, a psalm through which we come to know Jesus, our Savior and our King.

The application of this psalm and its usefulness for Christian ministry certainly includes an encouragement to the Christian to thank God when he delivers us from our own mundane trials. But when read in light of the canon as a whole, we cannot stop at such a narrowly self-focused application. Instead, our eyes are drawn off ourselves, to Jesus, the sufferings he knew at the cross, and the deliverance he experienced in the resurrection. And we see that his suffering and his deliverance were not merely for our forgiveness, but to obtain a kingdom.

Only after having seen this do our eyes return to ourselves. But now we see ourselves differently, for we have been reminded that whatever trials we have experienced in this life, they are as nothing in comparison to the glorious deliverance from death that Jesus has accomplished for us. We're reminded that though we may know the opposition of men now, the day is coming when "the kingdom of the world [will] become the kingdom of our Lord and of his Christ" (Rev. 11:15). When we read the Bible in light of the whole, not only do the horizons of our interpretation expand, but our own horizons expand as well.

CHAPTER THREE

Biblical Theology Tools 2: Prophecy, Typology, and Continuity

How do you feel about preaching from the Old Testament? If you're like many evangelical pastors, chances are you feel a lot more comfortable in the Pauline epistles than you do in the minor prophets, and not just because you don't remember a lick of Hebrew from seminary. When was the last time you gave an evangelistic talk from the Old Testament rather than from one of the Gospels? If your answer is "Never," don't worry because you're not alone.

On the other hand, if you're asked to develop a six-week class on biblical leadership, can you think of a better text than Nehemiah? Or how about planning a weekend workshop on biblical money management? Sure, there are lots of texts to draw on, but the Proverbs would work well as a core resource, wouldn't they? And can you even imagine teaching a class on parenting that doesn't begin with Deuteronomy 6?

I think for most of us in church leadership, particularly those of us who teach, the Bible divides fairly neatly into those portions that proclaim the gospel and build up the church, and those portions that teach us how to live ethical, godly lives. And while there's some overlap between the two, that divide, for the most part, seems to run between the Old and New Testaments. There are a lot of reasons for this division—some historical and some theological. My point isn't to explain the phenomenon, but simply to comment on how pervasive it is. Recently I even heard one well-known Bible church pastor affirm that he never has and never intends to preach from the Old Testament on Sunday morning, for the simple reason that he's a gospel preacher. The Old Testament is reserved in his church for Sunday evenings and other contexts.

I applaud his commitment to being a gospel preacher, and yet I cannot help but wonder at his assumption—shared with so many evangelical church leaders—that gospel preaching and teaching means New Testament preaching and teaching. To begin with, God gave us the whole Bible, not just the New Testament. Surely he meant the first three-quarters of the Bible to be used for more than moral stories and historical background? Even more to the point, Jesus and the apostles did their entire gospel preaching from the Old Testament. Of course, they also wrote the New Testament as a result. But I'm convinced that their gospel preaching from the Old Testament wasn't merely because they hadn't yet written the New Testament. I think they were able to preach the gospel from the Law and the Prophets because that's what they found there. My goal in this chapter is to help us find it there too, and so recover the whole Bible for gospel teaching.

In the previous chapter, we considered the details of the story, the various covenants and the epochs they formed. But how do we put the details together? What tools help us read the story as a single story about Christ and the gospel?

First of all, in saying that we can find the gospel in the Old Testament, I don't mean to say the New Testament is unnecessary. As Hebrews 1:2 says, "In these last days, God has spoken to us *by His Son*." The point is that this revelation is definitive and final. Peter tells us that through the revelation of Christ, "we have the word of the prophets *made more certain*" (2 Pet. 1:19). And yet, isn't it interesting that Peter connects the revelation of Christ to the word of the prophets? And isn't it significant that the book of Hebrews goes on to explain Christ through an extended sermon on the Pentateuch? What both authors are illustrating is that in the Old Testament we have the gospel promised, the gospel foretold, the gospel in seed form. In the New Testament that seed comes into full flower, as the promises are kept and the prophecies are fulfilled.

The relationship between the promises made in the Old Testament and the promises kept in the New Testament brings us to the crucial problem we face if we are to read all of Scripture as Christian Scripture: how do we understand the biblical dynamic of prophetic promise and prophetic fulfillment? Understanding this relationship, and getting it right, is what allows us to read and teach every text as something written not just for those people back then, but for us today as well. It's what allows us to affirm that Paul had not just the New Testament, but the Old Testament in mind when he said, "all Scripture is God-breathed, and is useful for teaching, rebuking, correcting, and training in righteousness" (2 Tim. 3:16). He even meant the genealogies and lists.

The Prophetic Character of Scripture: Promise-Fulfillment

You cannot read far in the Bible before encountering one of the most fundamental characteristics of God's self-revelation. Not only is God a speaking God, he is a promise-making God. From the promise of judgment in Genesis 2:17 to the promise of salvation through judgment in Genesis 3:15, through the promises made to Noah and Abraham, Moses and David, right through to Jesus' final words to his disciples before he ascended to heaven in Matthew 28:20, God makes promises to his people.

God Keeps His Promises

Now if God were like us, all this promise-making would be nothing more than a curiosity. In fact, God is not like us. He always keeps his promises. And this conviction of God's faithfulness underlies the biblical authors' frame of mind as they write. They understand themselves not only to be recording the oracles and promises of God, but they also understand themselves to be witnesses to God's faithfulness in fulfilling those promises. And that same perspective gives them faith and hope concerning promises yet to be fulfilled, a faith to which they call us as well.

Here, in the character of God, is the glue that holds the diverse parts of the canon together; and trust in that glue allowed the biblical writers to write—and us to read—the Bible expecting that promises once made already are, or will someday be, promises kept.

God Fulfills His Plans According to a Pattern

There are several things we need to understand about God's promises. First, his promises are not simply random good intentions. Rather, God's promises together point to and delineate a divine plan for history—a plan to rescue a people for the praise of his glory, and to effect that rescue, that salvation, through a judgment that God himself would bear on our behalf. In other words, history is not cyclical, a "mere repetition" of archetypal patterns.[1] Rather, history is heading somewhere. It's linear. It's developing and progressing toward an end that God has already prepared.

Second, God's plans are fulfilled according to various patterns. In other

---

[1]Richard Lints, *The Fabric of Theology: A Prolegomenon to Evangelical Theology* (Grand Rapids, MI: Eerdmans, 1993), 303.

words, the linear nature of history doesn't mean it's unpredictable. There is one God and one plan to solve one problem with one solution. History, as Scripture presents it, follows a pattern or framework. It progresses and develops, but not randomly. God works out his *plans*, yes, but since his ways do not change he works out his plans according to certain *patterns*. This means that the present is tied to the past in Scripture, but not as an endlessly repeating cycle of karma. Rather the connection between past and present is more like the development of a Bach fugue or the construction of a soaring skyscraper. The initial theme, the original shape, is present from the beginning. But by the end, it has been developed so that the finished product is so much more than the initial pattern seemed to promise.

Let me illustrate what I mean. In Genesis 2:17 God promised that sin would bring death, which it did beginning with Adam and Eve's sin. Gratefully, God also promised to save the woman and her seed in Genesis 3:15. How would he save? In due time, God would give his people the system of animal sacrifice as an atoning substitute for their sin, which we see happening with Abraham and Isaac in Genesis 22, with the Passover night in Egypt in Exodus 11–12, and with the whole system of Levitical sacrifices. (Martin Luther thought it was even evident in the death of the animals that provided the clothing for Adam and Eve in Genesis 3:21.) But wait a second: do you see the pattern at work here? There's a promise to judge and the promise to save, but to fulfill these promises God established a pattern of death for sin unless a substitute is offered. Ultimately, however, the pattern and plan are both fulfilled in the atoning sacrifice of Jesus Christ on the cross. There, as Hebrews 9 tells us, a better sacrifice was offered, one that does not need to be repeated because it was perfect and sufficient. At the cross, then, God's *plan* of salvation is accomplished and fulfilled, but so is the *pattern* of sacrifice that gives meaning to the plan. Animal sacrifices and all that surrounded them cease in the New Testament church, not simply because they are not necessary, but because they have been fulfilled in Christ. The implicit promise that a substitute would be provided for God's people has been kept.

Multiple Horizons of Fulfillment

The character of Scripture as recording a redemptive history that's both linear and that proceeds according to a pattern helps us recognize that God's promises (prophecies in the broadest sense of the term) typically have multiple horizons of fulfillment. What's more, each successive fulfillment occurs not only later in time chronologically, but is greater in significance both theologically and historically (see chart 3.1).

Chart 3.1: Multiple Horizons of Prophetic Fulfillment

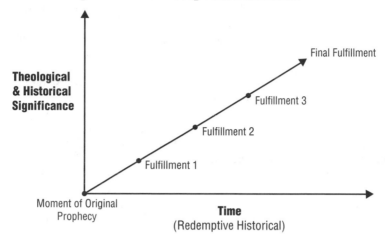

This pattern of fulfillment does at least two things for us as we try to read the Bible canonically. On the one hand, the various fulfillments help us see the way in which the pattern is developing and the plan is progressing. On the other hand, the various fulfillments help us to be sensitive to the distinct epochal emphases along the way, helping to safeguard us against hoping in the wrong fulfillment for our own epoch.

Let me give an example that illustrates both the multiple horizons and the ever-greater character of God's promise-keeping. Consider God's promise to Abraham in Genesis 12:1–3.

> The LORD had said to Abram, "Leave your country, your people and your father's household and go to the land I will show you. I will make you into a great nation and I will bless you; I will make your name great, and you will be a blessing. I will bless those who bless you, and whoever curses you I will curse; and all peoples on earth will be blessed through you."

God promises that childless Abram will be the father of a great nation that will bless the nations of the earth. A few verses later, in Genesis 12:7, God promises to give Abram's offspring the land of Canaan. So those are the promises. Got them in your head? Now, watch how God keeps his promises as redemptive history unfolds:

- The promise of descendants and a great nation begins to be fulfilled with the miraculous birth of Isaac, and then takes on steam with Jacob and his twelve sons. Centuries then pass, but God isn't done fulfilling his promise.

- A new epoch dawns with Moses and the covenant of Sinai. And there Israel, the descendants of Abraham, is constituted by God, not simply as Abraham's family, but as a nation holy to God. The book of Joshua then records the first fulfillment of God's promise concerning the land, as the nation goes in and conquers. But God still isn't done.
- Both the promise of land and the promise to be a blessing to other nations finds yet further and greater fulfillment under King Solomon. Under Solomon, we see the nations being blessed by his wisdom, and we see for the first time the entire Promised Land, from the Euphrates to the Mediterranean Sea, from Lebanon to the Sinai, under Israel's control. There is rest on every side. But God *still* isn't done.
- As Paul makes clear in Galatians and Romans, the true promised offspring wasn't Isaac or Jacob or David or Solomon. It was Jesus. And through faith in Jesus, men and women from every nation are blessed, as they become children of Abraham. This spiritual family is also a spiritual nation (1 Pet. 2:9) that spreads to the very ends of the earth. And yet, like Abraham, this nation is once again homeless, living as aliens and strangers in the world (Hebrews 11). If the pattern of fulfillment is to hold true, we know that there must be yet more. Even after the cross and resurrection, even after Pentecost and the spread of the gospel throughout the world, God still isn't done.
- In fact, there is more. According to Hebrews 4 and Revelation 21–22, the promises of a great nation in the land under God's blessing and rule find their final fulfillment in a new heaven and new earth, in which all the people of God, both Old Testament and New, form one new humanity (Eph. 2:14–22) in God's perfect new creation (see chart 3.2).

Chart 3.2: An Illustration of How Prophecy is Fulfilled Over Multiple Horizons

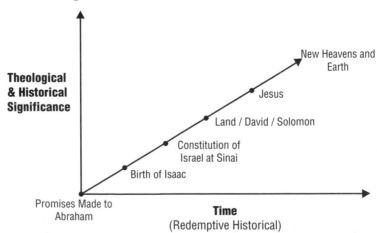

So I ask you, how many times was the promise to Abram in Genesis 12

fulfilled by God? I'm not known for my math skills, but I count at least five times, all clearly identified in Scripture. Each is a real fulfillment, and each is greater than the one before.

Typology

But there is more to the prophetic character of Scripture than the direct fulfillment of spoken promises. God not only speaks, he is also the Lord of history. This means that God providentially orders events and individual lives so that they serve to prefigure what is yet to come. The Scriptures therefore record the lives of real people and the course of real events, and yet these people and events serve as historical analogies that correspond to future fulfillment.

What Types Are and What They Are Not

The biblical language for this is "types," which simply means "pattern" or "example."[2] One theologian describes it this way: "Typology is simply symbolism with a prospective reference to fulfillment in a later epoch of biblical history. It involves a fundamentally organic relation between events, persons, and institutions (type) in one epoch and their counterparts (antitype) in later epochs."[3]

But to refer to types as symbols doesn't mean that they are nothing more than fanciful, arbitrary allegories or vague expressions of general truths. Someone might allegorize the parable of the Good Samaritan, for instance, by saying that the inn is the church, the innkeeper is Paul, and the oil and wine are the sacraments. In other words, arbitrary connections are made between symbols and the things symbolized. With a biblical understanding of types, on the other hand, there is an organic "relationship between some 'essential' aspect of the type and antitype."[4] What's more, unlike a fable, the type wasn't invented by the author in order to make a symbolic point. Rather, a type is an actual historical person or event that God has providentially ordered in order to use that person or event to point beyond himself or herself. In the type-anti-type relationship, there is a comparison of *historical* realities that establish an analogy or pattern, which then organically develops and expands.

Again, let's consider an example from Scripture. In Romans 5, Paul is

---

[2]A good, basic introduction to this idea can be found in David L. Baker, *Two Testaments, One Bible: A Study of the Theological Relationship Between the Old and New Testaments*, rev. ed. (Downers Grove, IL: InterVarsity Press, 1991), 185–189.
[3]Lints, 304.
[4]Ibid., 304n17.

concerned to explain how it is that Christ's obedience to death on the cross could bring the gift of life to sinners like us. In Romans 5:14, he refers to Adam as a pattern or type of Christ:

> Nevertheless, death reigned from the time of Adam to the time of Moses, even over those who did not sin by breaking a command, as did Adam, who was a pattern [type] of the one to come.

This is no random coincidence or arbitrary imposition of Paul's on the accidents of history. Paul is asserting that God set the whole thing up. And it's on this typological foundation, Paul says, that the gospel hinges. Here's how he develops the point in the next verses.

> But the gift is not like the trespass. For if the many died by the trespass of the one man, how much more did God's grace and the gift that came by the grace of the one man, Jesus Christ, overflow to the many! Again, the gift of God is not like the result of the one man's sin: The judgment followed one sin and brought condemnation, but the gift followed many trespasses and brought justification. For if, by the trespass of the one man, death reigned through that one man, how much more will those who receive God's abundant provision of grace and of the gift of righteousness reign in life through the one man, Jesus Christ.

Just as Adam represented the human race, and so brought the whole race into condemnation through his act of disobedience, Paul says that Christ, the second Adam, stood as a federal representative too. But instead of rebelling against God, Christ obeyed. And his obedience now brings life and forgiveness for those who are in Christ.

Paul is not simply drawing a comparison or allegorizing Adam. He's arguing for a historical correspondence in which the type, Adam, points forward to and finds its redemptive fulfillment in the antitype, Christ. The former helps us to understand and even defines for us the work and meaning of the latter. But Christ is not merely a repetition of Adam. Like the multiple horizons we saw earlier, the fulfillment in the antitype involves a difference in degree. The type points forward to something greater than itself! (See chart 3.3.)

We could multiply the examples—Moses, Joshua, David, Solomon, Samson, and Jonah, just to name a few. All of these, in one way or another, serve as types of Christ, and are explicitly identified in the Scriptures as pointers to Christ. By making these connections, the epochs of the past are linked to the present by the New Testament authors, and vice versa. Types literally stitch the Bible together as a single narrative.

Chart 3.3: Typological Fulfillment

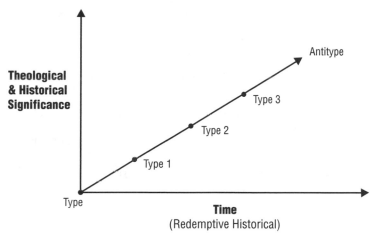

But it's not just the New Testament that uses typology. The Old Testament explains itself in these terms as well. In the prophets, for example, the Babylonian captivity and subsequent return from exile are repeatedly explained in terms of the exodus (e.g., Isaiah 49 and Jeremiah 16). Even more significantly, Jesus' redemptive activity in the Gospels, together with the apostles' proclamation of Christ, are explained as a second exodus (e.g., Mark 6 and 2 Corinthians 3). Like God's prophetic promises, the type in Scripture often finds its fulfillment in multiple antitypes, each pointing beyond itself to one still greater that is yet to come. And that's true until we get to Jesus, who declared that he was the fulfillment and the point of the Law and the prophets (Matt. 5:17; Luke 24:27).

How to Identify Types

Are there any restraints on identifying types? Yes, there are. Are there any interpretive rules for recognizing and interpreting the relationship between type and anti-type across the epochs of Scripture? Yes, there are. Of course, sometimes, the biblical writers themselves make the connection between type and antitype. That's what most of the book of Hebrews is doing, as it explains how the Old Testament temple, priesthood, and sacrificial system all pointed as types to Christ. It's what Paul does in Romans 5 and 1 Corinthians 10. Once a biblical author makes a typological connection explicit in one text, it's fair to see that connection in every instance of the type.

But do we have any basis for recognizing types not explicitly identified by a biblical author? I think we do, but only when we follow the pattern already set by Scripture itself. Pastor and scholar Gordon Hugenberger, following Louis Berkhof, has offered the following guidelines:[5]

1) There must be a real, historical, and essential resemblance or analogy between the type and antitype.
   EXAMPLE: King David, who was really God's anointed king over his Old Testament people, and King Jesus, who is the King of kings, God's anointed King over his universal people. Jesus is descended from David and heir to the promises of the Davidic covenant in 2 Samuel 7.

2) The type must be providentially designed to foreshadow God's ultimate redemptive activity in Christ. This means that accidental or even thematic similarity is not enough to make a type/antitype connection. "There must be some Scriptural evidence that it was so designed by God."
   EXAMPLE: Balaam's ass rebukes a false teacher. Jesus rebukes false teachers. But this by itself doesn't make Balaam's ass a type of Christ. The point of the donkey speaking in Numbers 22 is to highlight Balaam's obtuseness, rather than in some obscure way to point forward to Jesus.

3) Unlike a mere symbol, which represents a general truth or idea, a type by its very nature must look forward to its specific and greater fulfillment in the anti-type.
   EXAMPLE: In the Old Testament, blood is a symbol for life in general. Christ gives life, but blood isn't a type of Christ. It remains a symbol for life. However, the sacrificial lamb, whose blood is shed as a substitute for the sinner, is a type. This is because, as Hebrews points out, the type pointed forward to a greater sacrifice, one that would be truly effective and finally sufficient.

How to Move and Not Move from Text to Application

One other benefit of understanding typology is that it keeps us from moralizing and allegorizing the Old Testament. Every time we interpret an Old Testament text, we basically have four options for application. Our first option is to decide there is no application. This text was for "them" alone. It should already be clear that I don't think this is usually an option. The other three options are moralism, allegory, and typology. I've tried to graphically represent these three options in the illustrations that follow. I was introduced to this as Clowney's Rectangle,[6] and I've used it repeatedly over the years to demonstrate just how rooted in the text typology is.

Too often, we move directly from Old Testament type to personal appli-

---

[5]Gordon Hugenberger, "Introductory Notes on Typology," in G.K. Beale, ed., *The Right Doctrine from the Wrong Texts? Essays on the Use of the Old Testament in the New* (Grand Rapids, MI: Baker, 1994), 338.
[6]Ibid. It's a reference to Edmund Clowney, who first drew something like this for Gordon Hugenberger, who taught it to me. It has since been published in Hugenberger, 339–341.

cation by way of moralism. For example, David and Goliath becomes a morality tale on finding courage in God. No attempt is made to understand the text in its original context, or to relate it to Christ. The movement is direct from Old Testament text to contemporary application (see chart 3.4).

Chart 3.4: Moralism and Personal Application

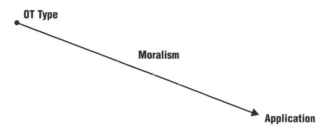

More common in the Middle Ages, but not unheard of today, is the approach of allegory. In that case, we start with preconceived ideas of application, and then turn the details of the Old Testament story into symbols that represent our application. For example, David's five smooth stones in his battle with Goliath become the five tools of a faithful pastor: Scripture, prayer, the sacraments, and two other things you think would be useful for a pastor to focus on! The movement is from today back to the text via arbitrary symbols that the original readers would not have recognized as significant (see chart 3.5).

Chart 3.5: Allegory and Personal Application

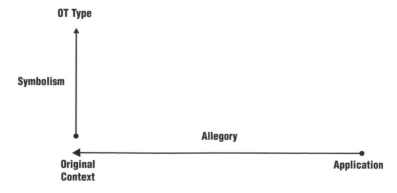

Typology actually safeguards us from moralism and allegory, as well as assuring us that the Old Testament was not written just for "them." This is because it starts with the Old Testament and seeks to understand the significance of the type in its original context, and in terms that would have been significant to the original readers. Then it moves not to us, but to the type's fulfillment in Christ and his redemptive work as the antitype. Only then does typology make the move to contemporary application (see chart 3.6).

Chart 3.6: Typology and Personal Application

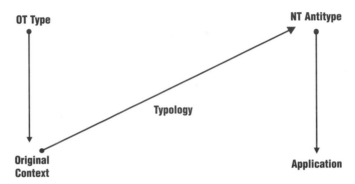

The story of David and Goliath therefore is neither an allegory on pastoral leadership nor a morality tale on courage, nor an interesting but finally useless bit of ancient history. Rather, this real Old Testament event gives us insight into what Christ accomplished for us in our salvation, as God's anointed but veiled king, a mediator who delivers God's people through individual mortal combat with our greatest enemy. The primary point of application thus moves from moral effort on our part to worship and faith in Christ our champion!

Continuity and Discontinuity

So far I've been stressing the fundamental unity of the grand narrative of Scripture, as prophetic promises are kept and as types are fulfilled in antitypes. But if you've been paying attention, I've also repeatedly mentioned that this movement from promise made to promise kept, from type to antitype, is an organic movement in which the fulfillment is always greater than the original promise or type.

However, the difference between promise and fulfillment cannot simply be explained as a difference of degree. Despite the continuity of the story of God's saving plan and actions, the movement from promise to fulfillment is described in Scripture as the movement between shadow and reality (Col.

2:17), between a mere copy and the genuine article (Heb. 8:5). What this means is that, in addition to continuity, there is significant discontinuity as we move across the epochs from one horizon of fulfillment to another.

Sometimes the discontinuity that we encounter is required to ultimately fulfill the promise. For example, in 2 Samuel 7, God promises David that a son from his own body will sit on his throne forever. In its original context, that could easily be taken to mean an unending dynasty. But in its ultimate fulfillment, the promised son is not only the descendant of David, but the eternal Son of God, incarnate of the Virgin Mary, resurrected to an immortal body, and given an eternal dominion as the ascended King, enthroned at the right hand of God the Father. It turns out that the promise of an unending dynasty is finally fulfilled through the reign of an undying King!

In other cases, the discontinuity itself is the fulfillment of the promise. For example, in Jeremiah's prophecy of the new covenant, Jeremiah explicitly says, "It will not be like the covenant I made with their forefathers, when I led them by the hand out of Egypt" (Jer. 31:32). How will it be different? For one thing, it will be unbreakable (v. 32). For another, all the members of that covenant will be regenerate, the law written on their hearts (v. 33). Yet another difference will be that the covenant will not operate according to natural lines of birth and descent, but through spiritual birth (vv. 29–30).

Here the discontinuity between the new covenant and the Mosaic covenant is enormous: a covenant of grace, not works; a covenant that regenerates rather than kills; a covenant entered into through spiritual rather than natural birth. And yet for all this discontinuity, Jeremiah is clear that this new covenant is the ultimate fulfillment of God's promises to Israel, made to their forefather Abraham.

How do we make sense of discontinuity? The New Testament gives us the key. On the one hand, the old covenant could not bring life (Gal. 3:21). It was not effective. And so a better, more effective covenant had to be made. On the other hand, the new covenant is not just more effective, it's superior because it's the real thing. As glorious as the Old Covenant was, Jesus is superior to Moses, and the covenant in his blood is superior to that of a covenant sealed with the blood of animals (see Hebrews 9). These things were simply shadows that pointed to the real thing. Jesus fulfills all that came before and in doing so reveals the fullness of the glory of God. He is the ultimate and final Word of God, because he is the true High Priest and the true Lamb of God. He is superior because he is the true temple, where God and man actually meet. He is superior because he brings us into the true rest of God, an eternal rest, not in Palestine, but in the new creation itself.

When we consider the grand sweep of redemptive history, we realize that, were there no discontinuity between promise and fulfillment, our basis for hope in the midst of the trials and tribulations of this world would disappear. As Paul says, "If only for this life we have hope in Christ, we are to be pitied more than all men" (1 Cor. 15:19). But that is not our condition. Aaron's line of priests points to Christ, but Jesus does not descend from that line. Why? That line failed. The sacrifices they offered did not bring life. The covenant they mediated could not save. Instead, as Hebrews declares, "on the basis of the power of an indestructible life . . . [Jesus is] declared a priest forever, in the order of Melchizedek" and on the basis of his priesthood, "we draw near to God" (Heb. 7:16–19). Praise God that he keeps his promises, and praise God that he keeps them even better than we expected, or could even have imagined!

Conclusion

We've covered a lot of ground in the last two chapters, and some of it has been pretty rough terrain. So it's time to take a break and see how far we've come toward constructing a biblical theology that is truly useful for pastoral ministry. I started this chapter by asking you to think about how you approach the Old and New Testaments. The main take-away at this point I hope is obvious. The tools of biblical theology give your whole Bible back to you—from Genesis to Revelation—as a powerful source for profoundly Christian preaching and teaching. For example, I'm getting ready to preach through the book of Numbers at my church. The title of the series is "Marching toward Heaven/Wandering on Earth." And my first sermon is confined to Numbers 1 to 10. That's right—the lists, the order of encampment and marching, and the laws of purity. How do you preach a Christian sermon on material like that? You do it only when you recognize the typological correspondence between Moses and Christ, and between Israel and the Church. Hebrews 4, 1 Corinthians 10, and many other passages should inform our interpretive approach. Therefore, we can recognize that these things were written down, not to teach us how to draw up a battle plan for Armageddon, but to point us to Christ and the victory he has won on our behalf—a victory that gains for his people far more than Middle Eastern real estate, but heaven itself.

But I also want you to see that the tools of biblical theology not only give you a whole Bible to preach from, they give you a whole Bible to do all of ministry from. So when a church member comes to your office, struggling with fear, you can turn to the story of David and Goliath. But instead of using David as a moral club to urge them to courage, which will probably just make them feel guilty, you use David to point them to Christ, who has overcome their fiercest enemy of sin and death. Or when a teenager comes to you with questions about sexual purity, you can take them to the story of David and Bathsheba. But instead of using the story's horrible consequences as a scare tactic to demand purity, you can explain to them that David's failure, like our own, points to the need for a better King, one who does not fail, but then who uses his purity to rescue us from our own impurity. In the gospel context of David's failure and Christ's righteousness, you can explain the incredible privilege we have in the church to be the bride of Christ, and so to use our bodies, whether in singleness or marriage, as a display of Christ's pure and exclusive love for his people.

Biblical theology is practical theology, because it gives us the whole Bible to use as God intended it: gospel-centered, Christ-exalting, life-transforming Scripture. It doesn't get any more practical, any more useful, than that.

CHAPTER FOUR

Biblical & Systematic Theology: Do We Really Need Both?

In the first three chapters we've considered some of the specific tools for building a biblical theology. We've tackled the topics of

- *exegesis*, and reading a text in context.
- *genre*, and the impact various literary forms have on meaning and interpretation.
- *the covenants* of Scripture and the structure they give to the Bible, both historically and theologically.
- *the various horizons of interpretation* at the level of text, epoch, and canon.
- the glue that holds the whole story together—the *prophetic nature of Scripture* and its *dynamic of promise and fulfillment*.
- *typology*, which is grounded in the providentially prophetic ordering of history itself.
- *the tension between continuity and discontinuity* as God's revelation progressively and yet organically unfolds and develops from seed form to full flower.

Our Work Isn't Over

We've done a lot of work, and it's tempting to think that our preparation is over and we're ready to start building. If we put all these tools to work, so that we come to understand the story of the whole Bible and how each part relates to the others and culminates in Christ, won't we have a faithful biblical theology? Won't we have what we need in order to live faithful lives in light of the biblical story and help others do the same? No, we won't. We need systematic theology as well as biblical theology if we're going to construct something that's really useful for ministry.

There are some who believe systematic theology is not only unnecessary, but downright unhelpful. Take Rob Bell's *Velvet Elvis*.[1] Throughout

---

[1]Rob Bell, *Velvet Elvis: Repainting the Christian Faith* (Grand Rapids, MI: Zondervan, 2005).

the book, Rob affirms much of orthodox Christianity. But it's also clear that he is far more comfortable with the category of "meaningful story" than he is with the category of "propositional truth." For Bell and many others in the emerging, postmodern mind-set, the idea of propositional truth is offensive. It's so narrow, so static, so final. And nothing else needs to be said on the matter. In contrast, they point to the open, dynamic, and relational character of story. Story conveys truth and meaning, but it also invites you in and asks you to respond, so that your response becomes part of the significance of the story. The same story can be heard by different people in different ways at different times, and doesn't require that one be better or more right than the others. In fact, it's said that story and narrative, unlike propositions, produce a conversation that leads to new and further insights. On the other hand, propositions go nowhere and generally produce argument, division, and oppression, as I try to force you to agree with me and you do the same to me.

This is why Bell titled his book *Velvet Elvis*. It's a book about Jesus, the gospel, and the Christian life. But just as no velvet Elvis painter thinks he's produced the definitive portrait of Elvis, so Bell's not claiming to say anything definitive about Jesus or the Christian life. It's just his perspective, and he's inviting you to bring your perspective to the conversation too.[2] It sounds pretty humble, and if you have an intellectual temperament like mine, it sounds downright attractive.

If Rob Bell's *Velvet Elvis* captures something about our cultural context, which I think it does, you can imagine why biblical theology is often preferred over and against systematic theology. Biblical theology is all about the story of the Bible as a whole. Systematic theology, which is about drawing propositions out of that story, is thought of as narrow and dogmatic. Lots of folks these days are fond of pointing out that God didn't reveal himself to us in a systematic theology, but through history. They point out that the majority of the Bible is narrative and that many of the concerns of systematic theology seem distant from the texts of Scripture themselves. So, it's said, we don't come to know and understand God by memorizing his attributes as outlined by systematic theology. We come to know and understand him by encountering him in the stories of the exodus and the exile, stories that allow us to experience his power, his faithfulness, his love, and his terrible wrath.

Well, as attractive as this sounds, and despite the fact that there is some truth in what's being said, it has been the conviction of Christians

---

[2]Ibid., 10–14.

since "Day One" that biblical theology is not enough if we are to know God and live lives that are faithful to his self-revelation in the Bible. Even if you've never thought about this question before, you experience the need for systematic theology every day in ministry. It's systematic theology that you draw on when you

- need to counsel a pregnant teenager to keep her child rather than abort.
- teach on our responsibility to be good stewards of the world God made.
- comfort parents whose adult child has abandoned the faith he was raised in.
- train other church leaders in how the local church should be organized and governed.
- explain to a visitor that Jesus intends us to be members of local churches, and not just the universal church.
- explain what baptism and the Lord's Supper mean.
- explain to the local chairman of the Republican/Democratic party why he can't have ten minutes to address your members at the next business meeting.
- need to help your elders think through what it means to love the illegal immigrant neighbors in your town.

You see what I mean. I could make that list go on almost forever. All of these are questions that we face all of the time, and yet there's not a simple narrative in the Bible that we can turn to for an answer. No, if we're to have a theology that is biblical and that can be applied to all of life and every area of human thought and endeavor, we'll need more than just the tools of biblical theology. We'll need the tools of systematic theology, too.

How Biblical and Systematic Theology Relate

Before we go any further, we need to establish some definitions. What is biblical theology? What is systematic theology? How are they similar? How are they different? How should we think about relating the two of them together?

Biblical Theology

We'll start with biblical theology, since that's what we've been talking about, more or less, since the Introduction. I've already said that biblical theology is not only concerned with what the Bible teaches, but how that teaching is progressively revealed and progressively develops over the course of history. Now it's time for a more precise and formal definition. If it only it were that easy. If you look up the history of the term, you'll find that almost as much has been written about what biblical theology is as there has been biblical theology written.

I'm not going to bother with the definitions that are largely confined to scholarly debate and the academy. If that's of interest to you, you should invest in the *New Dictionary of Biblical Theology*.[3] Instead, let me offer you a few that seem to cover the waterfront among those who hold to a high view of Scripture. Each of them tells us something important about what biblical theology is.

The grandfather of biblical theology amongst evangelicals, Geerhardus Vos, defined it this way: "Biblical Theology is that branch of Exegetical Theology which deals with the process of the self-revelation of God deposited in the Bible."[4] So what does that mean? It means that biblical theology does not focus on the sixty-six books of the Bible—"the finished product of [God's self-revelation]," but on the actual "divine activity" of God as it unfolds in history (and is recorded in those sixty-six books). This definition of biblical theology tells us that revelation is first what God says and does in history, and only secondarily what he's given us in book form. That means that one of the fundamental characteristics of biblical theology is that its principle of organization is historical. Biblical theology moves along the axis of redemptive history. It's particularly concerned with development and therefore with questions of continuity and discontinuity, the movement from seed to tree.

Here's another definition. Don Carson says that "biblical theology . . . seeks to uncover and articulate the unity of all the biblical texts taken together, resorting primarily to the categories of those texts themselves."[5] So what does that mean? It means that biblical theology is particularly concerned with the diverse literary and historical contexts of the story, and so attempts to relate the meaning of the story in the terms of the story itself. For example, biblical theology traces out the development of sacrifice and covenant, not because those are particularly relevant contemporary terms, but because these are the terms and agenda that the story itself gives us. As Tom Schreiner has summarized, biblical theology "asks what themes are central to the biblical writers in their historical context, and attempts to discern the coherence of such themes."[6]

---

[3]T. Desmond Alexander, Brian S. Rosner, D. A. Carson, Graeme Goldsworthy, eds., *New Dictionary of Biblical Theology* (Downers Grove, IL: InterVarsity Press, 2000).
[4]Quoted in Vern Poythress, "Kinds of Biblical Theology," *Westminster Journal of Theology* 70 (2008): 130.
[5]D. A. Carson, "Systematic Theology and Biblical Theology," in *NDBT*, 100.
[6]Thomas Schreiner, "Preaching and Biblical Theology," *The Southern Baptist Journal of Theology* 10 (2006): 22.

Here's one more definition. Steve Wellum says that biblical theology "contends that to read the Bible as unified Scripture is *not* just one interpretive option among others, but that which best corresponds to the nature of the text itself, given its divine inspiration. As such, [biblical theology], as a discipline, not only provides the basis for understanding how texts in one part of Scripture relate to all other texts, but it also serves as the basis and underpinning for all theologizing. . . . "[7] What's the point of this definition? It means that biblical theology is interested not merely in the fact of prophetic promise and fulfillment, type and antitype, but in the demonstration of these things so that, despite the diversity of literature, history, and human author, the reality of a single story emanating from a single Divine mind according to a single divine and sovereign will is plain for all to see. As Don Carson rightly observes, this means that, like systematic theology, biblical theology is not merely descriptive. Rather it is making "synthetic assertions about the nature, will, and plan of God in creation and redemption, including therefore also the nature, purpose, and 'story' of humanity."[8]

As you can see, none of these definitions are mutually exclusive, but each of them emphasizes a different aspect of what we call biblical theology. Perhaps the best way forward is to stick with the simplest definition I've come across (because it's my own). Biblical theology is the attempt to tell the whole story of the whole Bible as Christian Scripture. It's a story, therefore, that has an authoritative and normative claim on our lives, because it's the story of God's glory in salvation through judgment.

Systematic Theology

What about systematic theology? A definition comes a little bit easier this time.

Perhaps the simplest definition is what I use when I teach this topic in the classroom. Systematic theology is *the attempt to summarize in an orderly and comprehensive manner what the whole Bible has to say about any given topic.* In other words, systematic theology isn't concerned with how a topic is developed over time or across the history of the Bible. It's concerned to take all that's said on the topic, collect it, collate it, relate it, and then comprehensively summarize it. Systematic theology isn't concerned with the storyline so much as it's concerned with the bottom line.

But of course, systematic theology does more than summarize the Bible's teaching on random topics. If the topics were random, we might call

---

[7]Stephen J. Wellum, "Editorial: Preaching and Teaching the Whole Counsel of God," *SBJT* 10 (2006): 2–3.
[8]Carson, *NDBT*, 100.

it disorganized theology.[9] Traditionally, systematic theology has sought to organize the topics themselves, making sure that all the major and most of the minor topics of Scripture are covered, and then relate the topics to each other logically, so that an entire system of thought is established. In that sense, systematic theology is not an encyclopedia of the Bible, giving us articles on every topic imaginable. Instead, it's an attempt to make explicit what we might call the Bible's worldview.[10] When such a framework for understanding who God is, who we are, where we came from, and where we're heading is in place, it quickly becomes apparent that systematic theology allows us to think biblically about all sorts of things that the Bible does not directly address. So, for example, what does the Bible teach about psychology, about electrical engineering, or about the social welfare state? Well, nothing directly. But it teaches quite a bit indirectly, because the Bible, through systematic theology, gives us a worldview through which we can think through those issues.

We can go even one step further. Systematic theology not only summarizes the Bible's teaching on any given topic, and then organizes those topics into a coherent framework or worldview, but it also seeks to formulate those summaries into precise and accurate doctrines that define the boundary between truth and error, between orthodoxy (right belief) and heresy. Systematic theology seeks to make normative statements. Here's an example from Wayne Grudem: the statement that "the Bible says that everyone who believes in Jesus Christ will be saved" is a "perfectly true summary" of the Bible's teaching on salvation.[11] But if that's all we have to say on that topic, then everyone from evangelicals to Roman Catholics, Mormons, and thoughtful Muslims can line up behind that statement. Why? Because we haven't said what faith is, who Jesus Christ is, what salvation is, what we're being saved from and to, and what it means to believe in Jesus. To protect against error and to communicate the truth that actually saves, systematic theology goes beyond general summaries to precise and detailed doctrinal formulations. This isn't an effort to improve the Bible, but to be fully faithful to what the Bible teaches.

Finally, systematic theology not only summarizes, organizes, and defines, but also seeks to apply these truths to our lives today. John Frame defines systematic theology as "the *application* of the Word by persons

---

[9]Wayne Grudem, *Systematic Theology: An Introduction to Biblical Doctrine* (Grand Rapids, MI: Zondervan, 1994), 24.
[10]Stephen J. Wellum, unpublished Systematic Theology 1 Class Lectures (2006).
[11]Grudem, 24.

to the world and to all areas of human life."[12] Wayne Grudem notes that "application to life is a necessary part of the proper pursuit of systematic theology."[13] Don Carson puts it this way: "systematic theology worthy of the name . . . seeks to articulate what the Bible says in a way that is culturally telling, culturally prophetic." Its interests are neither antiquarian nor traditionalist.[14] Rather systematic theology has a strong concern for contemporary relevance. Its goal is to teach us not just timeless truth, but what it means to believe and obey that timeless truth today.

Why do theologians put application at the heart of systematic theology? For the simple reason that "nowhere in Scripture do we find doctrine studied for its own sake."[15] In that sense, systematic theology is really nothing more than an attempt to obey the Great Commission. If biblical theology tries to understand how the Great Commission fits into God's overarching plan of redemption, systematic theology tries to spell out just what it means for us to teach and obey everything that Jesus has commanded.

Relating the Two

If these are the definitions of biblical and systematic theology, then how do they relate to each other? We can think about this in at least two different but helpful ways.

First, they are related through a common trajectory of authority. That trajectory begins in Scripture, the authoritative and normative source for all our theologizing. It then moves from Scripture through our exegesis of a particular passage. As we put all the passages of the Bible together it takes shape in our biblical theology. Finally, the trajectory culminates in systematic theology, as we try to summarize and apply the truth of Scripture to our lives today. In that sense, biblical theology tends to be more foundational, while systematic theology both builds on the results of biblical theology and is itself guided by the interpretive horizons established by biblical theology. As Carson has put it so well, "unlike biblical theology, systematic theology is not so much a mediating discipline as a culminating discipline." And yet, since both find their source of authority in Scripture itself, both are normative theology for the Christian church.[16]

But second, they are also related through a trajectory of use (or end). Biblical theology immerses us in the storyline of the Bible in order to

---

[12]John Frame, *Salvation Belongs to the Lord: An Introduction to Systematic Theology* (Philipsburg, NJ: P&R, 2006), 79.
[13]Grudem, 23.
[14]Carson, 101.
[15]Grudem, 23.
[16]Ibid., 101–102. Cf. Schreiner, 23.

describe the Bible's teaching in its own terms. It is a hermeneutical discipline; a way of reading and studying the Bible. The end of biblical theology,
therefore, is an internally coherent understanding of the Bible. Systematic
theology synthesizes the Bible's worldview. It's an applicatory discipline, a
way of summarizing and representing the Bible's teaching in "self-conscious
engagement with [our] culture."[17] The end of systematic theology, therefore, is an externally rational articulation of truth.

In the end, we can't have one without the other. Biblical theology is how
we read the Bible. Systematic theology is how the story of the Bible is shown
to be normative in our lives. To say you want one but not the other simply
shows that you understand neither. Everyone has both a systematic theology
and a biblical theology, whether they realize it or not. What we want, though,
is for both to be faithful to the Scriptures—the biblical story and the biblical
worldview. We won't understand that worldview if we don't understand the
story out of which it arises. But if all we have is a story, how will that story
ever engage the contemporary concerns of our own lives?

Why Systematic Theology Is Important
for Biblical Theology

When I first discovered faithful biblical theology, I was blown away. It
made the Bible come alive for me all over again and put a lot of things
together for me. I confess that I was so taken with biblical theology that, for
quite a while, I didn't have much time for or interest in systematic theology.
It's not that I thought it wasn't needed. I just thought I'd moved beyond it,
to something better.

I wasn't alone in that idea. From the mission field to the postmodern
church scene, more and more voices have been joining a diverse chorus that
increasingly rejects systematic theology in favor of the "storied narratives"
of biblical theology. Some have pointed to the fact that when Jesus taught,
he used stories (parables), not theology lectures. Others have pointed out
that when God decided to reveal himself through Scripture, he didn't do it
in the form of a systematic theology, but mostly in the form of narrative.
Still others have suggested that language simply isn't capable of proposi-
tionally conveying who God is, and yet the narratives of Scripture allow
for a rich, profound, multi-layered communication of his character. Finally,
lots of people are claiming that our postmodern age just doesn't like theology the same way it likes stories.

---

[17]Carson, 102–103. I'm also indebted to Stephen Wellum for stimulating and helpful dialogue on the
question of how these two disciplines relate.

Thankfully, my own neglect of systematic theology in favor of biblical theology was relatively short-lived. I wised up before I got into real trouble in ministry. But for those of you who are still wondering, I want to try and make the case that as good as biblical theology is, our ministry in the local church will be incomplete and impoverished without sound systematic theology as well.

Ligon Duncan has laid out from Scripture six things for which sound doctrine (the fruit of systematic theology) is essential:

1) John 17:13–17 says that doctrine is for joy and growth.
2) Matthew 28:18–20 says that we make disciples (in part) by teaching truth.
3) 1 Timothy 1:3–5 says that bad doctrine destroys but good doctrine produces love.
4) 1 Timothy 1:8–11 says that doctrine cannot be separated from ethics.
5) 1 Timothy 6:2–4 says that doctrine promotes godliness.
6) Titus 1:1 says doctrine is vital for godliness.[18]

Several things strike me about Duncan's list. First, notice where all the citations are taken from. They are either from the pastoral epistles—Paul's instructions to people like us about what we should be doing—or they're from Jesus' prayer for or instructions to the apostles about what their ministry should be all about. I don't know about you, but I'd be thrilled if my ministry even distantly approximated the ministry of the apostles. So, if both Paul and Jesus said we should teach doctrine, regardless of whether we like it or what we think our postmodern age will think, it seems to me we should probably teach doctrine.

But I'm also blown away by what Paul and Jesus say doctrine is for, as Duncan observes. Joy. Growth. Godliness. Discipleship. Love. Life. Just about everything, it seems. These are things I'm supposed to pursue in my pastoral ministry, and doctrine promotes them all, as well as fending off immorality, heresy, disunity, discouragement, and so forth—the things that want to destroy joy, growth, godliness, etc.

Now, I'll grant you that Duncan didn't offer any verses that promised that sound doctrine would promote bigger crowds at your church. He didn't offer any assurance from Scripture that sound doctrine would entertain people or make them feel better about themselves or like you more as their

---

[18]J. Ligon Duncan III, "Sound Doctrine: Essential to Faithful Pastoral Ministry: A Joyful Defense and Declaration of the Necessity and Practicality of Systematic Theology for the Life and Ministry of the Church," in Mark Dever, J. Ligon Duncan III, R. Albert Mohler Jr., C. J. Mahaney, *Proclaiming a Cross-centered Theology* (Wheaton, IL: Crossway, 2009), 36–44.

pastor (though I did find one passage that suggests the opposite—2 Tim. 4:3–4). And, as far as I can tell, sound doctrine doesn't guarantee better programs or more efficient management structures or an answer to the age-old problem of which came first—the bigger sanctuary or the bigger parking lot. If it's answers to questions like these you want, you're going to have to look elsewhere. Doctrine isn't very useful in a ministry of crowd management.

But if you want practical help in promoting godliness in your church, fostering love and unity, making disciples, and growing in grace, there's nothing more practical than sound theology. Could it be that some of us in ministry have lost our interest in sound theology because we're not really doing Christian ministry anymore?

Test Case: The Gospel

Let's consider for a moment how both biblical theology and systematic theology are important and relate to each other when we try to answer the most basic of ministry questions: What is the gospel? What is the good news that the Bible reveals to us?

When biblical theology comes to this question, it lays out the grand sweep of God's actions in history. That sweep might be described as the movement from Creation ➔ Fall ➔ Redemption ➔ New Creation. I don't want to take the time to tell the story in full now. Chapters 6–10 are going to do that. But what I want you to notice is that this outline follows the narrative of Scripture itself. It explains what God is doing across redemptive history as that history moves from the garden of Eden to the new heavens and new earth.

Biblical theology also talks about the gospel in terms of the kingdom of God. George Eldon Ladd has forever changed the way all of us think about this kingdom.[19] As Ladd observed, the Bible generally uses the language of kingdom to speak not of God's realm, but of his reign. Of course God is always reigning. He's the sovereign Lord of the universe that he made. But when Scripture speaks of the kingdom of God, it's typically referring to his redemptive reign. It's the reign that we see among those who are truly his people, those who obey.

When Mark 1:14–15 says that Jesus came preaching the gospel of God that the kingdom of God is near, this is what biblical theology says that gospel is all about. It's the cosmic good news of what God is doing through Jesus Christ. The kingdom was lost to us at the fall and pictured for us as a

[19]George Eldon Ladd, *The Gospel of the Kingdom: Scriptural Studies in the Kingdom of God* (Grand Rapids, MI: Eerdmans, 1959).

shadow in the history of Israel. But now, through the life, death, and resurrection of Jesus, the kingdom of God has been inaugurated anew. Sin has been defeated. The church lives out the life of the kingdom by the power of the Spirit. And we look forward to the day when the king returns and consummates his reign, a reign that will know no end.

This is a fantastic message. It's an extraordinary story, as we'll see in the chapters to come. It captures the imagination and reorders the way we think about everything. It is incredibly good news!

Except for one thing.

Me. And you.

Where do we fit into the story?

The grand story of creation, fall, redemption, and consummation, the story of the coming of God's kingdom, tells me what God is doing and how he's doing it. But how is that good news for sinners like you and me? The coming of the kingdom of God might be good news to the cosmos, but it's bad news for sinners, because the coming of the kingdom means judgment and wrath, as well as renewal and re-creation. So does the story of God's coming kingdom apply to me so that it is personally good news?

To answer that question, we need systematic theology. When systematic theology answers the question, "What is the gospel?" it talks in the four categories of God → Man → Christ → Response. Here's how the cosmic good news becomes personal good news, a gospel for you and me. The coming of the kingdom of God (biblical theology gospel) is bad news for sinners. But in view of Christ's work on the cross as a penal substitute, and God's provision so that we can benefit from that work through repentance and faith (systematic theology gospel), we now have good news. Here is a message that doesn't merely describe how wonderful the kingdom is. No, here is a message that brings you and me personally into that kingdom. Some people these days want to denigrate such formulation as overly individualistic, overly defined by Western legal notions of guilt and punishment. But the fact is, unless the gospel has something to say about my individual salvation, it remains merely a story that can inspire us to good deeds and noble thoughts, but cannot rescue *us* from God's wrath (whatever else it has to say about God's rescue of the cosmos). Systematic theology lands the plane;[20] it connects the story of God's kingdom with the story of your life and mine.

---

[20]Jonathan Leeman, "Biblical and Systematic Confusion Yields Gospel Delusions," 9Marks e-journal (Nov/Dec 2006), http://www.9marks.org/partner/Article_Display_Page/0,,PTID314526%7CCHHID7759 82%7CCIID2277978,00.html (last accessed June 4, 2009).

Does this mean we don't really need biblical theology after all? No! As soon as I've said the word "kingdom," I've returned to the biblical theology gospel and the hope of a salvation that is defined by an eternal kingdom. Without biblical theology, I'm much more prone to reduce salvation to a privatized, existential experience, cut off from what God is doing corporately amongst his people. Without biblical theology, I'm unlikely to grasp the future hope that is held out for us in the new creation. Without biblical theology, I'll be tempted to understand the plan of salvation as being about me, rather than about God's glory. You see, I need both, and they need each other. To be right with God for this life only doesn't amount to much, says Paul (1 Cor. 15:19). The hope that the gospel brings us into is "a living hope through the resurrection of Jesus Christ from the dead, and into an inheritance that can never perish, spoil, or fade—kept in heaven for you, who through faith are shielded by God's power until the coming of the salvation that is ready to be revealed in the last time" (1 Pet. 1:3–5).

Conclusion

I haven't given you any systematic tools to work with yet. Instead, I've simply made the case for why we need the tools in the first place. Having spent the better part of the book so far singing the praises of biblical theology, I didn't want the tools of systematic theology to be neglected, like a poor cousin. As great and important as biblical theology is, it's not enough if we're going to have a biblical theology that's truly practical and related to all of life. For that we need systematic theology as well.

I was recently reminded of this as I sat down to mediate conflict within a nuclear family. The question at hand was how a group of adults who were all related interact with one another without descending into conflict. In the back of my mind, and informing everything I said, was the Bible's rich biblical theology of speech. God is the original speaker in Scripture, and our words and speech are patterned off of his. His Word creates, convicts, and conforms his people. His Word reveals himself and creates relationship and intimacy with his people. His Word is always true, always loving, and always right. And it is finally and fully revealed in the Word made flesh, Jesus Christ. This perspective was important, even essential, if I was to engage with any sort of hope for resolution.

But frankly, that wasn't enough if I was going to engage the very practical issue of controlling the tongue. I needed not only a biblical theology of speech, but also a systematic theology of speech that was rooted in my biblical theology. Knowing that we are created in the image of God, whose speech is always a reflection of his character, I needed to remind everyone that our tongues always speak from the overflow of our hearts (Mark 7; James 3). Knowing that our own lives are constantly recapitulating and reconfirming the fall, I needed to remind them that when we speak words of anger, or manipulation, or deception, we are speaking the language of the serpent in the garden and revealing our own fallen nature (John 8:44). Thus, the first step in conflict resolution wasn't better communication strategies, but self-examination and repentance.

I also needed to instruct everyone on God's purposes for our speech. Again, the background is biblical theology and the revelation of God's Word, ultimately seen in Jesus Christ. Jesus himself reveals the pattern of speech as God intended it. It's not to get what we want (James 4:1ff.), but to build others up according to their needs and for their good (Eph. 4:29). In this way, our speech reflects God's speech, as we are recreated by his grace in his likeness "to be like God in true righteousness and holiness" (Eph 4:24). At this point, acknowledging that the problem was internal (my heart), not external (my family member), and depending on the grace of God in Christ to renew and change us, we could talk about specific steps that each person needed to take.

Here is the proper work of systematic theology. Undergirded and surrounded by biblical theology throughout, systematic theology applied the truth of God's Word to the specific, contemporary situation of a family in conflict. Without biblical theology, I might have been tempted to merely give them rules and moral guidelines. But without systematic theology, all I could tell them was a story.

CHAPTER FIVE

Systematic Theology Tools: How and Why to Think Theologically

The deacon who is in charge of our church library keeps statistics on which section of the library gets the most use. Theology isn't at the top of the list.

I'm not surprised. I have a PhD, and I don't always jump at the chance to dive into the latest work of systematic theology. It seems to drip with the idea of philosophical complexity and dry technicalities. Most of us don't know any professional theologians personally, but we all have an idea of what they must look like. Dry and slightly shriveled, the corners of their mouths constantly turned down, wire-rimmed spectacles, musty clothes, and faint wisps of hair on a balding head sums up my image.

But even if we don't know any professional theologians, we've all run into people who love to talk theology. And most of us have learned to steer a wide passage around them. People just seem to get hurt in conversations with them.

Yet I'm here to tell you that, despite the vague unease and intimidation you might feel at the thought of engaging in systematic theology, and notwithstanding the unfamiliarity you feel toward theologians, you in fact have been hanging out with theologians your whole Christian life. What's more, you've been engaging in theological discussion since the day you became a Christian.

Everyone Has a Systematic Theology

Why am I so confident of that fact? Because I'm confident that you've either asked or attempted to answer the question, "What does the Bible teach us about [fill in the blank]?" Yes, like it or not, whether you mean to or not, you are more or less doing systematic theology every time you make a statement about what the Bible teaches, or what Christians believe, or how Christianity relates to the world around it. You simply cannot self-consciously be a Christian without being a systematic theologian. And if that's true for you, a church leader, it's just as true for every other member of your church.

That, at least, was the conviction of one of the earliest Christian theologians, the apostle Paul. People have long noted that most of Paul's letters break into two parts. He generally opens his letters with an extended theological meditation. He then concludes them with lots of practical advice and instruction. But the two halves are not unrelated. Almost every time, Paul places an important hinge in the letter—a massive "THEREFORE" between the theology he's been explaining and the practical instruction he's about to give.

What makes this structure so striking is that the reasons that prompted Paul to write each of his letters can almost always be found in the second half. Paul may have been a theologian, but he didn't sit down one day and say, "You know, I think I should write the Ephesians an extended treatise on our election in Christ, and the Philippians could really use a meditation on the divinity and humanity of Jesus." No, he wrote the Ephesians because they were struggling to know how Jews and Gentiles should relate in the church, and the Philippians were struggling with persecution from outside and quarreling within.

Practical, even mundane problems prompted Paul to write to these churches. Yet what he offered them was not merely practical advice on conflict resolution or community life. Instead, he offered them profound theology. As one theologian has put it,

> [Paul is convinced of] the applicability of the profoundest theology to the most mundane and most common-place problems . . . [Paul] is telling them: You have these practical problems; the answer is theological; remember your theology and place your behaviour in the light of that theology. Place your little problems in the light of the most massive theology. We ourselves in our Christian callings are to be conscious of this. We must never leave our doctrine hanging in the air, nor hesitate to enforce the most elementary Christian obligations with the most sublime doctrines.[1]

---

[1]Donald Macleod, *The Humiliated and Exalted Lord: Studies in Philippians 2 and Christology* (Greenville, SC: Reformed Academic Press, 1994), 4. Quoted in J. Ligon Duncan III, "Sound Doctrine: Essential to Faithful Pastoral Ministry: A Joyful Defense and Declaration of the Necessity and Practicality of Systematic Theology for the Life and Ministry of the Church," in Mark Dever, J. Ligon Duncan III, R. Albert Mohler Jr., C. J. Mahaney, *Proclaiming a Cross-centered Theology* (Wheaton, IL: Crossway, 2009), 43.

Practical problems have theological answers. So the question is not whether or not you're going to be a theologian, but what kind of theologian you're going to be. Will you be a good theologian or a bad one, a consistent theologian or an inconsistent one, a systematic theologian or a haphazard one? To help you be a better theologian, I want to consider what doctrine is, how to think theologically, and why we should be engaged in such study in the context of the local church. Here, finally, are the tools of systematic theology.

What Is Doctrine?

In the previous chapter I said that doctrine is simply a precise and accurate summary of what the Bible says on a topic and is used to define the difference between truth and error, orthodoxy and heresy. It's time to flesh that out a bit more. In fact, doctrine has at least three aspects to it, all of which are important if we are to understand what it means to think theologically.[2]

Biblical Knowledge

Fundamentally, theological knowledge is knowledge of God. As Scripture presents the idea, knowledge of God is more than simply having a head full of facts about God. God is not like a bug that we put under a magnifying glass, an object of our study and examination. God is a person. And so to know God is to know him as you would know another person, a friend, or a family member. But God is not a person just like you and me. And so our knowledge of him is neither casual nor familiar. Even more important, our knowledge of God is not intuitive. We can't deduct who God is from what we're like. God is spirit and God is holy. He is our Creator and our Lord. That means that knowledge of God will demand of us reverence, obedience, and worship. It also means that such knowledge will have to be given to us. We won't be able to discover it on our own. If we are to know God, God must reveal himself. And the place he has revealed himself is through the inspired revelation of Scripture.

All of this leads us to the first aspect of doctrine, which is, doctrine begins with biblical knowledge. As we've said before, the Bible is God's inspired self-revelation. It therefore is authoritative, not just about God, but about any question that theology asks and seeks to answer. The Bible provides us a normative perspective on God, ourselves, and our world. And

---

[2]The sections that follow are deeply indebted to John Frame's discussion of epistemology in *The Doctrine of the Knowledge of God* (Philipsburg, NJ: P&R, 1987). While I don't agree with all of Frame's epistemology (e.g., his insistence that some language about God is non-analogical), I have found his three categories of normative, existential, and situational perspective helpful, and have adopted them in what follows as biblical, personal, and situational knowledge.

this perspective demands our submission and our obedience. To know God from the perspective of biblical knowledge is to be subject to the Lordship of God, bringing every thought captive to Christ (2 Cor. 10:5).

To make this more practical, let's take an example. What does the Bible say about stem-cell research? It doesn't say anything using those terms. But in fact it says quite a bit, when we begin to think theologically. To begin with, it tells us that God is the Creator and giver of life (Ps. 139:13–16), and that human life was formed in God's image (Genesis 1). Therefore we do not have the authority to usurp God's prerogative over human life (Ex. 20:13), no matter how good our purposes are. According to God's Word, the creation of human embryos for the purpose of harvesting their stem cells, which results in their destruction, is murder. Despite our attempts to do good for others through that act, it is an affront to God's exclusive claim as the Lord of life.

But in telling us that we are made in God's image, the Bible also tells us something about ourselves, which leads us to the second aspect of theological knowledge, or doctrine.

Personal Knowledge

If theology is knowledge of God, and such knowledge is gained authoritatively through Scripture, we might be tempted to think that theological knowledge and biblical knowledge are identical. Once we have one, we have the other. But in fact it's not that simple. As soon as we speak of knowing God, we also find that we are saying something about ourselves, as the ones who know and are known by God. John Calvin understood this, and opened his *Institutes of the Christian Religion* with this observation:

> Nearly all the wisdom we possess, that is to say, true and sound wisdom, consists of two parts: the knowledge of God and of ourselves. But, while joined by many bonds, which one precedes and brings forth the other is not easy to discern . . . the knowledge of ourselves not only arouses us to seek God, but also, as it were, leads us by the hand to find him. [But] it is certain that man never achieves a clear knowledge of himself unless he has first looked upon God's face, and then descends from contemplating him to scrutinize himself.[3]

Theological knowledge, and therefore doctrine, always involves us in personal, or existential, knowledge. In light of who God is, and what he has revealed about himself and his will, the question immediately arises,

---

[3]John Calvin, *Institutes of the Christian Religion*, I.i.1–2.

who am I? How are theological and personal knowledge related? Here is the connection that we talked about at the beginning between theology and life. To know God is to be subject to his authority and to be brought into his presence. True theology, worthy of the name, can never be mere abstract, academic, theoretical language. Rather, it relates you and me to God as subjects, as worshipers, and as creatures. Of course, as we focus on ourselves in this aspect of theology, we don't do so independently of Scripture or in contradiction of it. Unlike liberal theologians who would substitute the categories of existential philosophy or communitarian sociology for God's revelation, faithful theological thinking remains submitted to God's Word. But it does not do so with the assumption that we can approach our knowledge of God as disinterested observers. Rather, our knowledge of God through his normative Word confronts us with knowledge of ourselves as simultaneously noble image-bearers and ignoble rebels of the Most High.

How does this speak to our example of what the Bible says about stem-cell research? Well, it helps us understand why we desire to study and research such things. We are image-bearers, made to be like God, to explore and understand the world he made, which includes our bodies. But his image in us extends beyond creativity and curiosity. It also includes compassion. We desire to heal the sick, to cure the diseased because of the image of God in us.

But we are not only image-bearers. We are also sinful rebels. That means that even our best intentions and highest skills are likely to be twisted to selfish and self-serving ends. As sinners, we are likely to evaluate the harm done to others not in absolute and principled terms, but according to a political calculus of cost and benefit. Our friends, neighbors, and family members with incurable diseases seem more deserving than the unborn. Put bluntly, they vote, earn money, and pay taxes, and the unborn don't. We are easily influenced by imbalances of perceived power and perception. Furthermore, we are motivated by the pride of accomplishment, a pride that brooks no restraint. If we *can* do something, we *should* do it.

And so you see how systematic theology, drawing upon knowledge of ourselves in light of the knowledge of God, explains why some humans would define other humans as nonhumans, in order to use them for themselves in a program designed, ironically, to heal and restore. Systematic theology also provides a distinction between embryonic stem-cell research and adult stem-cell research. It explains both our longing to research and to heal, and why we should place limits on those longings. Finally, it provides a way for us to think about the value, dignity, and hope for human life in the midst of suffering and disease. For such value and hope is not found in utilitarian or functional categories, but in our relationship to God.

So doctrine, or theological knowledge, involves both biblical knowledge that gives a normative perspective, and personal knowledge that provides an existential perspective. And the two are interrelated. They don't cover different fields of knowledge, but consider the whole field of knowledge from different angles. However, if you've been following closely, you'll realize there is yet another aspect of theological knowledge. When we come to a knowledge of God and of ourselves, we don't do so in a vacuum. Rather, we know God in the midst of this world that he made, at a particular point in history, and in a particular cultural context. And that's the third aspect we need to consider.

Situational Knowledge

All of us know ourselves and know God, not as timeless abstractions, but as people who are thoroughly situated in a context—a reality that is external to ourselves. Paul tells us in Romans 1 that some of what can be known of God is revealed through the natural order, which means that we come to that knowledge of God by knowing and observing the world around us. But when I refer to situational knowledge, I don't just have in mind what theologians call natural theology—what can be known of God through nature. I also have in mind what sociologists call culture—the way in which we make sense of the reality around us, including ourselves and God as actors in that reality.

Abraham Kuyper, a Dutch theologian and statesman of the early twentieth century, once famously said, "There is not a square inch in the whole domain of our human existence over which Christ, who is Sovereign over *all*, does not cry: 'Mine!'"[4] This truth has important implications for theological knowledge. To begin with, to know something about the world and to know something about human culture is to know something about the Creator and sovereign King who made both and who rules over all. It's also to know something about ourselves as creatures who know God.

But there's even more. To know our situation is to know a world that was made good, but now rests under God's curse. This world is twisted, hard, and marked by tragedy and horror. And yet it is not merely a world under God's curse. Both common grace and saving grace are at work

---

[4]Abraham Kuyper, "Sphere Sovereignty: The Inaugural Address at the Opening of the Free University of Amsterdam, 1880," in James D. Bratt, ed., *Abraham Kuyper: A Centennial Reader* (Grand Rapids, MI: Eerdmans, 1998), 488.

in it. So the curse is not carried out to its ultimate degree, yet. Life goes on; beauty and love exist side by side with ugliness and hatred. Work is toilsome, but not entirely without productivity and satisfaction. Human culture and civilization provide a framework of meaning that makes God seem absent and belief irrational, and yet rationality has not entirely disappeared, and the products of human culture still reflect the marks of the good, the true, and the beautiful. The world is corrupt and corrupting, but not as corrupt as it could be. What's more, forgiveness and reconciliation have broken into this world through Jesus Christ. The reality of the age to come, characterized by newness of life, peace with God, and the beauty of holiness, has dawned even in the midst of the darkness of this fallen world.

Now, what does this situational knowledge mean for our discussion of what the Bible says about stem-cell research? A lot. For one thing, it gives us an understanding of the ultimate causes of disease (the fall), and the ultimate cure (re-creation). It therefore prevents utopian agendas. Furthermore, situational theological knowledge gives us categories with which to understand science, technology, and medicine. Each of these is more than mere intellectual process and product. We see that technology is a component of culture, and fallen human culture, in all its various manifestations, is dedicated to the denial of God and the deification of man. In fact, fallen human culture is precisely that which makes belief seem irrational and unbelief seem rational and normal. In such a context, technology may easily masquerade as helpful, while in fact perpetrating great evil.

But situational knowledge also keeps us from rejecting this world out of hand. Our call under God is not to be Luddites who refuse and reject all technology, nor to be Amish and withdraw from culture altogether. Rather, our call is to explore this world and develop human culture to the glory of God. That will include technology and science, which as gifts from God are capable of accomplishing great and profound good for humanity.

How to Think Theologically

If those are the three aspects of theological knowledge—knowledge of God, knowledge of self, and knowledge of the world—how then do we put all of that together so that we can think through a topic theologically?

I tried to give examples and summaries as we went along, but let me attempt now to put it all together. What *does* the Bible say about stem-cell research? Remember, I'm not a professional theologian, so my apologies in advance to those of you who are. On the other hand, to the regular pastors and church leaders out there like me, I say that if I can do it, so can you!

Our answer must begin with the authoritative and normative Word of God. God is the Author and Creator of life, and he has uniquely created humans in his image (Genesis 1). Therefore human life itself is uniquely set apart for the glory of God (cf. Gen. 9:4–6). And yet, as we turn to our situation, we find ourselves in a world that is cursed, wracked not only by pathogens that attack from outside our bodies, but by corrupted genetics, so that our bodies turn on themselves in disease and decay. This is not the result of random accident, but the outworking of God's curse for our sinful rebellion (Gen. 3:19). Because human life is made in the image of God, there is a moral obligation on us to use the knowledge and resources at our disposal to preserve, promote, and heal that life (cf. Luke 10:25–37). When we do so, we are acting not only as image-bearers, but as agents of mercy in a world subjected to the curse of God (Matt. 5:43–48).

But the obligation to heal is not the only obligation we bear. We also bear the obligation to protect human life (cf. Ex. 21:28–32). God's Word tells us that all human beings are made in his image, and therefore there is an equality of right to life that is not conditioned on ability, capacity, or usefulness. This means that there are limits on our obligation to heal, if the exercise of that obligation entails the deliberate killing or maiming of another. As we turn to personal knowledge informed by Scripture, we recognize that, in our fallen state, we are prone to the selfish use of others for our own ends, and that we are utterly capable of constructing moral rationalizations for our sinful motives and actions (cf. Acts 16:16–21). Furthermore, we are the producers *and* the products of a fallen human culture that's committed to denying any and all limits that God would place on us. As gods, we want to set our own limits, and in fact we live as if there are none (Gen. 3:1–7).

Finally, as we consider the reality of sin, as it impacts both our bodies and our cultural agendas, we recognize that physical healing is not an ultimate good, nor even a universally attainable goal (2 Cor. 12:7–10). We also recognize that physical suffering is not an ultimate evil (Matt. 10:28). So, as humans, we are called to reject the idolatry of a modern medical utopia, and instead put our ultimate hope in the redemptive power of God, demonstrated through Christ's defeat of sin on the cross and his defeat of death in the resurrection.

All of this leads us as Christians, thinking theologically, to reject any and all forms of embryonic stem-cell research, since it deliberately creates human life only to destroy it, even though it professes to do so for the sake of other human lives. It also means that we can and should support other forms of stem-cell research based on adult cell lines. But as we consider the aims and goals of such research, we understand that its purpose should be to heal and restore. Any attempt to use such research to reengineer life, to create hybrid forms of life, or "designer babies," must be rejected as an infringement on God's rights as the Creator and Lord of life, and as a debasement and assault on the image of God in man.

Give Them Meat, Not Milk

By some accounts, John Piper, pastor of Bethlehem Baptist Church in Minneapolis, has done more to motivate a new generation of young American Christians into fields of missionary service than anyone else alive today. How has he done it? Has he inspired them with stories of heroic sacrifice? Has he brought the plight (and guilt) of the dying masses to bear on the tender consciences of America's youth? Has he articulated a mission strategy so compelling that people simply must get on board?

The answer to all of those questions is, "No." He hasn't done any of those things. What he has done is give people profoundly deep theology. He's confronted them with the awesome God-centeredness of God. He's challenged them with the difficult but biblical truth that God's greatest love is God, that God's supreme goal is his glory, and that God's ultimate purpose in both creation and re-creation is his worship and fame. What's more, he's demonstrated that there is nothing wrong, and everything right, with the God-centeredness of God. And then he has brought together two very practical truth-applications. First, "missions exists because worship doesn't."[5] Second, "God is most glorified in us when we are most satisfied in Him."[6] When these two truths come together in a regenerate, grace-filled heart, grounded in a profound theology of God, people reorganize their lives, change their ambitions, and give themselves to the God-glorifying work of world evangelization.

I think it's easy for many of us to look at the impact of John Piper and think, "I could never have that kind of impact, because I'm not John Piper. I don't have his gifts. I don't have his energy. I don't have his brain!" I understand the feeling.

But I don't agree with it.

And neither would he. John Piper would be the first to tell you, he's just a man, with failings and fears and quirks like you and me.

---

[5]John Piper, *Let the Nations Be Glad! The Supremacy of God in Missions*, 2nd ed., revised & expanded (Grand Rapids, MI: Baker, 2003), 17.
[6]John makes this point everywhere. This particular quotation is from *Brothers, We are Not Professionals. A Plea to Pastors for Radical Ministry* (Nashville: Broadman & Holman, 2002), 45.

No, what I think accounts for the way God is using Piper today is that, like a modern-day Paul, he has taken the gifts God gave him, and put them wholly at the disposal of the truth of God's Word. And in doing so, he is a model to us of what it means to be a servant of the truth. More important than his style, his delivery, or even his personality and passion is his belief that God's Word, all of it and every part of it, is true and meant as food for the sheep of God's pasture.

That's the model Piper gives us. That's what we should be about as church leaders. "If we are going to feed our people, we must ever advance in our grasp of biblical truth. We must be like Jonathan Edwards who resolved in his college days, and kept the resolution all his life, 'Resolved: To study the Scriptures so steadily, constantly, and frequently, as that I may find and plainly perceive myself to grow in the knowledge of the same.'"[7]

It should be our ambition to grow in our ability to carefully and faithfully articulate biblical doctrine, and then to communicate it with clarity, precision, and passion. Not so that we can impress our fellow pastors or awe our church members. But so we can feed the sheep. Our people need meat to grow strong and mature, but too often we have been responsible for their arrested development, since all we've been feeding them is milk. Many of us, I think, fear that doctrine will simply become the dead wood of orthodoxy in our church, and so we cut it out whenever we can. In fact, doctrine is the fuel God has given us that, when lit by the fires of grace, burns in a white-hot devotion of Christian worship and discipleship.

This is what I meant when I compared John Piper to the apostle Paul. When Paul was confronted with lack of generosity or quarrelsome divisiveness in the local church, he was dealing with the sort of mundane problems that you and I face every day. But his response was anything but mundane. His response was profound theology. "Who would ever imagine that the response to the glory of the incarnation might be to give to the collection for the poor? Who might imagine that the application of the glories of New Testament Christology might be to stop our quarreling and our divisiveness in the Christian *ekklesia*?"[8] And I might add, who would have ever thought that the response to the unrelenting God-centeredness of God would be twenty-somethings changing their career plans and heading to the mission field?

---

[7] Ibid., 74.
[8] J. Ligon Duncan III, "Sound Doctrine: Essential to Faithful Pastoral Ministry: A Joyful Defense and Declaration of the Necessity and Practicality of Systematic Theology for the Life and Ministry of the Church," in Mark Dever, J. Ligon Duncan III, R. Albert Mohler Jr., C. J. Mahaney, *Proclaiming a Cross-centered Theology* (Wheaton, IL: Crossway, 2009), 43.

I'll tell you who thought of it. Long before John Piper, Jonathan Edwards, or the apostle Paul, God thought of it. He knew what we would need, and he gave it to us in the Scriptures. Not just stories, but God-breathed truth, "useful for teaching, rebuking, correcting, and training in righteousness, so that the man of God may be equipped for every good work" (2 Tim. 3:16).

This was brought home to me a few years ago when I was called to the house of a young family in our church. A young mother had been diagnosed with a fairly advanced cancer. As I sat on their couch and first listened to them and then cried with them, I had a choice to make. I could say vaguely comforting and spiritual words, assure them that God would take care of them and urge them to have faith. Or I could address the hard reality they faced with the uncompromising truth of God's Word. I chose the latter. I looked the young mother and her husband in the eye and told them of God's love, a love that was not grounded in their circumstances, but in the cross of Calvary. I told them of God's sovereignty, that it was God who ordained that she have this cancer, and that God intended to use it in her life to teach her to depend upon him and to find him sufficient. And I told her, even as I wept with her, that I was excited to see how God would glorify himself in her through this trial that he had appointed for her.

As they told me later, they were slightly shocked at my words, even though they were delivered with gentleness and tears. But they also told me that they clung to those words, and the Scriptures I shared with them that night. In the dark and uncertain days of chemotherapy and surgery, they needed more than milk. They needed the meat of God's sovereign love and his commitment to be glorified in the lives of his people. In the end, she survived the cancer, but their lives are not the same. The truth of God's Word, brought to bear in the crucible of trial, has completely reordered their lives.

Theology and the Local Church

It used to be, a century or two ago, that theology was primarily done in the church and for the church. It's not that Christian theologians were uninterested in engaging non-Christians. It's simply that they understood that the primary audience of theology, and the primary constructors of theology, were Christians gathered in the local assembly. Somewhere along the way, however, that ceased to be the case. David Wells has even made the case that not only is theology not done in the local church, it's increasingly not welcome there.[9]

Instead, the church has become enamored with business practice and psychological method. Her leaders are expected to be CEO's, not pastor-theologians. The church's public gatherings are designed to be events that appeal to the outsider, rather than assemblies that give corporate expression to our identity as the people of God.[10] And our habits of thought tend to be shaped more by polling data, the blogosphere, and the image-driven nature of television than they do the Bible. The thoughts of God and his glory, our nobility and depravity, and this world's value and transience—thoughts that shaped and characterized the minds of previous generations of Christians—rest lightly, if at all, on the church today.[11]

The Church Must Not Abandon Theology

If we are to faithfully give witness to Christ, the Lord of Life, in this age, then we must recover not simply the ability to think theologically, but the commitment to do so together in the life of the local church. Until we recover theological vision in the church, the nerve that gives rich and profound biblical life to our worship and mission will remain cut. Our public worship will remain shallow and entertainment-driven. Our mission will either be indistinguishable from the methods and goals of any sales organization, or it will be co-opted by the agenda of an ultimately hostile culture. This culture will encourage us to do good things like caring for the poor, but it will only applaud us if we agree to leave Christ out of it.

"The church abandons theology only at great peril to herself,"[12] says theologian Richard Lints. Without theological vision, a vision that wrestles with what it means to be God's people, in God's world, under God's rule, the church inevitably loses both its *identity* as God's possession and its *purpose* as the people and place where God's glory is displayed in the gospel and God's praise is declared.

---

[9]David Wells, *No Place for Truth, or Whatever Happened to Evangelical Theology?* (Grand Rapids, MI: Eerdmans, 1993).

[10]This, of course, is one of the key principles of the seeker-sensitive church growth movement. Its exponents are so numerous and well-known that I need not point to examples.

[11]I owe the idea of God "resting lightly on the church" to David Wells. This is a theme he has explored in great depth in the project that began with *No Place for Truth* and recently concluded with *The Courage to Be Protestant: Truth-lovers, Marketers, and Emergents in the Postmodern World* (Grand Rapids, MI: Eerdmans, 2008). For a fuller discussion of this idea, see, *No Place For Truth or Whatever Happened to Evangelical Theology?* (Grand Rapids, MI: Eerdmans, 1993), 106–114 and *God in the Wasteland: The Reality of Truth in a World of Fading Dreams* (Grand Rapids, MI: Eerdmans, 1994), 88–113.

[12]Richard Lints, *The Fabric of Theology: A Prolegomenon to Evangelical Theology* (Grand Rapids, MI: Eerdmans, 1993), 319.

Theology Must Not Abandon the Church

At the same time, Lints has also written, "theology abandons the church at great peril to itself."[13] Outside the church, theology is disconnected from the context of worship, mission, and discipleship. It therefore becomes nothing more than another academic discipline talking to itself. Outside the church, theology knows no boundaries, no accountability, and most importantly, no practical application. Sometimes this leads to heresy. Often, in our age, it has led to a withering of theology among evangelicals, as increasingly nothing can or need be said beyond a few essential doctrines, at which point the real work of technique and management is taken up.[14]

What may be most important, however, is that theology done outside the church is bereft of the means that God has provided to illustrate and display not just the truth, but the application of truth to life. The church is to be the display of the gospel (Eph. 3:10), a living, breathing, growing colony of heaven,[15] a community of people who are living out the worldview that sound biblical theology articulates. Without the church, how does anyone know that theology has something to say that's worth listening to?

Conclusion

Why do we do systematic theology? Because theology is the application of truth to life; because theology is the foundation for every good work; because theology provides the framework and the worldview that allows us to make sense of our lives and this world in relation to God and the gospel of Jesus Christ.

We live in a fallen world, a world now shaped by fallen human beings to make the theological project seem like an irrelevant waste of time. But systematic theology prepares us for that, tells us to expect it, and then invites us to pursue thinking theologically about this world anyway. Further, we should not do this thinking on our own, but in the context of the church, with an ear open to what Christians who have gone before us have said, and with an eye to bringing that thinking to bear on what it means to follow Christ in our own age.

We now have the tools we need to construct a theology that tells the whole story of the whole Bible, and that, in doing so, orients us in this world to live as Christians, men and women who know God. It's time to try our hands at building.

---

[13]Ibid.
[14]Wells, *No Place*, 101.
[15]Edmund P. Clowney, *The Church: Contours of Christian Theology* (Downers Grove, IL: InterVarsity Press, 1995), 13 (chapter title).

SECTION TWO

The Stories to Be Told

CHAPTER SIX

The Story of Creation

W e're changing direction now. We've been preparing. Now we're going to build. But before we do, let me summarize what we've done so far. The goal of this book is to first convince you and then to help you. I've been trying to convince you that, if you're serious about Christian ministry, you need a biblical theology that's both faithful to the story of Scripture and sound in its application. Nothing is more practical than this. The first section of this book has been all about convincing you that the tools of theology, both biblical and systematic, are tools that you can use. In fact, they are tools you must use if you want to be a faithful church leader.

Why do I say that you *must* use them? I say it for the simple reason that God has a viewpoint on your life, and on my life, and on all of life. Now, maybe that sounds obvious. But think about it for a second. God has a viewpoint on what love really is, on how we speak, on what we do with our possessions, on how we relate to our neighbors, on how we relate to him. In our flesh, we might say we're interested in his viewpoint, but actually we dismiss it. We're only interested in our own viewpoint, and we spend just about every moment of every day justifying that viewpoint—sometimes consciously and sometimes unconsciously.

The Bible presents us with God's viewpoint. Yet as we've seen, the Bible's a different sort of book. It doesn't present God's viewpoint on things in a straightforward manner. It's part historical, part propositional, part poetic, and so forth. It gives us history, like many other books give us history. But unlike any other history ever written, this history is authoritative for our lives. That's why it also gives us propositions of absolute truth in the midst of the historical narrative. The Bible also gives us poetry, which guides us in singing and feeling and grieving, like so many other books of poetry. But unlike any other book of poetry, it's authoritative. Here is how you *should* grieve, rejoice, express fear, and so forth.

The Bible is utterly unique, designed to do what no other book in history has done—reveal God to people by God himself. The Bible is written for human beings, for persons like you and me. As persons, we grow to trust and believe in other persons as we walk with them—as we see them act, as we hear their words, and as we observe and eventually share their hearts. But in this case, the person we're getting to know isn't another person like you and me; it's the triune God, Lord of heaven and earth. Obviously, this is no ordinary book.

What the Bible does, really, is not just give us God's viewpoint; it allows us to walk with God through the course of human history. That way we can come to believe and trust the words, the viewpoint, and the heart of this One who is leading history. The Bible enables us, in David Powlison's phrase, to see with new eyes.[1] It enables us, in the Apostle Paul's phrase, to *see* with a new heart (Eph. 1:18).

In the first section of this book, we've been trying to understand the nature of this book called the Bible. So we're not just asking the exegetical question, "What does it say?" (That is, "What's the content of the book?") Nor are we just asking the systematic theology question, "What should Christians believe about topic '*x*'—God, man, sin, the end times, stem-cell research, government, and so on?" Rather, we're also asking something in between those two questions—a question in the middle—which is a biblical theology question: "*How* does the Bible say what it says?" If we don't understand *how* the Bible says what it says, we're likely to make mistakes about the other two questions. We're going to misunderstand the content, and we're going to misapply that content to what we should believe.

To answer that biblical theology question, we've considered a lot of concepts and introduced a number of tools:

- the authorial intent of the text
- the epochal and canonical horizons of any text
- the Bible's covenantal storyline
- matters of promise-fulfillment, which includes multiple horizons of fulfillment
- the role of typology
- matters of continuity and discontinuity

Next, we looked at the nature of systematic theology and considered how to construct doctrine, that is, what we believe. Good systematic theology consists of biblical knowledge, personal knowledge, and situational

---

[1]David Powlison, *Seeing With New Eyes: Counseling and the Human Condition through the Lens of Scripture* (Philipsburg, NJ: P&R, 2003).

knowledge. In essence, we've been thinking about how the bridge is built from *what the Bible says* over to *what we believe.*

That's what we've done so far. What are we going to do now? In this and the next four chapters, we're going to apply everything we've been talking about. We're going to consider five different stories that the Bible tells—five different biblical theology storylines. In fact, we're going to tell the whole story of the whole Bible five times, each time from a slightly different vantage point. And then we're going to consider some of the doctrines that arise out of those stories, and how those doctrines shape what we believe and how we are to live.

The first story we're going to tell is the story of creation. God's story begins with creation, and it ends with a new creation. If nothing else, this fact alone suggests that creation is crucial to understanding who God is and what he is about.

The Story of Creation

In the Beginning

"In the beginning, God created the heavens and the earth" (Gen 1:1).

Genesis 1 provides the cosmic overview. Everything that exists comes into being at God's command.

As we move into Genesis 2, the story focuses tightly on the details of the creation of mankind, the very first marriage, and the responsibilities entrusted to men and women. Everything is good. Everything is perfect. Everything is just as it should be.

Then tragedy strikes. Incredibly, Adam and Eve rebel against the One who gave them Paradise. In judgment and mercy, God thrusts them out of the perfection of his presence in the garden of Eden, into a created world that is now cursed and fallen.

The Cycle Continues

As chapter follows chapter, things go from bad to worse. Then finally we hear again God's words of judgment.

> The LORD saw how great man's wickedness on the earth had become, and that every inclination of the thoughts of his heart was only evil all the time. The LORD was grieved that he had made man on the earth, and his heart was filled with pain. So the LORD said, "I will wipe mankind, whom I have created, from the face of the earth—men and animals, and creatures that move along the ground, and birds of the air—for I am grieved that I have made them." (Gen. 6:5–7)

The actions of God in Genesis 3 are repeated in Genesis 6. God brings the flood. It was judgment day for what Peter called "the world that then existed" (2 Pet. 3:6, RSV).

But God also shows mercy by saving Noah and his family. With Noah's salvation comes an act of re-creation. Once again, the earth was formless and void, covered by the waters of the deep (cf. Gen. 1:2). What's more, outwardly the earth had been washed clean of mankind's sin. A new world, the present world, emerged as God once again put boundaries between the land and the sea. God now commissions Noah and his family just as he had commissioned Adam. He even echoes Genesis 1 by telling them, "Be fruitful and increase in number and fill the earth. . . . Everything that lives and moves will be food for you. Just as I gave you the green plants, I now give you everything" (Gen. 9:1–3).

But though the world is externally cleansed and re-created, internally the hearts of men and women are not changed. Sin intervenes once more. Within a few short years, Noah's family is torn apart and one of his grandsons cursed. By Genesis 11, we are once again witnessing humanity's prideful wickedness and God's merciful judgment, as he confuses their language at Babel and scatters them across the face of the earth in order to slow the progress of their wickedness.

At this incredibly low point in the story, with mankind not only alienated from God but also permanently alienated from one another, God's creating activity marks a profound change in the course of human history. Once again, God speaks and he creates, not a new world, but a new man. He takes the pagan idolater Abram and, by his irresistible call of love, changes his heart and his name. Abram becomes Abraham, the man who believed God and followed him. And God didn't stop speaking. He promises childless Abraham that he will make his family into a great nation. Then, according to his promise, God creates life in barren Sarah's womb. A generation later, their grandson has twelve sons. Before long, you can't even count all their descendants. From a single man and woman, they had multiplied and been fruitful.

The story rushes on. Abraham's descendants are enslaved by another nation. And so God sends his prophet, Moses, to speak God's words to Pharaoh. God speaks, Egypt is judged, and the nation of Israel is liberated. Only they aren't quite yet a nation. They are more a loose collection of tribes. But at Mount Sinai, God speaks again. In Exodus 19–20, God audibly speaks to the people, and creates Israel as his special people, his chosen nation out of all the peoples of the earth.

Then Moses went up to God, and the LORD called to him from the mountain and said, "This is what you are to say to the house of Jacob and what you are to tell the people of Israel: 'You yourselves have seen what I did to Egypt, and how I carried you on eagles' wings and brought you to myself. Now if you obey me fully and keep my covenant, then out of all nations you will be my treasured possession. Although the whole earth is mine, you will be for me a kingdom of priests and a holy nation.' These are the words you are to speak to the Israelites. . . . And God spoke all these words: 'I am the LORD your God, who brought you out of Egypt, out of the land of slavery. You shall have no other gods before me.'" (Ex. 19:3–6; 20:1–3)

But God doesn't just create the nation. God also promises to settle the people of Israel in a land flowing with milk and honey. It's described as a veritable garden of Eden, a place where former slaves can finally rest in the presence of their God.

Incredibly, the people rebel, not just once, but again and again (Exodus 32; Numbers 11–14, 16, 21, 25). God judges one generation, letting them die in the desert. Then he re-creates the nation again with their children. He establishes them in their own land, the promised land of rest, and eventually raises up for them a great king, David, who gives them rest on every side from their enemies. But they too eventually sin, and on and on the story goes. Like the generations before them, like Adam and Eve at the beginning, the nation rebels. This leads first to division and finally to judgment and exile. Scattered among nations whose speech it does not understand, Israel has recapitulated in its own history the first eleven chapters of Genesis.

Once again, God's creating grace intervenes. A remnant of the nation is brought back from exile. The temple is rebuilt and the walls of Jerusalem are restored. But something is missing. The temple is rebuilt, but it's empty. God is not there. Jerusalem's walls are restored, but the throne of David is a shadow of its former glory, and soon sits vacant. By the time the New Testament opens, the people of Israel are slaves once again, only this time, they are slaves in their own land. And there hasn't been a prophet in centuries. The God who speaks and creates had fallen silent.

The Inauguration of a New Creation

God remains silent, until one amazing day—the Creator himself appears in the form of a man. Echoing Genesis 1, the apostle John tells us,

In the beginning was the Word, and the Word was with God, and the Word was God. He was with God in the beginning. Through him all things were made; without him nothing was made that has been made. In him was life,

> and that life was the light of men. . . . The Word became flesh and made his
> dwelling among us. We have seen his glory, the glory of the One and Only,
> who came from the Father, full of grace and truth. (John 1:1–4, 14)

That Word was Jesus, God incarnate. In his life, he spoke and the blind
could see and the deaf could hear. And though wicked men crucified and
buried him, he rose from the dead and, with his resurrection, inaugurated
the new creation, a work that continues even today. Through his Word, the
gospel, Jesus resurrects dead sinners in newness of life and makes them new
creatures (Eph. 2:1–9). Through his Word, the gospel, he calls his people
into a new humanity, a holy nation. The author to the Hebrews, echoing
Exodus 19–20, calls this people the assembly and church of the firstborn
(Heb. 10:22–23).

The New Creation Consummated

And through his Word, the gospel, Jesus the Creator will finish his work
of new creation. Evil and sin will be finally and forever judged, and God's
people will be purified from all their wickedness and dwell with him in rest
forever in new heavens and a new earth. As John saw it,

> Then I saw a new heaven and a new earth, for the first heaven and the first
> earth had passed away, and there was no longer any sea. I saw the Holy City,
> the new Jerusalem, coming down out of heaven from God, prepared as a
> bride beautifully dressed for her husband. And I heard a loud voice from
> the throne saying, "Now the dwelling of God is with men, and he will live
> with them. They will be his people, and God himself will be with them and
> be their God. He will wipe every tear from their eyes. There will be no more
> death or mourning or crying or pain, for the old order of things has passed
> away." He who was seated on the throne said, "I am making everything
> new!" Then he said, "Write this down, for these words are trustworthy and
> true." (Rev. 21:1–5)

Patterns in the Storyline

That was a quick overview of the storyline of creation and re-creation. I'm
relying on the fact that you know at least some of the details of the story
that I didn't have time to spell out.

But before we consider what the story teaches us, consider *how* it
teaches us.

First, notice what I've already said—the whole thing plays out as a
story. Now when I say story, I don't mean it's fictional, any more than the
story of your life is fictional. What I mean is that, like all stories, God's

story of creation has a narrative structure. There's a beginning—creation. Tension comes into the plot with the fall. In the middle, the plot gets interesting through all the cycles of creation, sin, judgment, re-creation, and so forth. Along the way these cycles provide mini-climaxes and new developments. Finally, there's a truly climactic ending—the new heavens and the new earth.

Second, there is a clear pattern of promise and fulfillment throughout. God promised Abraham many descendents, a land, and that he would be a blessing. Clearly, God fulfilled this promise with Isaac, then the twelve sons of Israel, then the whole nation. But this promise was fulfilled at multiple levels. These many descendants not only include the old covenant nation of Israel, they include the new covenant church. And the Promised Land turned out to be not only Palestine, but the new creation itself.

Third, we find the covenantal storyline of Scripture here as well. In fact, if I had time, I would have explained the covenants with Noah, Abraham, and David. Taking note of all these covenants is important because our precise location in the covenantal storyline will affect our systematic theology conclusions. For instance, suppose someone wanted to argue for the legalization of marijuana by saying that everything God created "was good." Therefore, plants like marijuana are good. Well, everything God created *was* good . . . in Genesis 1. But then Genesis 3 happened, and that changed not only us, it significantly changed the world as well. You can't just proof-text like that.

Fourth, notice also God's use of typology in the storyline of creation. Re-creation after the flood was a type of creation. Calling the nation of Israel out of slavery into the Promised Land was a type of creation. But these types always pointed forward toward the antitype, the new creation inaugurated by Christ. Through the repetition of the types, we learn something of how God works and what he cares about.

Fifth, you probably noticed other patterns to this story as well. For instance, the fact that God always creates and re-creates through his Word, or that he creates and re-creates for his glory. You might also have noticed that re-creation always revolves around a single, representative man, no matter how many other people might be involved. This man always stands like Adam as a representative mediator for those who follow. The story of creation and the story of the son of God are inextricably intertwined. My goal here isn't therefore to exhaustively list all the patterns, but to prompt you to start looking for them.

Systematizing It All

We've heard the story. We've briefly considered how the story works. How then do we put all this together and apply it to the Christian and to the church?

As we think about the creation story's significance, I think that several doctrines become apparent. I want to highlight a few of these and consider how we might think about them in light of how the story works.

1) God Creates from Nothing

To start with, *God created everything from nothing.*

> In the beginning God created the heavens and the earth. (Gen. 1:1)

> Through him all things were made, without him nothing was made that has been made. (John 1:3)

What this means is that God is the owner of creation. He made it, so it's his. That means you and I are his, too.

Consider the systematic applications we can draw from this.

1) *God is all-powerful. He is creative. He is Creator. And he is Lord.* This has real application in our evangelism. In a postmodern context, people don't mind if we believe in God. If it works for you, that's great. What they mind is our attempt to impose our belief on them. So we must be clear, we aren't imposing anything. Christianity isn't a social project aiming at cultural hegemony. It's a declaration that God has a legitimate claim on all of our lives. This is why there is so much heat in the public debate over evolution and intelligent design. Fundamentally, it's not a battle over science; it's a battle over independence from God. The problem is, independence from God means slavery to everything else—our passions, our desires, our failures. The creation story makes this clear.

2) *Creation had a beginning. It has a purpose. It is good.* This has application for environmental stewardship, the humane treatment of animals, and the possibility and appropriateness of scientific research. But it also has application for our worship. Creation is not ultimate, and God is not the same as his creation. Any way of life that seeks to find final fulfillment in the creature rather than the Creator is idolatrous and rightly attracts God's judgment.

Yet it's as we're considering the typological pattern of creation throughout the storyline that we realize we're not just talking about a doctrine of creation. When we get to the New Testament, we're also talking about the doctrine of salvation. God creates our salvation out of nothing, as it were. We were dead, but he makes us alive. So we're called "new creations." Here's how Paul puts it:

> For God, who said, "Let light shine out of darkness," [*that's creation*] has shone in our hearts to give the light of the knowledge of the glory of God in the face of Jesus Christ [*that's new creation*]. (2 Cor. 4:6)

Do you see? God teaches us about our salvation and how it works through Old Testament patterns of creation. Are you tempted to think that you chose God, or that you saved yourself in any way at all? You might even have a New Testament proof-text to back you up. But hold on; look at the storyline of the whole Bible. Consider the fact that God creates out of *nothing* and how that might affect your understanding of salvation. That's exactly what Paul wants you to do in 2 Corinthians 4:6.

2) God Creates by His Word

Here's another theme worth pondering. Not only did God create everything from nothing, *God also created everything by his Word.*

> And God said, "Let there be light," and there was light. (Gen. 1:3)

If you and I make something, we need raw material to work with. Not so with God. As Paul says in Romans 4:17, "He calls things that are not as though they were," and then they are. God creates by speaking.

Whenever and whatever God creates, it's an act of powerful, irresistible grace. Nothing forces God to speak. He only speaks when he wants to. But when he does speak, things happen. And it's not just that he creates the potentiality for things. No, things happen. As we said in the introduction, God's words are not just true, they are effectual. God speaking *is* God acting.

- In Genesis 1, the void could not resist him.
- In Ezekiel 37, when Ezekiel calls out to the valley of the dry bones with God's Word and Spirit, the bones didn't say to Ezekiel, "We don't want to get up."
- In John 11, when Jesus calls out to the corpse of Lazarus, Lazarus didn't say to Jesus, "Not now, ask me again next year." No, when the voice of God rings out in gracious, creative power, not even death or unbelief can resist him.

God's voice is irresistible because it is powerful and because it is the voice of love.

Do you see a typological pattern developing here? Could it be that God is doing things among physical realities to teach us something about spiritual realities? If God's Word effectually creates every time, what do you think happens when Jesus calls out to sinners to come to him in repentance and faith? Does his Word all of a sudden become less effective, less powerful, just because he's talking to us?

Also, if God's Word effectually creates every time—"my word will not return back to me void," he says in Isaiah 55:11—what do you think churches should do when they gather? Should they concentrate on entertainment or on preaching the Word? I suppose it depends on whether they want a ministry designed to amuse the dying or a ministry aimed at raising the dead.

Notice what's happening with these various examples I'm giving you. I told you a story about creation. Then I pointed out *how* the story unfolds. And by doing that, we're able to draw systematic theology conclusions. More to the point, we're able to apply this story to our personal lives and our church life together today.

3) God Creates for His Glory

Another theme in the story of creation we should notice is that *God creates everything for his glory.*

God didn't need to create anything. There is nothing necessary about this universe. But in love and grace, he chose to create everything so that his glory might be the joy and delight of others. As Revelation 4:11 declares, "You are worthy, our Lord and God, to receive glory and honor and power, for you created all things, and *by your will* they were created and have their being."

Now it's easy to read that verse and think, "God created things for his glory. That makes sense. We go to church every Sunday and sing hymns of praise. God is all about worship. Fine." But if we stop there, we've really missed what this doctrine is saying to us.

Go back and look at the entire story again. In Genesis 1, we're told that the creation of human beings was different than the rest of creation. Unlike the animals, people—that is, you and me—were created to reflect the very character and glory of God.

> Then God said, "Let us make man in our image, in our likeness, and let them rule . . . " (Gen. 1:26)

Our lives have been created and purposed to image, or reflect, the glory of God. That's why we exist. In fact, the fall, the giving of the law, David's kingdom, the exile of Israel, and Christ's coming are all about this particular storyline, which is summarized in Revelation 4. All of life and history is about glorifying God. My very reason for drawing breath today is to glorify God.

When I build my systematic theology on a more comprehensive biblical theology, I discover that Revelation 4:11 is about much more than what I sing on Sunday morning or what I'll be singing in eternity. It all deepens and broadens, incorporating the whole of history and the whole of your life and mine. Does it offend you that we and all the rest of creation exist for God's glory? It certainly runs counter to everything inside us.

But when we understand that God freely created us for his glory, we finally realize that the story of creation is fundamentally a love story. God didn't have to create us, but he did. He didn't have to create us as bearers of his image, but he did. And in doing so, he gave us a unique ability—the ability to take joy in the highest, most beautiful, most desirable thing imaginable, the glory of God. God himself loves nothing more than his own glory. There is nothing better or higher to love. There is nothing more beautiful to fall in love with.

What's amazing is that, out of that same love, he created you and me to participate in his glory as image-bearers. Our own stories are swept up into the greatest love story that will ever be known, the story of the unending and unsurpassed glory of God.

4) Creation Is Frustrated in Its Purpose and Subjected to Death

There's one last theme I want us to notice in this creation story. If we're to understand the story of creation, we need to understand the effect our rebellion has had upon it.

1) *Because of sin, creation is frustrated in its purpose to display God's glory.* Paul puts it this way in Romans 8:20:

> The creation was subjected to frustration, not by its own choice, but by the will of the one who subjected it.

Who subjected creation? God did. In response to Adam and Eve's sin, creation would no longer be the pure stage of God's glory. Instead, creation would be both the context of our judgment and at times an agent of God's wrath against us. Far from being an ever-expanding garden of Eden, the world became a place of weeds and thorns, toil and frustration.

But God's curse on creation goes beyond frustrating its purpose.

2) *Because of sin, creation has also been subjected to death.* This is precisely the sentence God passed.

> For dust you are, and to dust you will return. (Gen. 3:19)

Paul put it this way:

> Therefore, just as sin entered the world through one man, and death through sin . . . in this way death came to all men, because all sinned. (Rom. 5:12)

This world is not the way it's supposed to be. God created it to be a place of joy; instead, we know it to be a source of constant frustration. God created it to be a habitat of life; we know it to be a crucible of death. God created it to be our home; we know it to be our graveyard.

We are dead spiritually, and we're going to die physically. There's nothing we can do to change that. And we have no one to blame but ourselves.

Now, all of this bad news was at least latent if not explicit in Genesis 3. But then the storyline plays out these themes of frustration and death over and over as the story continues:

- Cain murders Abel in Genesis 4.
- The world of Noah's day is destroyed in Genesis 6–8.
- The Tower of Babel leads to division in Genesis 11, and on and on it goes.

In some ways the storyline of the entire Old Testament focuses on explaining the sinfulness of humanity and the absolute futility of any solution to creation's demise and human sin that we might conjure up—whether towers, or mighty nations, or rigorous self-discipline.

And from all of this, we draw conclusions for our theology. It helps us understand human nature, the futility of work, even government and the corrupting influence of power. We could get a doctrine of sin simply by looking at Romans 3:23—"all have sinned," it says. There it is. Isn't that really the bottom line?

Well, remember what I said at the beginning about the fact the Bible gives us an opportunity to walk along with God and humanity, so that we might learn to see what he's like, and what we're like? Read the book of

Numbers and put yourself in God's shoes as the Israelites complain over and over and fail to trust God when he has proven over and over that he is trustworthy. Read the histories of 1 Kings and 2 Kings, and watch the nation turn away from him again and again, while God lovingly sends prophet after prophet to warn them. Following along the storyline like this deepens and broadens the bottom line of your theology because it deepens and broadens your understanding of God, yourself, and the world in which you now live. You'll see patterns emerge and repeat themselves over and over, and those patterns will change the way you think and the way you see.

So when your own child turns two and begins to throw temper tantrums when he doesn't get his way, you may think of Romans 3:23. But you'll also think of the book of Numbers and thousands of years of Israelite history, and you'll know what's behind Romans 3:23 and what exactly your child is doing. He's worshipping an idol. Its name isn't Baal, but it might as well be. Of course, this isn't just useful for explaining your two-year-old's heart; it's useful for explaining your own heart as well.

At the same time, the Old Testament offers us a promise of one who would come and release creation from its captivity. We're promised a time when the wolf would lie down with the lamb, and the leopard with the young calf. And it promises a king who will come to usher in this new creation. How will the king accomplish this great rescue?

3) *Because of sin, the Creator dies as a substitute for his creatures.* Given the scope of the problem, we're not really surprised when the King who shows up is the Creator himself. Remarkably, the Creator-King comes and dies in order to usher in his new creation.

Is his death totally unexpected? Not if you've been reading your Bible typologically. The idea is there from the beginning:

- God kills animals to cover (same word as atone) Adam and Eve's nakedness.
- God calls Abraham to sacrifice his son, but then offers a ram.
- Joseph was left for dead, and his "sacrifice" was used to save the world.
- The Passover lamb is sacrificed so the Israelite firstborn are spared.
- The Levitical sacrifices are offered repeatedly for the forgiveness of sins.

The idea of substitution was there from the beginning. The amazing, unexpected twist in the story is that the final substitute is the Creator himself. We couldn't have invented this idea even if we'd tried.

I could keep going. Throughout the story, God was teaching about himself, about us, and about how salvation would come. He could have just given us the bottom line. But he didn't because he wanted to give us so much more. He wanted to give us himself.

Conclusion: Creation's Goal

As I said before, the story of creation really is a love story, the story of a bridegroom who will stop at nothing, not even the cost of his own life, to win for himself a bride, and to present her to himself radiantly beautiful, spotless, and pure. The story ends with the bridegroom preparing a new home for the new couple—a new heaven and a new earth. Unlike Adam with his bride, this bridegroom promises that he will exclude everything from that new home that might spoil or detract from their love.

In that place, there will be no more crying or pain, because there will be no more sin and evil. Only love will be there, as Christ and his bride display the glory of God's redeeming grace, and the angels watch in awe.

We're not there yet. But we will be. Are you living for that day? Will your story be included in that story? It can be. God's grace is sufficient, and the call of his love is irresistible. Pray that you will have ears to hear God's voice of love in Christ. Pastor, pray that your people will have such ears. Do not rest content until you are sure that the only voice they hear from your pulpit is that singular voice, that matchless and irresistible voice of love.

CHAPTER SEVEN

The Story of the Fall

Suppose a friend or church member were to ask you questions like these:

> What's wrong with this world—that my niece has cancer?
> Why do people do bad things, like the terrorists we read about in the newspaper?
> Are people basically good or bad? I feel like I'm good, but sometimes I do things I regret.
> Why do people die? My mother is about to die.
> Why does it seem like there's so little true justice in this world? I just read about all those people starving in Sudan because of an unjust government.
> Can I trust the God whom you claim rules over this world?

Notice, this person is asking belief questions, questions that help him know what to believe about life here and now. He's not just asking you what the Bible says. He's asking you to engage his life, what really matters to him. How do we get from what the Bibles says to where life is lived?

The Bible answers those kinds of questions in crisp statements here and there. But most of the time, it answers those questions with history—history, and propositions, and poetry, and prophecy, and more. In other words, it offers not just answers, but a whole new perspective and worldview. And it does all this by telling the story of the fall. You're probably familiar with it, but let me tell it to you again.

The Story of the Fall

The story of the fall begins in Paradise. God has created Adam and Eve, and he has put them in a perfect world in order to be a reflection of his glory. He's provided them everything that they need. He's given them meaningful, enjoyable, and satisfying work. He's given them each other. And he has established them as rulers over all creation under him. There's only one limit he has placed upon their freedom and authority. There is one tree in the garden of Eden that they are not to eat from, the tree known as the Tree of the Knowledge of Good and Evil.

In comes Satan, tempting them to do the one thing, really the only thing that they should not do. Incredibly, they fall for his scheme. They choose to disobey God. In doing so, they fall from a state of moral innocence to a state of shame, disgrace, and condemnation.

In the Day that You Eat of It . . .

Immediately, everything changes. Because of their decision to rebel, God judges Adam and Eve. Life will now be filled with pain, toil, and sadness. What's more, they are kicked out of Paradise and exiled from their home. An angel wielding a flaming sword is put at the entrance to the gate to the garden to make sure that they will never return alive. But their physical expulsion is just the prelude to a far more profound exile that will affect not only them, but all of their descendants. Now these who were created to live forever, who were fashioned for eternity, as Thomas Wolfe famously commented, are subject to death—an exile that never ends.

. . . You Shall Surely Die

As the story proceeds, we find that the consequences of Adam and Eve's rebellion are even more profound than at first appearance. Children are born, but not in innocence. Adam and Eve's very nature has been corrupted and twisted. Augustine described it as a "turning in on itself," so that now their nature no longer truly reflects God's glory, but is distorted and marred. That nature, along with the guilt it earns, is passed on to their children.

And so the fall didn't simply happen and we move on. Rather it continues and deepens as creation succumbs to death and decay. Things fall apart. The center does not hold.

Satan had managed to murder the souls of Adam and Eve.

Cain actually murders his brother Abel.

Satan had managed to drive a wedge in between Adam and Eve.

Lamech abandons marital union and takes two wives.

Cain murdered out of jealous passion.

Lamech murders just because a guy injures him.

And so it goes, until humanity's wickedness had become so great that "every inclination of the thoughts of his heart was only evil all the time" (Gen. 6:5). God's patience eventually runs out. He decides that he must finally judge the very men and women he had created in his own image.

The Cycle Continues

God sends the flood to destroy humanity, sparing only Noah and his family. The world gets a fresh start. It would seem that Noah is a new Adam. The only problem is that Noah and his family still have the fallen nature they inherited from him. Once again the progress of sin picks up right where it left off and quickly gathers steam. Eventually humanity is right back where they started—well, almost started. We're right back to the eve of the flood. Only now God judges humanity not by destroying all of it, but by confusing humanity's language at Babel in Genesis 11. Divided from one another, scattered across the face of the earth, humanity's exile has only deepened.

In this context, God calls out for himself a special people. Beginning with Abraham, God separates from the mass of humanity a people of his very own. They are to obey him and know him as their God. But even here, the fall continues to make itself felt. Lot and his family choose the wickedness of Sodom and Gomorrah over the godly society of Abraham. Esau chooses the comforts of this world rather than the promises of God. Finally, the nation of Israel, even after God rescues it from slavery in Egypt and promises to bring it into the edenic Promised Land, abandons God for idols. And they can't even wait for Moses to come down from the mountain to do it!

We're back in the garden all over again. When Moses comes down and sees their idolatry he calls the Levites to his side at the gate of the camp. The camp of the Israelites was to be a holy place, a veritable, moving garden of Eden. But sin has now invaded the camp, just as sin entered the garden of Eden. Recalling the flaming sword of Genesis 3, Moses tells his brother Levites to strap swords to their sides, and to go throughout the camp and execute God's judgment.

You would think that God's people would have learned from this. Or from the fact that none of that generation was allowed to enter the Promised Land, but died in the desert. But they didn't. Generations followed, and at times it seemed as if each new generation competed with the one before to exceed them in wickedness. In response to this, God finally exiles the Israelites from the Promised Land, just as he had exiled Adam and Eve so very long ago.

Seventy years later, the southern kingdom of Judah comes back. But though their physical exile is over, it's clear that their spiritual exile continues. God does not reinhabit the temple; the Holy of Holies stands empty. Eventually, even the prophets fall silent. At the end of the Old Testament,

God's visible people seem no better off than the Gentiles. Jew and Gentile alike stand under threat of God's judgment. In fact, the final words of the Old Testament are an echo of Genesis 3, warning that God will come and strike the land with a curse.

The Fall's End

As the New Testament opens, a new prophet, John the Baptist, appears on the scene and picks up where Malachi left off, warning the people of the judgment to come. But it would seem that no one is listening. God sends his own Son, Jesus, who leads a life of perfect love and perfect obedience, a life that should have offended no one. But humanity has become so wicked that now Jew and Gentile plot together to put to death the only man who never deserved to die. They nail him to a cross, and declare that their only king is Caesar.

That was two thousand years ago. Since then, humanity's corruption and evil has known wider scope and greater efficiency. But nothing has really changed. All the wars, including the ones going on now, all the assaults and murders, the slavery, the genocides that have marked the last hundred years, the exploitation of women and children for purposes of sexual gratification, even the cruel indifference of the rich for the poor, all of that has just been commentary on that first rebellious declaration of independence from God.

What will be the end of the fall? What will be the end of this story? In Revelation 18 we see the final fall. It is a day yet in the future when this world will fall under God's final judgment, never to rise again. Those who chose to worship idols rather than God will be left outside of heaven, and the tormented anguish of their exile in hell will last for all eternity.

Patterns in the Storyline

That's the story of the fall as the Bible tells it. It's a sobering story. But before we consider what it means and how it applies to our life and ministry, we want to think again about what we can learn from *how* the story is told. What patterns do we see in this storyline?

First, the patterns of narrative structure, promise and fulfillment, covenant and typology that I identified in the creation storyline are also present here. I won't work each of those out. But I do want to point out that the fall marks one of the most significant divisions in history, and all of us stand on the wrong side of that division. Many things happen in the Bible that don't have a universal effect. The fall is not one of them.

Second, we see a pattern of *causes* of the fall.

On the one hand, the fall was *instigated* by Satan's malice and deception. From the beginning, the Bible makes clear that Satan has an implacable hostility toward God and an unending hatred for humanity. And he hasn't stopped his work of deception and temptation.

On the other hand, the fall was also freely *chosen* by Adam and Eve. Satan's line was as bold as it was false: "If you eat of this tree, then your eyes will be opened and you will be like God, knowing good and evil." Not content to be mere creatures; not content to have a mere relationship with God, reflecting back to God his glory, Adam and Eve desired to be like God. They desired to be gods themselves. This was not simple disobedience. As the story continues, we recognize their desire as idolatry: the substitution of the creature for the Creator as the object of our loyalty, desire, and worship. And with every mini-fall after that, we see the same thing. From Babel to the golden calves, from Moses' disobedience to David's fall, we see the desire to set our own rules and reach for our own glory. The fall is a historical event, but it's also the pattern of our lives.

Third, we see a pattern of *effects* from the fall.

Effect 1: We are *banished* from God's presence. At first we're not entirely sure why. But as the story continues, we learn that God is a holy God. We learn this especially in the Torah. He can neither tolerate sin in his presence nor can he allow sin to go unpunished.

Effect 2: We are also *corrupted* in our nature, which, again, becomes more and more clear as the story develops. Cain proves it. The Tower of Babel proves it. Israel, with all of God's blessings, proves it. The problem of sin is not fundamentally one of behavior or education. It is far more radical. The problem is our heart. The Psalmist said in Psalm 51 that we are conceived in iniquity and born in sin (Ps. 51:5). We come out of the womb as sinners. This means that we aren't sinners because we sin; we sin because we are by nature sinners!

Fourth, we see the pattern of the *progress* of the fall.

It's clear from the storyline that the fall was not *just* a one-time event. After the Chicago fire of 1871, the city was rebuilt. But all these millennia later, we still haven't recovered from the fall at the beginning of creation.

What's more, the fall is *progressive*, not static. Things didn't just go from good to bad. Rather, things continue to get worse. They don't stay the same, and they don't get better. It's like a fatal disease that begins at a point in time, but then progresses and runs its ever increasingly destructive course.

Before we answer the questions with which we began this chapter, notice how we're going about looking for our answers. We're looking at the characters and plot of the storyline. We're considering how it develops. We're assuming that, though the story spans millennia and was written down by numerous human authors, it's one grand story, with one divine author. So we're paying attention to its patterns and cycles across the words of multiple human authors. And we're making sure we know where we are in the story before we draw any hard and fast conclusions.

Systematizing It All

Let's return to that hypothetical friend's questions from the beginning of this chapter. Whether he knew it or not, he was asking doctrinal questions. He was asking what the Bible means for understanding the world today. Our goal is to help him and others see God's perspective on God, on himself, and on the world around him.

Only by taking care with the whole storyline can we responsibly answer him. Based on the story and the patterns we have observed, let me try to enunciate some basic lessons—doctrines that give us God's perspective on his questions.

1) We Do Not Live in a Spiritually Neutral Universe

This world and our lives are a battlefield, not a playground. True to his form as a liar from the beginning, Satan would deceive us into thinking that nothing is really amiss, at least nothing that we can't take care of ourselves. He would have us think that we're better off without God, that our best interests are served by pursuing our own desires and enlarging our liberty from anything that would restrict us from fulfilling those desires. But Satan was lying on that day when he deceived Adam and Eve, and he is still lying. Satan intends our enslavement, not our freedom. He doesn't intend to enhance our lives; he intends to hasten our death.

We need to warn people not to be lulled into a false sense of peace in this world. The peace they feel is not the peace of paradise, but the peace of the morgue. Our ears need to be saturated with the Bible and our minds shaped by the worldview the Bible creates, so that we will recognize the lie when it's whispered softly and sweetly in our ear.

2) God Is Not Morally Culpable for This Fallen World; We Are

Many are tempted to blame God for the mess this world is in. I understand the feeling, but we need to know that according to Scripture, that is just another one of Satan's subtle lies. Adam and Eve were created in such a way that they were able to say no to sin and Satan's temptation. They had every natural help and aid you could want. They were standing in Paradise. They had each other. They had a clear, unequivocal, simple command from God. It wasn't hard to understand. And they chose, in utter freedom, to sin. That's right. The finest examples of the human race ever to live made an utter and complete hash of it.

This realization should lead us to a profound humility. It is only arrogance that whispers in the heart, "If I had been there, I would have done better. I would have chosen differently." No, you wouldn't have. We are in this mess because we put ourselves there. And so when we witness someone else's sin, we know as Luther said, "There, but for the grace of God, go I."

3) People Do Bad Things Because They Want to Be God, and He Is Just to Condemn Them

Like Adam and Eve, most of the time the real object of our worship isn't some creature out there, it's this creature right here. In the end, my idolatry centers on me. What's more, if I can persuade you or bully you or manipulate you, my idolatry will include you worshiping me as well.

As long as we think of sin as simple rule-breaking, we will never understand the enormity of sin, the incredible offense that it gives to God, and the justness of his response. Fundamentally, sin is not a matter of our behavior, though it eventually shows up in our actions. Fundamentally, sin is a matter of our hearts, for as fallen creatures our ruling desire is to remove God from his throne and to sit there instead.

Were it not so devastatingly real, it would be laughable, like a child playing dress-up in his father's closet. Were it not so evil, it would be pathetic, like Don Quixote tilting at windmills. But idolatry is neither laughable nor pathetic, for its effects are devastating, and its course is terrifying. Sin is no trifling matter. There is no more deadly lie that Satan would have you believe.

4) God is Holy, and Can Have Nothing to Do with Sin

People are not helped if our churches and preaching allow them to think of God as they would like to think of him. People need to think of God as he really is, a holy God who judges sin justly. This is why the New Testament takes so seriously the character of our fellowship in the local church. Paul asks in 2 Corinthians 6:14, "[W]hat do righteousness and wickedness have in common? Or what fellowship can light have with darkness?" It's not that Paul didn't want believers to talk to unbelievers. Quite the contrary.

In every conversation, in every interaction, in every encounter, he wanted unbelievers to see the difference between the church and the world, so that God's character would be accurately displayed and known. One obvious point of application here is to be careful in our membership practices. When we admit someone to the church who gives little to no evidence of being regenerate, or when we allow someone to continue as a member despite persistent unrepentant sin, we blur the line between the world and the church, and dim our display of God's glory.

5) There Is No Area of Our Lives Unaffected by Sin; We Are Enslaved to It

This does not mean that the Bible teaches we are as bad as we could be. But it does mean that there is no aspect of our lives, no aspect of our thinking, desires, or behavior that is untouched by the stain of sin. Even our best deeds, says Isaiah, are as filthy rags since they come from hearts that are committed to our own glory rather than God's (Isa. 64:6).

This also helps us understand what the Bible means when it says we are slaves to sin, which is an image that Paul uses in Romans 6 and 7. Some people are fond of debating whether or not we have free will. The Bible's answer is that it depends on what you mean by "free." If by "free" you mean that we do what we want to do, that nothing forces us to believe or to act against our will, then the Bible's answer is "yes." Our will is always free to act in accord with its nature. But if by "free" you mean that somehow our will is morally neutral and above the fray, able to choose between good and evil on its own merits, independent of predisposition or motive, then the answer is a clear and unequivocal "no." Our nature is corrupted and, as Paul says, we are sold as slaves to sin. We can no more choose not to be sinners than a fish can choose not to be a swimmer. It's our nature.

This doctrine of the will's bondage (or the depravity of humanity) has enormous implications for our evangelism. Contrary to what many people think, it doesn't lead us to give up evangelism. Rather, it leads us to give up manipulative practices in order to elicit a decision. It encourages us to share the good news and then to pray that God will change the heart through the preaching of his Word by the power of his Spirit. Ultimately, understanding our inability to choose God unless God first chooses us actually frees the evangelist to evangelize, and leaves the converting to God!

6) We Cannot Save Ourselves; We Need a Savior

We need more than a self-help program. We need something far more radical than a make-over that helps us straighten out our lives. Self-help programs and make-overs only make for prettier, more presentable slaves. What we need is freedom. We need new natures that are freed from the corruption and bondage of sin. We can no more fix ourselves than a slave can free himself. A slave must be freed, and so must we.

This has application to everything from our evangelism and preaching to our understanding of the Christian life. It means that conversion is a work of the Holy Spirit changing our nature, not the result of a seeker making a decision. It means that real Christians have a new nature and new lives that look increasingly different than the world around them, a nature that says "no" to sin. It also means that the Christian life is a life of conflict, as the new nature battles against the old.

The Bible calls these two natures the "old man" and the "new man," and they are in deadly conflict with one another. I think we often grow discouraged that this war continues, but what we need to understand is that this war is not going on in the heart of someone who has not been born again. Conflict with sin is one of the best evidences that someone has been given spiritual life. This is Paul's point in Romans 7.

Rather than pretending there is no struggle, our churches should be places that encourage this conflict. Rather than shooting the wounded, our churches should be places that bind up those who are injured in the fight. Above all, our churches should be communities that hold out the hope of Christ, who alone can free us from these bodies of death.

7) God Will Restore All Justice to the Universe by Judging Sin

Jesus says that the day of judgment has already been set in the mind of God. The vision of that day revealed in Revelation 18 is terrible. The fall does not end in rehabilitation or gradual reform as things get slowly better in an unending vision of progress. No, the fall comes to a final judgment. Pictured as a great city, sinful creation falls under God's judgment, *never* to rise again.

> Then a mighty angel picked up a boulder the size of a large millstone and threw it into the sea, and said: "With such violence the great city of Babylon

will be thrown down, never to be found again. The music of harpists and musicians, flute players and trumpeters, will never be heard in you again. No workman of any trade will ever be found in you again. The sound of a millstone will never be heard in you again. The light of a lamp will never shine in you again. The voice of bridegroom and bride will never be heard in you again. Your merchants were the world's great men. By your magic spell all the nations were led astray." (Rev. 18:21–23)

Not only final, this judgment will be *just*. The same chapter tells us that God will remember the crimes of this idolatrous world and he will repay her for her crimes. He will give to each of us exactly what we are due.

So how do we answer our friend who asks about cancer, and death, and terrorism? How do we respond to the friend who is anxious over environmental degradation or economic collapse? What do we say when people ask us why there isn't justice in the world?

If we want to duck and dodge, and yet appear intellectually honest, we take the open theism route: we claim that God didn't mean for it to be this way, and that he didn't know it would happen like this. If we want to avoid responsibility altogether, we blame it all on someone or something else: Satan, capitalism, communism, feminism, patriarchy, the Republicans, the Democrats, etc.

But if we want to be fair to the Bible, and honest with our friend, we will tell it like it is. God didn't create the world to be ravaged by things like cancer and terrorism. But he did curse the good world that he made. Why would he do such a thing? Why would he ordain things like cancer, and mothers who die too young? Why would he curse the ground, so that crops fail and earthquakes destroy cities? He did it because of our sin. This is not to say that a person's cancer is a specific judgment for a specific sin. Rather, it's to acknowledge that we have all set ourselves up as gods in place of him, and in doing so we have attracted his just wrath. God has rightly cursed this world because of us. We have no one to blame but ourselves.

But this isn't all that we have to say in response to such questions. There is one important aspect to the story we have yet to consider, and it's this aspect that allows us to explain why, in the midst of a fallen world, we can trust the God whose judgment we stand under.

Conclusion: The Cure for the Fall

When we understand the story of the fall (and not until then), we understand why the message of Christianity is good news. In the gospel, God has accomplished a *cure* for the fall, a rescue from this horrifying, accelerating descent into hell.

That cure is Jesus. In Matthew 4, we see something absolutely extraordinary. The Son of God has become a man. Like unfallen Adam, Jesus was not born in sin, but was conceived directly by the Holy Spirit. Also like unfallen Adam, Jesus is called to obey God in the face of an extraordinary Satanic assault. But that's where the similarities with Adam end. Whereas Adam stood in Paradise with a full stomach, Jesus stood in the desert of our exile from God with a stomach shrunken by forty days of fasting. Whereas Adam had the help of a wife, Jesus stood alone. Whereas Adam had a single command to obey, Jesus had the whole law to keep and fulfill.

Beginning there in the desert and continuing all the way to Calvary, Jesus did what Adam failed to do. He resisted Satan's temptation to exalt himself on his own terms, whether that was to turn stones into bread or to come down from the cross. Jesus freely chose to obey God, even to the point of death (John 10:18). "Not my will but yours be done," he said.

Unlike Adam, Jesus did not pursue his own glory, but laid that aside in order to glorify his Father. The irony is deep and rich, for unlike Adam, Jesus was in very nature God. He had every right to pursue his glory! Yet as Paul tell us in Philippians 2:6, Jesus "did not consider equality with God something to be grasped, but made himself nothing, taking the very nature of a servant, being made in human likeness." And then he bore our sin and suffered the judgment of God for it. He did not deserve this judgment. Instead, he suffered it on behalf of those who did.

On the cross, Jesus faced God's flaming sword, guarding the way back into the garden and the presence of God. He walked through it at the cost of his own life. He did this so that any who repent of their idolatry and turn in faith to Christ might find forgiveness for sins and reconciliation with God. He did it so that he could welcome us back home.

Paul says in Romans 5, "If the many died by the trespass of the one man, how much more did God's grace and the gift that came by the grace of the one man, Jesus Christ, overflow to the many!" That gift is the opposite of the curse: forgiveness instead of condemnation, life instead of death, reconciliation instead of exile.

Here is the answer to how we can trust God in the face of so much evil and suffering in this world. Here is the answer of how we can trust the God who cursed us for our sin. He is the same God who suffered for us to conquer evil and sin. He is the same God who bore the curse for us, that we might know his blessing.

Think about how amazing this is. The cross was not "Plan B" for God. It was the plan from the very beginning.

On the day in the garden when God declared that the judgment for sin was death, on the day that the flaming sword was put in place, prefiguring the judgment each of us must face, on *that* day, the Son of God was there sharing in the decision. It was the decision of the Trinity to banish Adam and Eve from the garden. It was an act of judgment, yes, but also an act of mercy. To remain in God's presence as a sinner was to die. Banishment forestalled that sentence. And it was the decision of the Trinity to deny the Tree of Life to fallen humanity. Again, it was an act of judgment, but also an act of mercy. To live forever as an unredeemed sinner is surely the definition of hell. Once again, final judgment was forestalled. Why?

God did not intend this story to be brought to a premature conclusion. If the story of the fall reveals our own sin and guilt, it surely also reveals the amazing depths of God's love and mercy. It was the Son of God who placed a sword at the entrance to the garden of Eden. He did it not just to keep Adam out. He did it so that, at just the right time, he could walk through in our place, to satisfy God's just wrath and make a way for us to enter back in, through the gate, to eat from the Tree of Life and live forever in the glorious presence of God.

Here is the answer to how we can trust God in a fallen world. He is none other than "the Lamb that was slain from the foundation of the world" for sinners such as me.

CHAPTER EIGHT

The Story of Love

I pastor a church filled with twenty- and thirty-something singles, and the question of love comes up pretty often. How do you know when someone loves you? It's on their minds. A child knows his parents love him when they provide for him. You know your friends love you when they stick up for you against your detractors. But how do you *know* if that special she or he loves you?

The fact is, the most powerful way most of us know that we are really loved is marriage. On a wedding day, a man says to a woman and a woman to a man that, out of the all the possibilities and options, "I choose you." Families have to love us, and friends get to go home at night. But spouses are another matter altogether. My wife could have married anyone, or even chosen not to marry, rather than marry me. But she chose me until death us do part, and if you knew me, you'd know that's true love.

Deep in the human psyche, all of us long to be chosen by love. It hurts, because we know we don't deserve it, but we want it anyway. It's really this that gives all the best stories about love their power. Whether it's the comedy of confused choices in Shakespeare's *Much Ado About Nothing*, or the pathos of a doomed choice in *Romeo and Juliet*, the power comes from how much is riding on love's choice and how mysterious that choice is. As Pascal said, "Love has reasons which reason cannot understand."

Surely the greatest love story of all is the story of God's love, a story as wide as creation, as dramatic as anything Shakespeare ever thought up, and as personal as you and me. For our own love stories are really echoes of the far greater story of God's love for the world.

This is why it's especially important for us to get our biblical theology of love right. We want to know what to believe about God's love for us, and the love we should have for others. After all, we can all take our favorite love "proof-text" and use it to say, "This is what love is like," or "This is what God is like."

For some, John 3:16 is a favorite prooftext: "For God so loved the world that he gave his only begotten Son . . ." What they usually mean is, "God loves everyone equally. He doesn't choose some and not others to salvation." Love means equality of opportunity.

Probably one of the most popular prooftexts in the Bible must be 1 John 4:16—"God is love." Why is that so popular? We can use it to say whatever we want to about God's love.

Theologian Kevin Vanhoozer has observed that the topic of love, as much as any other topic, is susceptible to the temptation to project our desires onto God.[1] But what does the Bible mean when it says, "God is love"? To answer that question, we need to look, not at a verse, but at the entire story of love as God reveals it in Scripture.

Love's Story

The story of God's love is a fairly simple story, like the story of a man choosing one woman to be his bride. It's the story of God choosing to love his people, and that choice is repeated and clarified as history unfolds.

In the beginning, God displays his love for all humanity by providing a perfect and beautiful world for us. Beauty isn't necessary for function, but God's love went beyond the pragmatic. He made a beautiful world, and then created us to be attracted to that beauty. Adam and Eve loved one another, but ultimately they were created to be attracted to God, the most beautiful person in their experience.

Unbelievably, Adam and Eve reject God's love when they decide to reject his Word. What's truly unbelievable, though, is that their rejection of God's love doesn't bring the story to an end. God excludes them from the garden, but he continues to love them. He places enmity between them and their greatest enemy, the serpent who deceived them (Gen. 3:15). He reunites the two of them in love. Practically, he loves them in the simple act of covering their shameful nakedness with clothes.

God continues to love the descendants of those who first rejected him. Though Cain and his heirs are rejected by God, Seth and his sons after him are loved by God, down the long generations to Noah. While humanity's wicked hatred of God finally culminates in the flood, still God's love is not completely extinguished. He chooses to save Noah and his family from destruction, and then particularly blesses Noah's son Shem, and the line that descends from him.

---

[1]Kevin Vanhoozer, *Nothing Greater, Nothing Better: Theological Essays on the Love of God* (Grand Rapids, MI: Eerdmans, 2001), 2n1.

Notice the pattern here. God loves all by giving *all* life. But he also seems to love *some* specially. Seth, not Cain. Noah, not all those around him. Shem, not Ham.

In Genesis 12, the story comes into sharp focus with God's call of Abram out of idolatry and into friendship and covenant with him. He promises Abram that he has chosen him and that his descendants will become a great nation. And God fulfills that promise. He sets his love on Isaac, then on Jacob, and eventually on Jacob's descendants, the nation of Israel. He rescues them from their slavery in Egypt, and sets them apart. He also gives that nation a covenant and calls them to be a blessing, an expression of love to the whole world. At Mount Sinai, God betroths the nation of Israel to himself as his own special and uniquely loved people.

Again, notice the pattern: a covenant is given to the ones he specially loves.

Like Adam, Israel rebels against God by turning to other lovers, idols that their hands have made. God responds by judging Israel. But throughout the judgment, God continues to love his people. Perhaps the best picture of God's reconciling, patient, forgiving love occurs in the book of Hosea. There God tells the prophet to take a wife named Gomer. She is a prostitute. When she returns to her prostitution not long after their wedding day, God tells Hosea to go and reconcile with her. This, says God, is what his love for his people looks like and feels like.

Incredibly, God's people continue to spurn his love, preferring their idols instead. So God leaves them. He refuses to live in the house with her and her lovers, like a husband jealous for his wayward wife's affections. Ezekiel is given a vision of this heartbreaking event—God leaves the temple. As the Old Testament draws to a close, the temple stands empty, the prophets fall silent, and the throne is vacant. As the New Testament opens, almost all the tokens of God's love are gone.

Suddenly, into this seeming picture of love's labor lost, comes the greatest demonstration of love the world has ever seen. God sends Jesus, the Son he has loved from all eternity past.

Jesus lives the life of loving obedience toward God that we should have but didn't. Then he takes upon himself our penalty for spurning God's love by dying our death on the cross. He calls it a new covenant in his blood. Wonderfully, death cannot hold him, for "love is as strong as death" (Song 8:6). In love Jesus rises from the dead, so that whoever repents of their sin and turns in faith to this Savior will be forgiven of his or her sins and welcomed back into God's loving embrace. Through Jesus, God proves his faithful love to his unfaithful people. Again, there's a covenant for God's special people.

Interestingly, the New Testament, especially John's Gospel, lets us peek into the story behind the story. The story of God's love doesn't begin with creation, but with the eternal love that God the Father has for the Son, and that God the Son has for the Father. Jesus says in John 5, "The Father loves the Son and shows him all he does," and in John 17, "Father, glorify me in your presence with the glory I had with you before the world began." God's love for a special people, it turns out, is wrapped up in his love for his Son.

Today that love still transforms unlovely people, sinners like you and me, into the radiantly beautiful bride of Christ, the church. Now we wait in hope once more for the demonstration of God's love to return. On that day, Jesus will take his bride home to a new heaven and a new earth, truly a world of love.

That's the story of God's love. What does it teach us about who God loves, how he loves, and why he loves? Let's consider some patterns in the story.

Patterns in the Storyline

The Story Was about Marriage

We've noticed before how the Bible begins and ends with a wedding. In Genesis, we see Adam and Eve established as husband and wife. Then in the history of Israel, we hear God describe his relationship with the nation of Israel as a marriage covenant. The same terms are used for Christ and the church: Husbands, love your wives as Christ loves the church. Heaven itself is described as a wedding feast.

Before we even get to our systematic application, here is a major point of contemporary significance. Marriage, a picture of love between one man and one woman, is at the heart of the biblical story of God's love. Therefore, marriage matters for a whole host of reasons. It matters because God created it, not society, and therefore God and God alone defines it. It matters because it's a picture of God's gospel love, hard-wired into creation. Change or redefine marriage, and you've gone a long way toward defacing and obscuring one of the most significant common-grace pointers to the love of God in Christ.

So while we want to defend marriage for all the typical reasons you hear in conservative Christian circles—safety and nurturing for children, reproduction and stability for society, and so on—perhaps the most important reason is this: it's one of the primary pictures of the gospel. The story of God's love is a story about marriage.

The Story Was Structured by Covenants

Given that the story was about marriage, it's not surprising to see it structured by covenants. Marriage itself is a covenant. And God's love is pictured as a betrothing love. So God gave a covenant to Israel. Christ gives a covenant to the church.

What should this be telling us about God's love? Again, we haven't drawn our systematic conclusions yet, but weddings and covenants both speak of distinctive, particular love, don't they? On the one hand, I'm to love my neighbor as myself, which means there's a sense in which I'm to love all people, even all women. On the other hand, I've covenanted with my wife because I love her in a way that is distinct from all others and is particular to her alone.

We see distinction begin in Genesis 3, when God put enmity between the seed of the serpent and the seed of the woman—the world and God's people. The distinction then plays out in Genesis 4, when God rejects the line of Cain but loves the line of Seth. We see it again with Noah's sons, when God rejects the line of Ham and chooses to bless the line of Shem. Ultimately, we see it in God's choice of Abraham and his descendants in Genesis 12. But even then, not all of Abraham's descendants are chosen in love by God. Ishmael, Abraham's son by Hagar, is rejected, but Isaac is chosen. Esau is rejected, but Jacob, his twin brother, is chosen. King Saul is rejected; King David is chosen. Later the whole northern kingdom is rejected, while the southern kingdom is chosen.

Every time God makes his choice, the blessings of his love are attached to the beloved exclusive of all others. We may not like the pattern, but the patterns are clear.

The Story Had Discontinuity and Continuity

The story of love in the Bible also bears elements of continuity and discontinuity as we move from one epoch to another. One of the most significant discontinuities in the story of God's love has to do with this pattern of distinguishing love. The distinguishing love of God *continues* across the entire story, from Genesis to Revelation; but his love for the ethnic nation *discontinues*. Eventually, it's given to believers from every nation and from every age. Paul says in Ephesians 1,

> Praise be to the God and Father of our Lord Jesus Christ, who has blessed us in the heavenly realms with every spiritual blessing in Christ. [How can we know this?] For he chose us in him before the creation of the world to be holy and blameless in his sight. In love he predestined us to be adopted as his sons through Jesus Christ, in accordance with his pleasure and will. (Eph. 1:3–5)

Among other things, this change highlights the movement across the covenants from physical to spiritual, from external to internal. God's people across the covenants are to be known by their holiness, being set apart for God. In the Old Testament this was particularly marked by their distinct ethnicity, their distinct dress, and their distinct food. Under the covenant of the New Testament, however, holiness is not marked off by the food we eat, but by the lives we live in distinction from the world around us.

The Story Was Filled with Patterns (Typology)

All these observations we're making depend on patterns we're seeing. That's called typology. In the garden, you get a type of something—a marriage. Then that type is repeated, but this time between God and a group of people—Israel. Then, when the New Testament comes along and uses this same language about Christ's love for the church, instantaneously, as it were, we have a ton of historical data for helping us understand what this love means. What does it mean that Christ loves the church as a bridegroom? Well, go back to the Old Testament types. See what it says about marriage in Genesis and even Song of Solomon. Then look at God's special love for his people in the Old Testament. All this will inform what it means that Christ loves the church.

The same is true for New Testament statements like, "God is love." What does that mean? Go back and look at the whole storyline. Who did God love, how did he love them and why? The answers we find in the Old Testament— read through the lens of Christ—will tell us what we long to know.

Systematizing it All

As we observe all these things, we're able to see that the topic of love may not be as simple as we often make it out to be. It's actually quite complex, and God does seem to love people differently, and in different ways. This is why D. A. Carson actually wrote a book on *The Difficult Doctrine of the Love of God*.[2]

---

[2]D. A. Carson, *The Difficult Doctrine of the Love of God* (Wheaton, IL: Crossway, 2000).

God is love. But what does that mean? Let's do our systematic work by organizing our doctrines under the three questions we've already raised: who does God love, how does he love, and why does he love?

Who Does God Love?

The Father Loves the Son

We can't finally explain what it means that "God is love" until we've worked through the systematic application of the entire biblical story of love. But it's equally true that we can't begin to explore the story without at least a partial explanation of what it means that God is love. Why the conundrum? For the simple reason that there was never a time when God was not expressing love toward another and receiving love from another. The Father loves the Son, and the Son loves the Father. Love is bound up into the very nature of the Trinity. God cannot be God without love, because God is love.

It's not just that one of God's attributes is love. For example, God is wrathful toward sin, but Scripture never says God is wrath, because his wrath has reference to something outside of himself—our sin. There was a time in eternity past when God's wrath had no expression. But there has never been a time when God was not love, for the love of the Father for the Son and of the Son for the Father is eternal.

Absent sin, God could still be God without wrath. Absent sin, God could still be God without mercy. Absent sin, God could still be God without patience. But God cannot be God without love, for God is love, and there has never been a moment, and never will be a moment, when he is not.

Is this idea new in the New Testament? Yes, but the Old Testament prepares us for this idea, and even teaches us about it through God's love for David. Look at Psalms 2, 20, 110, and more. God gives a special covenant of love to David, which helps us to understand the covenant of love between divine Father and Son when it's finally revealed in the New Testament.

What difference does this make for ministry? To begin with, it is profoundly humbling and incredibly reassuring.

For some of us, it is easy to think that God and his love must revolve around me and my problems, and we evaluate his love based on how we feel he's doing at loving us. But God's love was perfect before we ever arrived on the scene, and it will remain perfect long after we leave. The eternal and therefore prior love of the Father and the Son for each other reminds us that at the end of the day, life and love is not about me. Though the love of God for me is real, it is also derivative, an overflow of this most fundamental love within the Trinity itself. This will make quite a difference in our preaching and teaching.

It's also reassuring. Some others of us look around, and wonder if John had it right. How could he say, "God is love," in the face of this world's tragedies? The answer to the question isn't found by looking around for evidence in the world. The answer is found by looking at God, and the revelation of his love for his Son, Jesus Christ. If we find love firmly established in the nature of God, then there is hope, despite what we encounter here. After all, the ultimate reality of the universe is God, and God is love.

God Loves the World

Second, God loves the world in two ways.

First, God loves creation, the work of his hands. Proverbs 8 tells us that he delights in every part of creation. Jesus tells us that a sparrow does not fall to the ground without God's loving notice and that he clothes the flowers in beauty (Matthew 6).

Second, God loves rebellious humanity. Even in his unswerving wrath against sin, God loves this world that hates him. So Ezekiel declares, "'As surely as I live,' declares the Sovereign LORD, 'I take no pleasure in the death of the wicked, but rather that they turn from their ways and live. Turn! Turn from your evil ways! Why will you die, O house of Israel?'" (Ezek. 33:11). We read in John's Gospel the proof that God loves the world: "For God so loved the world that he gave his one and only Son, that whoever believes in him shall not perish but have eternal life" (John 3:16).

Jesus is the display and demonstration of God's love for sinners. If anyone wants to know God's love, he must know Jesus.

What implication does this have for ministry? Among other things, it teaches us to ask the question, "Do I love the world the way God loves the world, or do I love the world the way the world wants to be loved?" There is a crucial distinction, you know. One leads to the world's salvation. The other leads to its destruction.

God Loves His Own People Distinctively

Not only does God love the world, God loves his people. Throughout the story of God's love, God makes a distinction between people and then places his love on the ones that he has chosen.

The biblical language for God's love for his people is *election*, the language of choosing. People sometimes recoil at this word because it seems to make God mean, narrow, and unloving. But in the Bible, to be chosen is the very nature of what it means to be loved by God, in the same way a man loves a woman by choosing her.

In Deuteronomy 7, Israel stands on the brink of the Promised Land. Moses explains that God is going to give them the land. He also warns them to remain faithful to God. Then in verse 6, Moses says,

> For you are a people holy [that means set apart] to the LORD your God. The LORD your God has chosen you out of all the peoples on the face of the earth to be his people, his treasured possession. The LORD did not set his affection on you and choose you because you were more numerous than other peoples, for you were the fewest of all peoples. But it was because the LORD loved you and kept the oath he swore to your forefathers that he brought you out with a mighty hand and redeemed you from the land of slavery, from the power of Pharaoh king of Egypt. (Deut. 7:6–8)

Why did God choose Israel? Did he choose them because they were better than everyone else? Because they were bigger than everyone else? Because they were more righteous than everyone else? No. No. No. God chose them simply because he loved them. And he loved them simply because he did.

God Loves Sinners

What all of this is driving us to see is that God loves sinners. Paul says in Titus 3:4, "But when the kindness and love of God our Savior appeared, he saved us, not because of righteous things we had done, but because of his mercy." God's saving, electing love is not only *not* merited, it's given in spite of reasons to the contrary. We've merited just the opposite—God's wrath. "But God demonstrates his love for us in this: while we were still sinners, Christ died for us" (Rom. 5:8).

God is not like us. We love people who deserve to be loved. But not God. God's love is free, it's gratuitous, it's unconditional. You cannot earn it. You can only receive it by faith in Christ Jesus.

Here, my minister friend, is balm for the anxious, troubled soul. And here is the real appeal that we must make to sinners. Not to their felt need for significance or peace or happiness. But to their real need for forgiveness. God's love in Christ is *wider* than the breach your sin has made with God; it is *long* enough to reach back into your past and forward into an eternal future; it is *high* enough to bring you to God;

and it is so *deep*, it will never run dry (see Eph. 3:18). In Christ, God loves sinners.

How Does God Love?

If that's who God loves, we need to consider more carefully *how* God loves.

God Loves Providentially

To begin with, God loves everyone *providentially*. That is, he shows it by providing for everyone. Jesus noted that God "causes his sun to rise on the evil and the good, and sends rain on the righteous and the unrighteous." His providential love is generous and impartial (Matt. 5:45–48). This is clearly a point of continuity between Old Testament and New.

If we are to understand suffering in this life, we must understand it in the context of God's providential love. This world is not a cruel joke. Rather, God orders our lives so that we will either learn to value him more than this world, or else be left without excuse for our unbelief. Suffering in this life is at least partly a warning to us, a foretaste of the eternal suffering we deserve outside of Christ.

God Loves Sacrificially

God also loves *sacrificially*. We see this typologically in the Old Testament (Abraham and Isaac, the Levitical sacrifices, etc.). But all these pictures point us toward and teach us about the costliest love that this universe has ever seen. On the cross outside of Jerusalem, God poured out his just wrath on the Son whom he has eternally loved. Christ became a substitute to pay the penalty for our sins. Why did God do this? He did it for his enemies! He did it for people who hate him, for sinners like you and me.

We as humans most clearly encounter the amazing love of God in the vicarious, substitutionary, propitiating sacrifice of Christ. Sacrificial love alone saves us, for it alone atones for our sins. But also, sacrificial love alone assures us—since we did not earn it, we cannot lose it.

How far such love is from the way people think God loves sinners! They imagine he loves with a wink and a nod, and a quick brushing of our unmentionables under the carpet. Nothing could be further from the truth or more unworthy of the God who loved sinners at the incalculable cost of his Son's blood.

God Loves Perfectly

Finally, God loves us *perfectly*. The Bible describes God as a perfect Father, who in love has adopted us in Christ, and then who always loves his children in exactly the way they need to be loved. In that process, his love perfects them. John puts it this way:

> How great is the love the Father has lavished on us, that we should be called children of God! And that is what we are! . . . Dear friends, now we are children of God, and what we will be has not yet been made known. But we know that when he appears, we shall be like him, for we shall see him as he is. Everyone who has this hope in him purifies himself, just as he is pure. (1 John 3:1–3)

God's love in Christ is changing us to be like Christ. So often, the people we counsel in ministry are tempted to question the wisdom of God's love based on the circumstances of their lives. Surely if God loved me, he wouldn't let my husband walk out on me? Surely if God loved me, he wouldn't let my child get involved with the wrong crowd at school? Surely if God loved me, he wouldn't have left me in this dead-end job?

But, in fact, the perfection of God's love for us isn't measured by how well he's managing our agenda for life. No, the perfection of God's love for us is seen in the goal he's set for our life, and that goal is nothing less than likeness to the Son he loves.

Why Does God Love?

Why does God love people like us in this extraordinary way? The answer is not hard to find. But it may be surprising, because in the end it has nothing to do with us.

Because God Chooses to Love

To answer that question, Paul clearly makes use of the Bible's typological devices. In Romans 9, he points to the example of Jacob and Esau, twin brothers. He recalls that

> before the twins were born or had done anything good or bad—in order that God's purpose in election might stand: not works but by him who calls—Rebekah was told, "The older will serve the younger." Just as it is written, "Jacob I loved, but Esau I hated." (Rom. 9:13)

Why did God choose to love Jacob and not Esau? For the same reason God chooses to love anyone. Not because he sees something in advance that is lovely and attractive. Not because there's anything about us that can coerce or demand his love. God loves his people . . . because he chooses to. And in that free and unconditioned choice, the glories of God's electing love are displayed.

Because God Loves His Son

In Ephesians 1, Paul says that the reason God elects some to adoption is "to the praise of his glorious grace, which he has freely given us in the One he loves." This is a truly amazing statement. God loves us, because ultimately God loves his Son. There is nothing that he desires more than to display his glory in and through his Son, which he accomplishes through our salvation.

Conclusion: God Is Love

What does the Bible mean when it says that God is love? To answer that question, we need to read the Bible's story of love. And in that story we see that a holy God chose to love an unholy people at the incalculable price of the life of the Son whom he has loved from all eternity. He did this so that he might transform an unlovely people into a radiantly beautiful bride for that Son.

Our salvation isn't finally about us. Our salvation is finally about the display of God's glory in this eternal love of Father for Son and Son for Father, as each tries to outdo the other in love. To our eternal joy and happiness, the good news is that our lives can be caught up in that incredible story of love.

How does that story touch down into the story of our lives? We noted earlier that the Bible begins and ends with a wedding. Yet if we really want to understand God's love for us, we need to notice an important difference between those two weddings. Do you realize the first marriage in the Bible was arranged? Adam had no choice in the matter. God just presented him with his wife.

But the last marriage is different. The last marriage is the marriage between Christ and his people. And as we've seen, we were chosen from before the foundation of the world. The last marriage in the Bible, the last marriage in all of history, isn't an arranged marriage. It's a marriage for love.

If you are a Christian, you are loved. Your spouse may not love you. You may not even have a spouse. Your friends may be fickle and your family may be hurtful. You may feel loveless. But you are loved. Christ has chosen you.

Because God is love.

CHAPTER NINE

The Story of Sacrifice

As a pastor or elder of our church, one of my regular responsibilities is to interview people for membership at our church. Perhaps the most important part of that interview is to ask the individual to briefly explain the gospel to me. I ask it for two reasons. First, I want to know if they understand and believe the gospel. That's fundamental to joining a Christian church. If a prospective member is trusting in something other than the gospel, like "being pretty good," I want to know this on the front end. It lets me know that the next step isn't membership; it's a Bible study on the gospel!

Second, I want to make sure that every church member knows how to explain the gospel so that he or she can share that good news with others. Sometimes it appears that members are trusting in the gospel, even though they cannot quite explain what makes the gospel good news. They will talk about "believing in Jesus" or "forgiveness for sin." But they will miss what Jesus did to accomplish our forgiveness. So I have to pull it out by asking, "What does the cross have to do with the forgiveness Jesus offers us?"

It seems that in large swaths of evangelicalism these days, the cross is either assumed (and so largely ignored) or redefined in terms less offensive to modern sensibilities. We talk about Jesus as our friend and helper. We talk about his victory over death and sin, followed by our reconciliation to God. We talk about the healing and purpose he brings to our lives. But we don't talk much about how he has done all these things for us. To do that, we'd have to talk about the bloody cross. If my membership interviews are anything to go by, you're more likely to see a cross on a necklace or tattooed on an arm than you are to hear about it in a sermon.

How different that is from the apostolic ministry. Listen to the preaching of Peter, Paul, John, and the author of Hebrews.

- "Therefore let all Israel be assured of this: God has made this Jesus, whom you crucified, both Lord and Christ" (Acts 2:36).

- "Jews demand signs and Greeks look for wisdom, but we preach Christ crucified" (1 Cor. 1:22–23).
- "I resolved to know nothing while I was with you except Jesus Christ and him crucified" (1 Cor. 2:2).
- "Before your very eyes Jesus Christ was clearly portrayed as crucified" (Gal. 3:1).
- "Let us fix our eyes on Jesus, the author and perfecter of our faith, who for the joy set before him endured the cross, scorning its shame, and sat down at the right hand of the throne of God" (Heb. 12:2).
- "He himself bore our sins in his body on the tree, so that we might die to sins and live for righteousness; by his wounds you have been healed" (1 Pet. 2:24).
- "This is love: not that we loved God, but that he loved us and sent his Son as an atoning sacrifice for our sins" (1 John 4:10).

The cross of Jesus Christ was the core of the apostolic preaching of the gospel.[1]

What did Christ's sacrifice accomplish? What was he doing on the cross? The answers to these questions are at the heart of Christianity, and so you can be sure that the doctrine of Christ's sacrificial atonement is target number one for the devil. You can also be sure that all sorts of controversies will surround the meaning of this central event in Christianity.

In fact, many of the most compelling answers given to the question "What was Christ doing on the cross?" will be compelling and true; they just won't be the whole truth. For example, did Christ die to demonstrate God's love for us? Yes! But is that all?

If we're going to preach and teach the gospel in our churches, the gospel that saves sinners, rather than some other gospel; if we're going to train our members to share the gospel faithfully; if we're going to take into membership people who trust in the gospel, and not something else, then we need to understand what Jesus was doing on the cross. The cross makes the gospel good news.

To understand the cross, we need to understand the Bible's story of sacrifice. Though Christ's sacrifice was the most important sacrifice ever made, it wasn't the first in the Bible. And the sacrifices that came before were given so that we would understand what happened at Calvary.

Story of Sacrifice

When we think of sacrifice, we often think in terms of self-denial. Ironically, the biblical story of sacrifice begins with a colossal failure of self-denial.

---

[1]For a strong defense of this statement, see Leon Morris, *The Apostolic Preaching of the Cross*, 3rd rev. ed. (Grand Rapids, MI: Eerdmans, 1965, repr. 2001).

When Adam and Eve indulged their desire to be God's equal, they plunged all of us into a world under God's curse, a world in which sacrifice would become the order of the day. Humanity would need to embrace not just self-sacrifice, but a judicial sacrifice, one that would repair the breech in our relationship with God made by sin. As the narrative of Scripture unfolds, the need, nature, and effects of sacrifice are slowly revealed. I'm going to divide up the storyline into six episodes.

1) The first sacrifice is offered by Cain and Abel in Genesis 4. There's no mention of sin or blood with this sacrifice. The Bible calls it an offering, a gift, and the idea is one of tribute to a great King and submission to his lordship. Right here in the fourth chapter of the Bible, God reveals to us what may be the most basic idea related to sacrifice: in sacrifice we offer back to God what is already his by right.

2) The next recorded sacrifice occurs in Genesis 8. After the flood, Noah offers up a variety of clean animals as whole burnt offerings. The context is thanksgiving, and the fact that they are whole burnt offerings communicates the idea of a gift because the whole animal is given to God. Scripture says this gift has an effect on God. The Bible tells us that

> The LORD smelled the pleasing aroma and said in his heart, "Never again will I curse the ground because of man, even though every inclination of his heart is evil from childhood. And never again will I destroy all living creatures, as I have done." (Gen. 8:21)

The sin that prompted God's judgment remained in the hearts of Noah and his children, but God promises to never again destroy all humanity. Here in chapter 8, then, we see something new in the story of sacrifice: some sacrifices have an effect on God and his attitude toward us.

3) Though we hear of the occasional altar being built, the Bible does not record another sacrifice until Genesis 22:2, when God speaks these shocking words concerning Abraham's seed, through whom he has promised to bless the nations:

> "Abraham, take your son, your only son, Isaac, whom you love, and go to the region of Moriah. Sacrifice him there as a burnt offering on one of the mountains I will tell you about."

Once again, horrible as it sounds, the idea seems to be that of tribute and lordship. It all belongs to God, and he has the right to take it back, even if it's your only son. At the last second, God stops Abraham, but provides a ram. The test of Abraham's devotion is over, but not the sacrifice. A ram is sacrificed, Isaac is spared, and the story of sacrifice has developed further. It turns out that God will accept a substitute for the life that is his to claim. What's more, he'll even provide that substitute.

4) The story of Abraham's family continues, but sacrifice again fades into the background until we find ourselves in Egypt, with the descendants of Abraham enslaved and oppressed. Pharaoh refuses to release the people, and so God warns that he will send the angel of death who will strike down the firstborn male of every creature in Egypt. And now a new sacrifice is introduced, the Passover lamb. In Exodus 12 the Lord promises to spare the firstborns of Israel if each family takes a year-old lamb without defect, sacrifices it, and smears its blood on the doorframe of their houses. God says that he will see the blood of the sacrifice and pass over their homes, sparing them the judgment that Egypt faced.

What's more, God says this sacrificial meal will be a sign that sets them apart, as God makes a distinction between Israel and the rest of the world, consecrating them as his special people. That very night, Israel is spared because of the sacrifice. Moses leads the people out of Egypt to Mount Sinai, where God covenants to be their God, and gives them his Law, that they might be a holy people, set apart for God. Here is yet another development in the story. Those who are spared by a sacrificial substitute are now forfeit to God, consecrated to and for him.

5) Up until this point, there have been less than a dozen instances of sacrifice recorded in the Bible. It doesn't seem to be a major theme. But that changes with the giving of the Law. An entire book of the Bible, Leviticus, is largely given over to detailing all the different sacrifices that Israel must offer God. There are fellowship offerings and whole burnt offerings, which we've already seen. But now there are more, the most important of which are sacrifices to atone for sin and guilt. Now, all the pieces that had been slowly revealed come together.

- Only clean animals without defect can be sacrificed.
- Every firstborn Israelite, who represent the nation as whole, must be redeemed with a sacrificial substitute.
- Prominent is the taking of life and the shedding of a blameless victim's blood.
- The idea of a substitution is also prominent. We're told that if anyone brings a sacrifice, "He is to lay his hand on the head of the burnt offering, and it will be accepted on his behalf . . ." (Lev. 1:4). It's a way of saying, "This sacrifice stands for me; what's about to happen to it should happen to me."

- Sacrifices now begin and end every single day in God's temple, presented by priests who serve as intermediaries between God and his sinful people.
- There are additional sacrifices that mark the beginning of each week, each month, and each season.
- And at the pinnacle of this entire system of sacrifice was the Day of Atonement. The high priest alone took the blood of the sacrifice into the Holy of Holies and sprinkled the blood on the mercy seat, the symbolic throne of God, to make atonement for his own sins and the sins of the people.

It's at this point in redemptive history that the story of sacrifice stops, or at least stalls. Century follows century, and nothing changes. No new sacrifices are introduced; the old ones are endlessly repeated, day after day, week after week, year after year. And therein lays the problem. They aren't getting rid of sin. In fact, they increasingly become a nauseating reminder of just how sinful the people remain. Through the prophets, God denounced the rote and superficial performance of these sacrifices. Repentance, not ritual, is what God desired. But for Israel, repentance had vanished and ritual was all that remained. And so God banished the nation to exile. Without the temple, there could be no sacrifice. Perhaps then the people would learn that what God wanted was repentance.

When God brings them back from Babylon, and the temple is rebuilt, sacrifices resume. But the people have not changed. Other things have changed, though. The Holy of Holies is empty. There is no mercy seat for the high priest to appear before and plead for forgiveness. There is just an empty room. Malachi, the last of the Old Testament prophets, declares, "'Oh that one of you would shut the temple doors, so that you would not light useless fires on my altar! I am not pleased with you,' says the LORD Almighty, 'and I will accept no offering from your hands'" (Mal. 1:10). Those are chilling words. If there is no sacrifice that God will accept, then God's people are as exposed to God's judgment as Egypt was on the night of the Passover, or as Isaac was as he lay bound on that altar.

6) Then something incredible happens—a sixth sacrifice to point out, a sacrifice like none before, and one that will make all future sacrifice unnecessary. God is true to his word to Abraham. He will not accept a sacrifice from the hands of his sinful people, and so he provides one instead. He sends his Son, who takes on flesh, and then offers his own life and blood as an acceptable sacrifice, as a substitute for his people—a people who belong not just to one nation, but to all the nations.

There at Calvary, Christ fulfilled everything the Old Testament sacrifices meant, and accomplished what they were unable to do. Through his blood, he made atonement for the sins of his people and reconciled them to God. And to demonstrate that God accepted this sacrifice, he raised Jesus from the dead, so that—starting now and continuing on into eternity—whoever repents of their sins and places their faith in Christ's sacrifice is redeemed from slavery to sin and is free to live a life of tribute and praise to God.

Patterns in the Storyline

That's the story of sacrifice. So what patterns do we see? What do we learn about Christ's sacrifice from how the story of sacrifice is told?

Typology of Sacrifice

The first pattern to notice is the pattern itself—the pattern of sacrifice. Once again, we're looking at typology. There's a type of something, then another, then another. God is telling us to fix our attention on this. The shedding of blood isn't something we think much about today, but the Bible is obviously interested in it. Why? What is it saying?

Also, we noticed a crescendoing trend with these types. Abel's sacrifice was about thanksgiving. Noah's sacrifice was about thanksgiving and assuaging the Lord. Abraham and Isaac's episode included all this, but also the ideas of utter devotion and a substitute. The Passover sacrifice introduced the ideas of a spotless lamb, the representative role of the first-born Son, and the distinguishing of a people. Then the Levitical sacrifices emphasized atonement for sin.

So, a pattern or type is repeated. But there's a crescendo within the pattern.

Discontinuity in the Pattern

But there's not just crescendo and continuity. There's discontinuity, especially when we get to Christ. The Levitical sacrifices were repeated endlessly, but Christ was sacrificed once. The Levitical sacrifices were for one ethnic nation, but Christ was sacrificed for all nations.

Promise and Fulfillment

One other pattern for us to notice in this storyline is that of promise/fulfillment. There are many promises I could highlight, such as God's promise to Noah. Let me point to two.

First, there is a connection between God's promise to punish sin through death, God's promise to rescue his people from the serpent, and the establishment of sacrifice. Sacrifices offer a vicarious (experienced through another) fulfillment of God's promise to punish sin. But because they are vicarious, they accomplish the promised rescue, at least temporarily. Thus, sacrifice actually ties together multiple promises in Scripture.

Second, there is a connection between God's promise to Abraham—that his seed would be a blessing to all nations—and Christ's sacrifice. Christ fulfilled this promise to Abraham not just through his birth and ministry as a genealogical descendant of Abraham, but especially through his sacrifice. Therefore, the cross of Christ, and not merely his person, is a blessing to all nations and is at the heart of the good news of the gospel.

Systematizing It All

What's the purpose in pointing out these patterns? They are instrumental in helping us to understand who Jesus is, what his sacrifice accomplished, and our need for his sacrifice. All these patterns point to Jesus, and help us understand Jesus. They set the context for his coming. They give us "pre-interpretation," if you will.

Over the years, some have suggested that Christ died primarily as an example for us, to inspire us to greater love for God. Others have suggested that Christ's death was merely a demonstration of God's hatred for sin. Still others have said it was a demonstration of his compassion and identification with sinners.

These days, some are saying Jesus died simply to declare victory over sin and death and to demonstrate his lordship. And we can point to verses in the New Testament that say all these things—that Jesus died as an example, to demonstrate God's hatred for sin, and to declare victory over sin and death. Well, all those comprise *a part* of why Jesus died. They comprise a part of what's wrong with you and me. We do need someone to set a good example. We do need someone to identify with us in weakness and to defeat death. But is that all we need?

What's more, an increasing number of people who claim to be evangelicals are not only saying these things, but are also denying other things about the cross. They are denying that Jesus died as a substitute—that he died to bear our sin and take our penalty. They are denying that there was a penal aspect to the cross at all.[2]

---

[2] A thorough treatment of these criticisms can be found in Steve Jeffery, et al, *Pierced for Our Transgressions: Rediscovering the Glory of Penal Substitution* (Nottingham, UK: Inter-Varsity Press, 2007; Wheaton, IL: Crossway, 2007). For an extended exegetical response, see Mark Dever and Michael Lawrence, *It Is Well: A Series of Expositional Sermons on Substitutionary Atonement* (Wheaton, IL: Crossway, 2010).

But given the storyline and the patterns we've observed, such explanations are not faithful to Scripture. What's more, they undermine the good news of the gospel itself. What follows, I believe, is a more faithful presentation of what the whole Bible says about the cross of Jesus Christ.

1) Humanity's Fundamental Problem: Sin and the Guilt it Incurs

It's not death. It's not a broken relationship. It's not our need for love or an example of love. The fundamental problem with the world and humanity is sin, guilt, and the wrath of God that sin incurred.

I'm talking about the need for sacrifice here. Before the fall, Adam and Eve had no need to kill an animal and offer it to God. They were in a right relationship with a good and holy God. But the moment sin entered in, Adam and Eve's lives were forfeit because of sin and guilt. Romans 6:23, echoing God's words to Adam in Genesis 2, tells us that the penalty for sin is death. Sin came first, then death.

Here is the problem that sacrifice in the Bible is designed to solve. We don't primarily need an inspiring example of love, or victory over the powers of darkness, or victory over death. Rather, the eternal and holy God is justly angry with us for our rebellion, and we need a way to escape the penalty of his justice, because we cannot bear that penalty ourselves. According to Scripture, we need a sacrifice.

2) Christ Came to Die as a Substitute

An effective sacrifice is a substitute. We saw a ram slain in the place of Isaac. We saw the Passover lamb slain in the place of the firstborn. And we see the same kind of substitute pictured in the book of Leviticus—a point punctuated when the person lays his or her hand on the animal. In the same way, Jesus provided an effective sacrifice for us by offering himself to God as a substitute.

3) Christ Came to Die as a Penal Substitute

The victim receives the penalty the sinner deserves. The sacrificial victim doesn't just die; it is judicially executed in the sinner's place.

Both the Old and New Testament clearly teach that, on the cross, Christ died as a penal substitute, taking the punishment that his people deserved. This is what the prophet Isaiah foretold. Speaking of the Messiah, Isaiah says,

Surely he took up our infirmities and carried our sorrows, yet we considered him stricken by God, smitten by him, and afflicted. But he was pierced for our transgressions, he was crushed for our iniquities; the punishment that brought us peace was upon him, and by his wounds we are healed . . . the LORD has laid on him the iniquity of us all. (Isa. 53:4–6)

Jesus said the same thing of himself: "I am the good shepherd. The good shepherd lays down his life for the sheep" (John 10:11). Jesus did not understand his own death as an example, or as a demonstration, or even as an open-ended general death with reference to nobody in particular. No, Jesus laid down his life as an effective sacrifice, a penal substitute for his sheep.

Paul affirms the same point: "God presented him as a propitiation through faith in his blood . . . to demonstrate his righteousness at the present time, so that he would be righteous and declare righteous the one who has faith in Jesus" (Rom. 3:25–26, HCSB). This brings us to the next lesson.

4) Christ Came to Die as a Penal Substitute to Propitiate the Wrath of God

Christ's sacrifice propitiates God's wrath. What do I mean by that? I mean simply that by enduring the penalty that our sin deserves, an effective sacrifice actually satisfies the demands of justice, removing the reason for God's wrath against the sinner. If you think back to the story of sacrifice, we saw a suggestion of propitiation in Noah's sacrifice. Noah's sacrifice was pleasing to the Lord. We also see it in the repeated reference throughout Leviticus that the aroma of a burning sacrifice was "pleasing to the Lord."

5) Christ Came to Die as a Penal Substitute to Propitiate the Wrath of God and Make Atonement for His People

The turning aside of God's wrath leads to another effect of sacrifice. An effective sacrifice atones for sin. We've already seen that the high point of the Jewish year was the Day of Atonement. What exactly is atonement? The Hebrew word for atone means "to cover." The English word simply means "to be at one with." So a sacrifice, you could say, covers our sin and makes us "at one" with God. Having assuaged God's wrath, the sacrifice obtains forgiveness for the sin that caused God's wrath in the first place, and it removes the guilt that sin had incurred.

6) Christ Came to Die as an Effective Penal Substitute to Propitiate the Wrath of God and Make Atonement for His People

While the Levitical sacrifices were repeated endlessly, the book of Hebrews draws our attention to the fact that Christ was sacrificed once.

> He sacrificed for their sins once for all when he offered himself. (Heb. 7:27)

> He entered the Most Holy Place once for all by his own blood, having obtained eternal redemption. (Heb. 9:12)

> Now he has appeared once for all at the end of the ages to do away with sin by the sacrifice of himself. (Heb. 9:26)

The whole sacrificial system had only been a picture, a teaching aid, designed, as Paul says in Galatians, to lead us to Christ, and to recognize him when he appeared. Now that he was here, the picture was no longer needed. Jesus Christ's death on the cross effectively turned aside God's wrath and satisfied it. As the writer to the Hebrews says, "it is impossible for the blood of bulls and goats to take away sins" (Heb. 10:4). But, he goes on to say, "we have been made holy by the sacrifice of the body of Jesus Christ" (Heb. 10:10).

The good news of Christianity is that on the cross Jesus Christ accomplished salvation. He turned aside God's wrath. He made atonement for sin.

The only question is, did he do this for you? Jesus said that he gave his life as a ransom for many. Are you among the many? Jesus said that he lays down his life for his sheep. Who are his sheep? They are those who listen to his voice, who respond to his call. John put it this way in John 3:18: "Whoever believes in the Son has eternal life, but whoever rejects the Son will not see life, but God's wrath remains on him."

Jesus Christ has accomplished redemption for everyone who listens to his call to repent and believe. We don't preach a potentiality or possibility. We certainly don't preach an atonement that needs to be completed with our response. Rather, we preach a salvation accomplished on the cross, and we call men and women everywhere to lean hard on Jesus with repentance and faith.

This leads us to the end of sacrifice in the Bible. In a story saturated with the repeatedly shed blood of sacrifice, it cannot escape attention that sacrifice comes to an end at the cross. There's no further sacrifice people can give to pay for our sins before a holy God.

7) We're Saved by Faith Alone

This is why the Bible talks about the necessity of personal faith in a crucified and risen Christ for salvation. It's not that faith itself is saving. It's that faith is the way you acknowledge Christ as your substitute. Like the Old Testament Israelite who laid his hands on the sacrificial victim, so faith leans on Christ and trusts that when Christ died on the cross, he was dying in your place, for you. It's not enough to be born into a Christian family, or to be baptized, or to go to church, or anything else. No, by faith you must believe that Christ was sacrificed for you.

8) We're Saved by Faith Alone in Christ Alone

It's not just that Christ is the best example of a substitute—he's the only substitute, for no one else has ever lived a perfect life. It's not just that his death approximates the judgment we deserve—it's that on the cross Christ endured the holocaust of God's wrath against our sin, and exhausted it. He is the last sacrifice, because in reality he is the first true sacrifice and the only effective sacrifice that has ever or will ever be made.

The exclusivity of this sacrifice is significant. There will be no second chances after death, no alternative means of getting to heaven. There is only one sacrifice that reconciles sinners to God, and so there is only one name under heaven by which we may be saved. We all need a sacrifice. The good news of Christianity is that God himself has provided that sacrifice. His name is Jesus, and to our everlasting joy we preach him crucified.

Conclusion: One More Sacrifice?

There is, however, one more sacrifice in the Bible to observe. It's not one that gains salvation or adds anything to salvation. It's one that follows salvation. When Jesus calls a person, he calls him to pick up his cross and to follow him. Paul uses similar language when he says in Romans 12:1 that Christians are to offer themselves as "living sacrifices." What does Paul mean?

Before the fall, Adam and Eve were made in the image of God. Their lives were meant to be a tribute, an offering of praise, back to God. Ultimately, the end or purpose of Christ's sacrifice is that we might once again offer our lives back to God as sacrifices, not as payment for sin, but as living sacrifices of praise to his glorious grace.

I think most of us struggle with sacrifice. It's hard to lay down your life for others, to love your enemies, to return kindness for insults, and to let go of this world's riches for the treasure of heaven. So long as we try to offer these sacrifices as payment for sin, to appease God and make him happy, we will fail. But when we faithfully teach ourselves and our flocks that God is not angry anymore because Christ has paid the penalty, something changes. Now these living sacrifices are not offered in fear, but in love. In one sense, they're not sacrifices at all. They are simply evidence that we have been loved in Christ and are now being conformed to the image of Christ as a living sacrifice, tributes of praise to God.

One of the most amazing pictures of sacrifice in the Bible is found in Revelation 5. There we learn that Jesus Christ, whose death was planned by God from before the foundation of the world, will for all eternity bear the marks of his sacrifice. More than anything else, those marks will be the object of our eternal wonder, adoration, and praise, since they are the marks of our salvation. The Lamb who was slain is the image to which we are being conformed. He is the destiny to which we are heading. Because of Christ's sacrifice, we will be an eternally living sacrifice of praise to the one who alone is worthy of praise, Christ, our Passover, the Lamb who was slain but now lives forevermore.

CHAPTER TEN

The Story of Promise

Some of the most difficult situations I deal with as a pastor involve the promises that people make. From big promises like "until death us do part" to little ones like "I'll be home by 7." Not only do people make them, other people count on them and build their lives around them. Yet inevitably, it seems, people break the promises they've made. Then come broken relationships, hurt feelings, and angry recriminations. Not a few of the people on the receiving side of a broken promise end up in my office, seeking help to put things back together again.

We habitually build our lives around promises. From mortgages to wedding vows, from Netflix to NATO, in large and small ways, our whole world is built around the idea that promises are made to be kept. Dr. Martin Luther King Jr. pricked America's conscience when he said, "Now is the time to make real the promises of democracy." And General MacArthur imbued hope in thousands when he promised, "I shall return!"

Why do we make promises? In Hannah Arendt's insightful prose, "Promises are the uniquely human way of ordering the future, making it predictable and reliable to the extent that this is humanly possible."[1] Promises bind us to each other, and to a common commitment for the future. Thus, as the American journalist Herbert Agar is oft quoted as saying, "Civilization rests on a set of promises."

What a fragile foundation for something so important. The fact that our lives, individually and collectively, rest on promises means that our lives are spent waiting, hoping, and believing. In between a promise and its fulfillment is a delay, and that delay requires us to live by faith.

What makes this so difficult of course is that we know that promises are broken all too often. As children, our friends broke their promises to us. So did our parents. As adults, it's more of the same, only the stakes are higher, as marriages and employment agreements fall apart.

---

[1] Hannah Arendt, *Crises of the Republic: Lying in Politics, Civil Disobedience, On Violence, Thoughts on Politics and Revolution* (New York: Houghton Mifflin Harcourt, 1972), 92–93.

But the amazing thing is that for every divorce, every betrayal, every contract broken or alliance undermined, we get up the next day and make promises again. In one way or another, the story of our lives is the story of promises made, promises kept, and promises broken.

Why?

Fundamentally, we make promises because we live in a universe created by a God who makes promises. If we want to know this God, then we must understand the biblical story of promise and our promise-making God. In a very profound sense, the story of the Bible is nothing more than the story of a single promise, made by God himself, and how he kept and will keep that promise. When we understand this story, we are also in a position to be able to help those whose lives have been wounded by the pain of broken promises.

The Story of Promise

So what's the biblical story of God's promise? It begins in the most unlikely of places. It begins in the words of God's curse after the fall. Adam and Eve had chosen to disobey God, and so he brought upon them the just punishment for their sin. But in the very sentence of condemnation, God makes a promise: "I will put enmity between you and the woman, and between your offspring and hers; he will crush your head, and you will strike his heel" (Gen. 3:15). God promises to create division and opposition between his people, the seed of the woman, and Satan's people, the seed of the serpent. And he promises that one day a son will be born who will defeat Satan and deliver his people from their sin. The promise comes out of the blue. Adam and Eve have done nothing to merit it, yet still he makes it.

Notice the promise has two sides: the seed of the serpent will strike at the seed of the woman; yet the seed of the woman will triumph. This promise and its various reoccurring fulfillments come to characterize redemptive history. Again and again the promise will be challenged, even apparently defeated, yet the promise will prevail.

Cain murders Abel, but God preserves Adam's line through Seth.

Humanity is captured by sin and deserving of God's judgment, but God's promise endures and he preserves Noah and his family. Then, to ensure his promise of deliverance is kept, God makes another promise—never again to destroy all humanity by flood.

Centuries pass. Humanity is no better than they were before the flood, but God has not forgotten his promise. In Genesis 12, he picks up that original promise and begins to flesh it out. He chooses Abram, an old childless man, and makes a promise to him:

> I will make you into a great nation and I will bless you; I will make your name great, and you will be a blessing. I will bless those who bless you, and whoever curses you I will curse; and all peoples on earth will be blessed through you. . . . To your offspring I will give this land. (Gen. 12:2–3, 7)

The threat of the serpent rises up again as Abram decides to take the promise of a seed into his own hands and produces a seed, Ishmael, through an illicit relationship. But God does not need Abram's help, and is adamant that his promise will be kept by grace, not human effort. He renews his promise and changes Abram's name to Abraham. Then "the LORD did for Sarah what he had promised" (Gen. 21:1). Barren Sarah gives birth to Isaac, the miracle baby.

A generation later, a rivalry ensues between Isaac's two sons, Jacob and Esau, with Esau trying to destroy Jacob. But Jacob is the chosen seed, and the Lord preserves him. Jacob has twelve sons, and it begins to look like the promise of becoming a great nation is on its way.

But once again, God's promise is challenged by jealous strife and attempted murder, by Joseph's slavery and imprisonment, and by a famine that threatens to destroy the whole family. But God is faithful. He sovereignly uses Joseph's suffering, which his brothers meant for evil, as the very means of salvation and deliverance not just for the chosen family, but for the surrounding nations as well.

Again, the seed of the serpent rears its head as the descendants of Jacob are enslaved by Egypt, and a whole generation of boys is slaughtered at Pharaoh's command. Again, God is faithful and remembers his covenant with Abraham (Ex. 6:5–8). He preserves the life of Moses, and then uses him to deliver his people from their slavery.

At Mount Sinai, God makes a covenant with Israel, in much the same way he did with Adam and Eve before the fall. If the people obey, they will stay in the Promised Land. But if they rebel, God will cast them out. Of course, their rebellion begins almost immediately. God judges his people, but he remains faithful to his promise to Abraham (Ex. 33:1).

A new generation, led by Joshua, is raised up, and God gives them the land he had promised their forefathers. Against all odds, they conquer the Canaanites. Though the people continue to rebel, and God continues to chastise them, he also raises up judges, successors to Moses and Joshua, who rescue the people and vanquish their enemies.

Finally, in an ultimate act of rebellion, the nation of Israel rejects God as their King, and asks for a king like all the other nations (1 Samuel 8). In mercy, God anoints a king after his own heart, David, who will be like a son to him. But the serpent even tries to chase down and destroy David from within Israel itself—first through Saul and later through David's son Absalom.

Yet God, who is gracious and faithful, makes yet another promise to David, a promise that is really just an extension of his promise to Abraham and that gives further shape to the promise of Genesis 3. God promises David that he will always have a son to rule on his throne, and that son will rule in righteousness (2 Sam. 7:11–16). The promised seed of Genesis 3 and Genesis 15 is in fact to be a king who will deliver his people.

At first it appears that son is Solomon. But it's not. Solomon proves unfaithful, and judgment follows. Division comes first. The kings in the north are progressively more wicked, until God sends the northern kingdom into an exile from which they never return. In the south there are periodic renewals, but the renewals are never complete, and they never last. Finally, God sends Judah into exile, and it seems that his promise has failed.

But even in the context of judgment and exile, God reveals that he has not forgotten and he has not failed. The prophets are given a message of hope, that God will make a new covenant with his people (Jer. 31:31–34).

After seventy years in exile, Judah returns to the Promised Land. The temple is rebuilt, and the walls of Jerusalem are restored. But the new covenant has not yet arrived. When will God finally keep his promise?

The answer comes many years later, one night in the town of Bethlehem, the city of David. A baby is born whose name is Jesus. Angels attend his birth. Kings come from afar to honor him. Could he be the promised son, the long-expected king who would deliver his people?

Again, the serpent snaps, and a whole generation of boys is killed. Yet the Lord preserves Jesus. Everything about his life suggests that Jesus is the long-awaited fulfillment to all of God's promises. His words have authority, and his work of healing and exorcism is nothing short of miraculous. It seems that God has not forgotten and that he's finally keeping his word.

Then the unthinkable happens. Once again, the sin and rebellion of the serpent seem to gain the upper hand. The religious leaders of Israel reject Jesus, and the Roman authorities crucify him. In a cold, dark tomb outside Jerusalem, God's promise seems to have finally and utterly died.

But nothing could be further from the truth. Three days later, Jesus got up from the dead and demonstrated beyond a shadow of a doubt that God keeps his promises. Through his sacrificial death on the cross, Jesus had crushed Satan's power and freed his people from their bondage to sin (Col. 2:14–15). Through his resurrection, Jesus guaranteed that the new life of the kingdom of God had finally dawned (Rom. 4:25).

Patterns in the Storyline

That's the biblical story of promise. What patterns do we see? How do we learn about our promise-making God from how the story is told?

The first pattern to notice is the promise itself. From the opening pages of Scripture to their close, the story of God's redemptive activity is structured by promises made and promises kept. You might even say that God making and keeping promises is the main plot device of the Bible. Without God's promise, there is no story after Genesis 3.

But it's not just that promise-making and promise-keeping moves the story forward. There is also apparent delay in God's promise-keeping, and it's this that brings tension and development to the story. God didn't just fix matters right there in the garden. He didn't send Jesus before the flood. And God hasn't sent Jesus back today . . . not yet, at least. What's striking when you consider that God is a God of promises is that it means our lives are, by design, lives of waiting. One of the main questions the Bible asks, and then answers in part, is "Why the delay?"

Second, notice that the promises God makes are not the sort we make every day: "I'll be home early" or "I'll come to your party." Instead, these promises always take the form of covenants. It's not that God doesn't make the sort of simple promises we do. He does, and there are instances of them all over Scripture. But the really big promises, the promises that give shape to the whole story, are different. They are promises that not only commit him to a future action, but that bind him in relationship to a particular people.

This tells us something about God. He's not only faithful, keeping his word; he's also personal, entering into relationship with others. It also tells us something about his purpose in making promises in the first place. The story of God's actions in history is not simply a story of God carrying out his agenda. It's a story of mercy and love, as he creates and redeems a people for himself.

Finally, notice that this story, like all the other storylines we've considered, has both continuity and discontinuity. The promise of redemption through a son continues. The promise of Satanic opposition continues. And the promise of the seed's triumph over Satan continues. But the full shape and scope of the promise of redemption isn't revealed all at once.

There are many discontinuities as well, and it's through these that the promise of redemption slowly unfolds. At one early stage, the promise is confined to a particular ethnic people. The division is essentially ethnic. But in Christ, that ethnic division has been erased, and the promise goes out to all nations. At first, the son is just a son. Later, the son is not only a son, but a king. In the end, he's not just a king, but God himself. These discontinuities not only help the story develop and move forward, they increasingly reveal what God intended from the very beginning. It's as if the story is slowly progressing from parable to reality. The entire story is history, but the ultimate reality to which it pointed doesn't appear until close to the end.

Systematizing it All

If those are some of the patterns of the story, what application does this story have for our lives and ministry? Why has God built delay into our lives and into his dealings with us? What difference does it make to our lives that God is a promise-making God?

Man Is Sinful

First, all of redemptive history is structured by a promise/fulfillment dynamic because man is sinful. We need to be redeemed. The very structure of the Bible says that there's a problem to be fixed.

Yet the fact that redemptive history is structured by a promise/fulfillment dynamic doesn't teach us about ourselves, it teaches us about God. It teaches us that he is a God of mercy as well as justice, a God of love as well as wrath.

We Live Amidst Spiritual Warfare

The storyline of promise teaches us that we live among spiritual warfare. Paul might as well be summarizing the storyline when he writes,

> We do not wrestle against flesh and blood, but against the rulers, against the authorities, against the cosmic powers over this present darkness, against the spiritual forces of evil in the heavenly places. (Eph. 6:12)

I don't point out the reality of spiritual warfare to absolve ourselves of blame for sin. No, it's simply that we need to recognize that this world, its powers and its cultures, are not neutral. Again and again in the story we saw the serpent strike out against the good purposes of God. Satan is at work through the seemingly innocent forces of this world, as well as through our sinful nature. Therefore, we need to be watchful and wary of worldliness in our hearts.

God Is Patient and Calls All People to Repentance

We struggle with what seems like God's delay in keeping his promises. But the fact is, delay displays God's patience, as he desires for all to come to repentance. Peter puts it this way:

> With the Lord a day is like a thousand years, and a thousand years are like a day. The Lord is not slow in keeping his promise, as some understand slowness. He is patient with you, not wanting anyone to perish, but everyone to come to repentance. (2 Pet. 3:8)

It's been 2,000 years, and still Jesus has not come back. Some would say that Christians are simply gullible. After all, how long does it take to prove a promise false? That's one way of looking at delay. But there is another way. It's that God is being patient and merciful toward sinners.

Looking back at God's patience with rebellious Israel, the book of Hebrews pleads, "Today, if you hear his voice, do not harden your hearts" (Heb. 4:7). This should give urgency to our evangelism. We do not know when God's patience will come to an end. Today, at this moment, his hand is stayed; he is exercising patience. Therefore, today, this moment, is the time to urge people to repent of their sins and place their faith in Christ.

God Is Gracious and Initiates Salvation by Grace

Not only is God patient, he is gracious. He doesn't just leave us to figure it out. He initiates salvation. God's promise in Genesis 3:15, along with every other promise he utters, is entirely of God's initiative; it is *grace*, pure and simple.

Did you notice the pattern as I told the story? Adam and Eve have just rejected God in the face of his abundant goodness, but God promises to deliver them and their descendants! What was Abraham when God promised to make him a blessing to the nations? An idolater. What was Moses when God set him apart? A murderer and fugitive from justice! What was David when God anointed him as king? A little shepherd boy who would grow up to be a murderer and adulterer.

And what are you when God's promise is held out to you in the gospel of Jesus Christ? As Paul says, "all of us . . . have gratified the cravings of our sinful nature and followed its desires and thoughts . . . [all of us are] by nature objects of wrath" (Eph. 2:3). God does not owe us salvation. The promise God has made to save is a promise of pure grace.

God Is Faithful and Keeps His Promises

We see God *faithfully* keeping his Old Testament promises in at least three ways. First, he's done it through the death and resurrection of Jesus Christ. Far from being merely the tragic work of wicked men, far from being Satan's triumph over Jesus, the cross was God's triumphant victory over sin and Satan's power. This was Peter's conclusion at the end of his sermon at Pentecost (Acts 2:36). And it was Paul's conclusion as well: "No matter how many promises God has made, they are 'Yes' in Christ. And so through him the 'Amen' is spoken by us to the glory of God" (2 Cor. 1:20).

Second, God continues to apply his promise to us through the Holy Spirit, whom Jesus has sent as a down payment and sign that the good things promised are true and already here. Paul goes on in 2 Corinthians 1:21–22: "Now it is God who makes both us and you stand firm in Christ. He anointed us, set his seal of ownership on us, and put his Spirit in our hearts as a deposit, guaranteeing what is to come."

How does the Holy Spirit do this? He applies the life of heaven to our lives here on earth. He produces in us the fruit of the Spirit, which is heavenly fruit. He confirms to us that we are indeed God's children, as he testifies to our own spirits and leads us to call God Abba, Father (Rom. 8:15).

How do we help believers struggling with doubt? One way is to point to the evidence of the Spirit in their life. I'm not talking about spectacular gifts, but the fruit of the Spirit: "love, joy, peace, patience, kindness, goodness, faithfulness, gentleness, and self-control" (Gal. 5:22). When these are present, and in increasing measure, then the professing believer can take heart. For it is the Spirit's work to give us confidence that God has kept and is keeping his promise, and that the day will come when he will redeem his down payment with payment in full.

Third, we see God faithfully keeping his Old Testament promises in that God has already bound Satan (Rev. 20:2). Satan cannot deceive God's elect even though he tries (Mark 13:22). We also know that God will ultimately defeat Satan and the powers of this world. As John prophesied, "And the devil, who deceived [the nations], was thrown into the lake of burning sulfur, where the beast and the false prophet had been thrown. They will be tormented day and night for ever and ever" (Rev. 20:10).

God Is Trustworthy and Will Fulfill What He Promises

We also learn that God is absolutely *trustworthy*. The problem with the promises that we make is that they are only as good as our intentions, and only as trustworthy as our ability to perform them. This means that even the best of us are by nature promise-breakers. But not God. When God makes a promise, you can take it to the bank. God cannot lie, so his promises never deceive. God is all-powerful, so his promises never fail. Consider Jesus' words in John 10:27-30:

> My sheep listen to my voice; I know them, and they follow me. I give them eternal life, and they shall never perish; no one can snatch them out of my hand. My Father, who has given them to me, is greater than all; no one can snatch them out of my Father's hand. I and the Father are one.

Anyone who truly repents of sin and trusts in Christ can be certain that God will preserve him until the end. That certainty has nothing to do with the strength of one's faith or the righteousness of one's life. It has everything to do with the power and faithfulness of God. As Paul says, "He who began a good work in you will carry it on to completion until the day of Christ Jesus" (Phil. 1:6). God keeps his promises. Always. You can count on it.

Does that mean that it doesn't matter how we live? Just make a decision for Jesus and go on as before? Not at all.

As we consider the fact that redemptive history is structured by this pattern of promise/fulfillment and that history is all about this delay in between the two, we not only learn about God, we learn about what he intends for us as Christians. We learn that it matters how we live.

God Intends for His People to Be Purified

One of the constant refrains in the Old Testament is that God uses suffering, and even chastisement, to purify his people. It's the image of smelting, in which the dross is removed and the pure precious metal remains behind. For example, the psalmist looks back on the wilderness wandering and the difficult days of the judges and acknowledges, "For you, O God, tested us; you refined us like silver" (Ps. 66:10). Zechariah, looking forward to the Messiah, says the same thing. God says, "I will bring [them] into the fire, I will refine them like silver and test them like gold" (Zech. 13:9).

As we minister to Christians who are suffering, we do them no good if we lead them to believe that God is ultimately concerned about their ease and happiness in this life. He is not. Though this world means it for evil,

God intends the suffering in our lives for good. He is not interested in the dross of our sin, or the worthless metal of our own efforts. No, he desires the pure gold of our unalloyed trust in him. Through suffering he sanctifies us. Just as Christ "learned obedience from what he suffered" (Heb. 5:8), just as he entrusted himself to God in the wilderness temptation, we too learn to put our faith solely in God through our suffering. "God's discipline produces a harvest of righteousness and peace for those who are trained by it" (Heb. 12:11).

But it's not just our purification that God is after. He's also patient in keeping his promise because he wants to reorient our hope.

God Intends to Reorient Our Hopes

This world constantly sings in our ears a siren song of hope, urging us to invest ourselves here, to live for this life, to save up earthly treasure, to cultivate the praise of men. It's a beautiful song, but like the song that captivated Ulysses, it is a song that will lead us to destruction. God knows this, and he wants us to come to the same realization. When he saves us, therefore, he doesn't whisk us off to heaven. He leaves us here, in part to learn that this world is not our home, and to grow our "longing for a better country—a heavenly one" (Heb. 11:16). His desire is that we would grow weary of the lies, pretenses, and broken promises that this world peddles, and instead, with Abraham, live here as an alien, all the while "looking forward to the city with foundations, whose architect and builder is God" (Heb. 11:10).

God Intends for His People to Persevere to the End

God's promise means it matters how we live. Jesus said his sheep listen to him and follow him. This means that it's the very nature of a Christian to repent and follow. True Christians may fall into real and grievous sin. True Christians may grieve the Holy Spirit, wound their conscience, and even lose all experience of God's grace. And that is a terrible and dangerous place to be, a place without assurance. Still, by God's grace, true Christians do not fall totally or finally. After all, true Christians are people who, by God's grace and because of his unbreakable promise, repent and follow Christ. Jesus tells us, "The one who endures to the end will be saved" (Matt. 10:22).

It is the grand mark of a Christian, not that he does not sin, but that he perseveres to the end. So we should not teach our people to put their confidence in some decision made yesterday or ten years ago. Rather, we should teach them, as Paul did the Corinthians, to "examine yourself today, to see if you are in the faith. Test yourselves" (2 Cor. 13:5).

Does all this talk of perseverance suggest that the Christian faith depends on our own efforts? No, it all depends on God. Yet God has determined to use our efforts, that our hopes might be reoriented and that we might grow in holiness: "work out your own salvation with fear and trembling, for it is God who works in you, both to will and to work for his good pleasure" (Phil. 2:12–13).

God Intends for Us to Work

What is holiness? It's not simply being set apart from sin. It's being set apart to the glory and love and work of God. Paul puts our lives in light of the story of God's promise when he writes,

> Now the Lord is the Spirit, and where the Spirit of the Lord is, there is freedom. And we, who with unveiled faces all reflect the Lord's glory, are being transformed into his likeness with ever-increasing glory, which comes from the Lord, who is the Spirit. (2 Cor. 3:17–18)

What is this freedom we've been given? It's not a freedom to live as we please, but a freedom to glorify God through lives that display his glory. We've been given work to do (Matt. 9:38). We've been given our marching orders (Matt. 28:18–20). We've been entrusted with a message (2 Cor. 5:14–21). And, as a result, our lives find purpose in God's delay, for

> as God's fellow workers we urge you not to receive God's grace in vain. For he says, "In the time of my favor I heard you, and in the day of salvation I helped you." I tell you, now is the time of God's favor, now is the day of salvation. (2 Cor. 6:1–2)

Conclusion: The End of the Delay

God has kept his promises in Jesus Christ. But there is one promise we are still waiting for him to keep. It's a day we still look forward to—the day when Christ returns and we enter into the full redemption, not just of our souls, but of our bodies, too. Though God is using the delay for our good, we still long for it to end. For God means to fully and finally deliver his people, not just from the guilt and condemnation of their sins, but from this very body of death.

Christ is coming back. And on that day, the trumpet of God will sound, the dead will be raised imperishable, and we will be changed. The dross will be gone. The sin will be gone. Sanctification and suffering will give way to glorification and joy. On that day, we will be like him, for we will see him as he is. As Paul declares with a shout of joy, "Thanks be to God! He gives us the victory through our Lord Jesus Christ" (1 Cor. 15:57).

So Christian, stand firm. Persevere. Your faith and labor is not in vain. Christ has kept his promise; he has delivered you from sin and Satan's power. And he has promised never to leave you, not even to the end of the age. It's a promise he will certainly keep. "For he who did not spare his own Son, but gave him up for us all, how will he not also, along with him, graciously give us all things?" (Rom 8:32). There is no better promise maker; there is no other promise keeper.

Putting It Together
for the Church

CHAPTER ELEVEN

Preaching and Teaching (Case Studies)

W e've spent the last ten chapters looking at how we construct a biblical theology (the whole story of the whole Bible) and then how we draw lessons (theology that is biblical) from that story. But now that we've built a biblical theology, what do we do with it? Does it go on the shelf, ready to be pulled out next time we find ourselves near a seminary campus or spoiling for a debate? I certainly hope not!

Introduction: So What Does Biblical Theology Have to Do With the Church?

As every workman knows, there are some tools that have a storage spot on the shelf and some tools that hang from your work belt. The highly specialized and expensive tools have a spot on the shelf. They're important, but you don't use them every day. The tools hanging from your work belt, on the other hand, aren't that expensive or much to look at. But you use them in almost every job. Biblical theology is like a tool that hangs from your work belt. It's one of the most practical tools a minister can have. In this chapter and the next I want us to consider how we can put our biblical theology to work in the local church.

In chapter 12 we're going to think about how to use our biblical theology in everything from counseling to world missions to a number of matters in between. But first we want to think about the main use for biblical theology in the church, and that's in our preaching and teaching. To do that, we're going to work through a series of case studies in different sections and genres of Scripture. But before we do, I want to summarize what we've done so far and then take a closer look at where the rubber hits the road: application.

A Quick Review of Where We've Been

For the last five chapters I've told the whole story of the whole Bible, each time picking up a different theme and telling the story from that angle. We've looked at creation, the fall, love, sacrifice, and promise. These aren't the only themes I could have used. For example, I could have told the story of the Bible through the theme of the son/seed, connecting Genesis 3:15 to Abraham, to the birth of Moses, to David, and finally to Christ, the true seed and divine Son through whom we too are adopted as sons and daughters of God. This is the way Paul tells the story in highly compressed fashion in Galatians 3–4.

There are many other themes as well. The whole story of the whole Bible can be told through the theme of the priesthood, or the king, or the bride, or the garden and the temple, just to name a few. There are lots of themes, lots of threads that are woven through the entire tapestry of Scripture that allow you to tell the whole story. I chose the five themes I did because, taken together, they allowed me to consider the doctrine of salvation from a number of different perspectives.

Having told the story and noted the structure and patterns in the story, I also tried to apply the story to our lives. Using systematic theology, I asked the questions, (1) What does this story teach us about God, about ourselves, and about the church? and (2) How does it apply to life right now? The answers were the points at which the biblical story touched down and intersected with our contemporary story. Or even better, the answers showed us the many ways in which our story is already incorporated into and interpreted by the biblical story, as an all-encompassing worldview that challenges the idolatrous worldviews of our age.

Each time I've told the whole story there have been two steps: (1) biblical theology—getting the whole story right, and (2) systematic theology—applying that story to our lives. In fact, each time there has been another step that I did ahead of time but didn't talk about. I simply announced the theme that I was going to trace through the Bible, and asked you to trust me that I got the theme right. But how did I get the theme in the first place? How did I come up with the additional themes I just mentioned? Is this really nothing more than a more sophisticated version of topical preaching? And whatever happened to the priority of expositing a passage of Scripture, which is where this book began?

How Do We Get from Here (Biblical Text)
to There (Biblical Theology)?

In fact, as we noted back in chapter 1, faithful biblical theology begins not with a theme or a grand storyline, but with a text. Chances are this is exactly where you start in your own personal Bible study, and where I start each week that I'm preparing a sermon or a Bible study. You start with a text, and you ask yourself, what's the point of this text? Paying close attention to grammar and syntax, genre and historical background, you attempt to understand the author's original intent.

But now I hope you see that the question, "What's the point?" is a bigger question than it first appears. Using the tools of exegesis, we look for the point in the context of the larger passage or biblical book. Using the tools of biblical theology, we then consider the point of the text in light of where the text falls in redemptive-history. In what epoch of God's saving work does it occur? Is there something new or distinct going on from what has happened before? Has a promise been fulfilled at one level? Has a type been developed or more clearly identified?

Then, using these same tools of biblical theology, we ask ourselves, what's the point of the text in light of the whole canon—that is to say, in light of Christ's work on the cross and his promised return? Do we see a final fulfillment of a promise or a type? Is discontinuity introduced that marks a change, development, or expansion of a previous promise? In what way is continuity maintained?

It's precisely at this point that biblical-theological themes become apparent, as we ask how the specific event or teaching relates to the ultimate revelation of Jesus Christ, his saving work, and his promised kingdom. Once we identify the key themes or threads that are running through our particular text, and once we're clear where in redemptive history our text falls, then we're in a position to trace the theme through the entire Bible. The result is that we are now able to teach or preach on our text, not as if it's a pearl on a string, unrelated to the rest of Scripture, but as it really is, one section of an entire tapestry that is inextricably and organically connected to the whole.

Finally, having placed and explained our text in its redemptive-historical context, we then ask the question, what's the point of the text for Christians and the church today? And we answer that question using the tools of systematic theology, applying the text not only to our individual lives, but to our corporate existence as a local church. Furthermore, since systematic theology allows us to develop a biblical worldview, we're able to apply our text to non-Christians, to issues of society and government, and to apologetic questions raised by competing worldviews. That's how we get from biblical text, to biblical storyline, to biblical Christian living.

Now, I want to walk you through the process with four different examples from Scripture. If you want, you can simply read through the case studies below. Or, if you'd like to make the exercise even more useful, take a moment now and think through each of the following texts on your own, and then read through the case studies:

1) The Levitical food and cleanliness laws found, for example, in Leviticus 11
2) The book of Joshua
3) Psalms 1–2
4) Mark 1:14–15

Take a pad of paper and write down what you think the main point of each text is, and how you would teach it or preach it in light of the entire canon of Scripture. How would you approach each text in a way that's sensitive to biblical theology as we've been talking about it? What would you emphasize? What would you avoid? How would you demonstrate the truth of the main point and apply it to your church today?

Before jumping into the first case study, let me point out a few steps that will be common to all of them. First, always begin with prayer. In the Old Testament we see that it is the Spirit of God who gives skill to the workman. Presumably Bezalel and Oholiab already knew the basic techniques of their craft. But when it came time to work on the tabernacle, God's Spirit filled them with "skill, ability, and knowledge." If the Spirit's intercession was necessary to produce what the book of Hebrews calls a mere "copy" of the heavenly things, how much more should prayer precede our handling of the very words of God, as we seek from God the wisdom and skill needed to faithfully feed his sheep!

Second, take the time necessary to observe and interrogate the text in order to accurately exegete the passage and so understand the author's original intent in its immediate context (see chapter 1). It is tempting, especially with familiar passages, to rush ahead to application, assuming that we understand what it means already. But God's Word is immensely rich and unfathomably profound. Even familiar passages repay careful observation for the sake of fresh exegetical insights.

Third, make sure you've correctly identified which redemptive-historical epoch your passage is located in. In addition, make note of whether it refers directly or indirectly to other epochs distinct from its own (see chapter 2). It will be difficult to relate your passage to the biblical story as a whole, and nearly impossible to correctly apply it, if you do not recognize where your text stands in the developing sweep of redemptive history (and where you stand in relation to it).

So, assuming prayer, correct and careful exegesis, and an accurate placement of the text within the redemptive-historical timeline, let's think about how we would understand (biblical theology) and apply (systematic theology) these texts.

An Application Grid

Before we get to our case studies, I want to introduce you to some practical tools that might help you be more thoughtful and deliberate in your application. There are undoubtedly a number of good ways to think through application. One approach that several of the pastors at my church have found helpful is called the "sermon application grid" (see chart 11.1). Some of us actually fill the chart out; others simply keep the categories in our head as we write our sermons. Either way, the grid helps us put the tools of biblical and systematic theology to work every time we preach or teach the Bible.

The grid is very simple. Running down the left side of the chart are the points of the sermon or lesson. These will have arisen out of our exegesis, as we've turned an exegetical outline into a preaching outline. Then across the top of the chart are different categories helpful for thinking through application.

- Where is this passage located in redemption history and how does it relate to us?
- What does this point mean for the non-Christian?
- What does it mean for us as citizens, as employees, and so forth?
- What does it teach us about Christ?
- What does it mean for us as individual Christians?
- What does it mean for our church as a whole?

These of course aren't the only categories you could list, but they are at least the main ones. For each sermon point (running down the left side of the chart), I try to think through the answer in each of these categories (running across the top of the chart). If I have a three-point sermon, when I'm done with the grid I've used the tools of biblical and systematic theology to develop at least eighteen potential points of distinct application. What's more, I haven't forced anything on the text. Rather, the application has arisen directly from the fruit of my exegetical outline, and in fact is tied to it.

Chart 11.1: Sermon Application Grid

Text:

Main Point of the Passage:

Categories / Outline	Epoch / Redemptive History	Non-Christian	Society	Christ	Christian	Church
Point 1						
Point 2						
Point 3						

My goal here is not so much to say that you should use such a grid, as it is to help us begin thinking in such categories so we'll put the tools of biblical theology to use. If you are interested in using a grid, it's the sort of thing you would do *after* devising a homiletical outline but *before* you write the body of the sermon.

Now, even when I preach hour-long sermons, I never use all the points of application developed in the grid. But having thought through each of the categories, I'm much more likely to avoid repetition and personal hobby-horses. I'm more likely to apply the text beyond the very narrow range most Bible teachers normally operate in: ethical application to the individual Christian life and gospel appeal to the non-Christian. And I'm more likely to apply the text to the corporate life of our church as a whole and to consider worldview implications for the non-Christian. Most importantly, I'm reminded by this grid that one of the most important "applications" isn't about me or us at all, but simply what the text teaches us about the Father, Son, and Holy Spirit, and how the Trinity has worked together to purpose, accomplish, and apply our salvation to their eternal glory.

A Shepherd's Taxonomy

But not only do we want to be deliberate in the categories of our application, we also want to be thoughtful about the people who are listening to us. What follows is a simple taxonomy of the sheep (and goats!), the ones who listen to you teach and preach every week. William Perkins, the sixteenth-century English puritan, developed a seven-point scheme in *The Art of Prophesying*.[1] What follows here is not nearly as complex. In a sense, I'm taking the single categories of Christian and non-Christian from the grid and exploring them a bit further.

First, everyone listening to you falls into the following three pairs:

- *Christian or non-Christian*: I want to address both in every sermon.
- *Complacent or Anxious*: The complacent need warnings more than promises, because God's promises don't mean much to them. They're content in this world, like the rich young ruler (Matthew 19). The anxious need promises, because they're already feeling what they lack, and they need hope: "Lord, help me to see. I do believe. Help my unbelief" (Mark 9:24). I don't want to tempt the fearful to discouragement or the proud to self-sufficiency.

---

[1] William Perkins, *The Art of Prophesying* (London, 1606; repr. Edinburgh: Banner of Truth, 1996), 54–63.

• *Legalistic or Licentious*: The legalistic will listen intently for anything you say about law and rules, but may overlook the gospel promises. The licentious will be eager to hear the gospel promises of grace, but may not appreciate your teaching on repentance and Christ's lordship. I think everyone tends in one direction or the other. I must apply the text to both.

Second, assume the following is true of everyone listening:

• *Idolatry*: Everyone is struggling with idolatry in one way or another. As John Calvin said, our hearts are idol-factories.[2] Therefore try to specifically identify some of the idols your passage speaks to, as they are expressed in our culture—power, pleasure, pride, security, wealth, and so forth.
• *Self-justification*: Ever since the Garden of Eden, we have attempted to justify our idols, to excuse ourselves from our sin and commend ourselves to God. We see it in our desire for praise from this world. But we need to understand that our desire for the praise of men is simply part of a larger conspiracy. Though we were made to give praise *to* God, in our hearts we long to receive praise *from* God based on our own merits.
• *Love of the world*: Love of the world takes a multitude of forms: sex, money, power, possessions, entertainment, beauty, and so forth. The list is endless, but underneath the variation lays the constant theme of worshiping the creature rather than the Creator (1 John 2:15–17).

Third, there are different kinds of errant sheep that need the Word (1 Thess. 5:12–14):

• *The idle*: These aren't lazy sheep so much as headstrong and impulsive sheep; they reject discipline and insist on going their own way. Paul says these worldly brothers and sisters need to be warned. This may well include preaching in the second person at times (You!), rather than always using the softer, gentler first-person plural (We).
• *The timid*: These are sheep who aren't obeying the Word, but not because they've rejected it outright. Rather they are fearful of the consequences, and perhaps responsibilities, that come with faithful obedience. These sheep need to be encouraged with the promises of the gospel and the worth of our inheritance in Christ.
• *The weak*: In one sense all of us are weak, but here Paul seems to have in mind those whose lack of faith and obedience stems from spiritual weakness that is the result of poor teaching. A diet of milk without meat might keep a sheep alive, but it won't grow them into the strength of maturity. These sheep need to be helped, says Paul, and we help them most through sound instruction.

---

[2] John Calvin, *Institutes of the Christian Religion*, I.xi.8.

Finally, pay attention to the physical, as well as the spiritual, circumstances of your hearers. How does the text speak specifically, and perhaps differently, to these categories?

- men and women
- single, married, and widowed
- the elderly, middle-aged, and children
- employed, unemployed, and retired
- wealthy and poor
- educated and un(der)educated
- employers and employees

How do we put these taxonomies to work? Perhaps the easiest way to answer that question is to offer an example. If I'm preaching on Romans 4:13–17, one of my main exegetical and theological points is going to be on justification by faith rather than through law. As I come to apply that, I'll want to think carefully about how people in different stations of life in my congregation might be tempted to justify themselves. Reflecting on American culture, I might note that men seek to justify themselves through their work, while women seek to justify themselves through their relationships. Men *tend* to idolize work. Women *tend* to idolize relationships. Of course there are exceptions to these generalizations. So I might not even identify these as male and female tendencies. But I'll want to address both kinds of people. I'll want to shine the light of Scripture on their idolatry, and then show them the better promises of God in the gospel. The "laws" of what a successful man looks like and the "laws" of what constitutes a meaningful relationship, like the Old Testament law of God, do not justify a person! Faith alone in Christ alone does.

What I won't do is simply appeal directly to their desires—for fulfillment, for happiness, for hope—and then invite them to find that in Jesus. Simply offering a congregation incentive to accept Jesus assumes that their desires are in good working order—that they're already wanting the right things. But if we believe in a doctrine of sin, we cannot assume that. Do non-Christians want a purpose-filled life? Of course they do. The problem is that, as idolaters, they want that purpose to center on themselves. And they'll be happy to even employ God and Jesus for filling that self-centered purpose.

All of this leads to the conclusion that we want our application to be gospel driven. A religious Jew or Muslim can preach on the eighth commandment and draw the application that we should not steal, that we'll be happier, more well-adjusted people if we don't steal, and that earning an honest income gives meaning and purpose to your life. But is that a Christian sermon? No!

A Christian sermon on the eighth commandment would point out that we are all thieves, whether or not we've ever robbed a bank. We've stolen from our employers and others what we rightly owed them. Most of all we've stolen from God, robbing him of his glory by claiming it for ourselves. And so we all stand condemned by God as thieves and robbers, both materially and spiritually. A Christian sermon then goes on to explain to the believer that Jesus Christ has brought him from death to life and given him an inheritance in heaven. Therefore, we have all we need in Christ. There is no reason to return to the old ways of stealing that lead only to spiritual poverty and therefore condemnation and death before God.

Four Case Studies

How does the application grid and shepherd's taxonomy work when we seek to understand and apply the four texts mentioned earlier in this chapter? Let's take them in turn. What follows are meant as suggestions and lines of approach, not exhaustive and definitive answers. Still, I hope they help you begin to think about using the tools of biblical and systematic theology in new and more fruitful ways as you seek to apply the Scriptures whenever you teach or preach.

Levitical Food and Cleanliness Laws

The Point

First, what's the point of these laws in their original context? Leviticus 11:44–45 sums it up. The people are to consecrate themselves to God. Because he is holy, they are to be holy and set apart for him, distinct from the surrounding nations. God's people are to be visible as God's people, separate from the surrounding world. One question we might want to keep in mind is whether this is a point of continuity or discontinuity as we move into the New Testament, and in what ways.

The Bible Storyline

How does this text fit into redemptive-history or the Bible's storyline? It's important to look backward to Exodus 19 where God promised to make these people a "holy nation," a set-apart nation. These laws then are the beginning of God's fulfillment of his promise. But does that mean that New Testament Christians should keep kosher? The answer is "No," and several New Testament texts are important in understanding why. One of them is Mark 7:15. Commenting on these very laws, Jesus said, "Nothing outside a man can make him 'unclean' by going into him. Rather, it is what comes out of a man that makes him 'unclean.'" The holiness of God does not disappear in the New Testament, nor does the need for God's people to be recognizably holy. Rather, the holiness code has become internal rather than external, a matter of the heart rather than mere ritual and law-keeping. Okay, so what points of *discontinuity* must we remember? These laws don't directly apply to the church today because God's holiness code has become internal, not external. The following categories, you might say, largely present points of continuity.

Non-Christian/Worldview

What does this mean for non-Christians and the reigning worldviews of the day? At the very least, the very specificity of these laws point out that God cares about every aspect of their lives: who they sleep with, how they treat their spouse and children, the ambitions of their hearts, what they do with their money. We are not as autonomous as we think we are. Also, God's holiness leads to judgment of all that's not holy. As one expression of the entire law of God, the food laws convict us of our own unholiness and the justness of God's judgment and wrath against us personally.

Society

What does this mean for us as a society? One application might be what this does *not* mean for us (another point of discontinuity). God was doing something unique in the political nation of Israel, setting apart an ethnic family as his visible people in the world. Whatever your eschatology and understanding of the relationship between Israel and the church, at least this much is clear. America is *not* the New Israel. Therefore we do not have a mandate to try to enact Old Testament laws. However, God's law, even his dietary laws, are a reflection of his character, and therefore there may be principles even here that would benefit the nation. God still cares about how the people of every nation live. Finally, we are reminded not only of the benefits, but of the limitations of law. Law does not, indeed cannot, make us good. Israel broke these laws, though given by God himself. In our own society therefore we need to recognize that cultural transformation happens not merely through better laws, but ultimately through transformed people.

CHRIST

What do we learn about Christ? Christ fulfilled these laws (Matt. 5:17). He was perfectly holy, and not simply because he ate the right foods. He was holy because his heart was characterized by what these external laws pointed to—a love for God and a consecration to his purposes (see Deut. 6:5; 10:12; 11:1; Matt. 22:37ff.). Wonderfully, in fulfilling the law, Christ has set aside the external and ritual particularities of Sinai and offered us a new covenant. This point was made dramatically to Peter by Christ himself in Acts 10. In Galatians 2:11ff., we read of Paul's sharp reminder to Peter of what good news this was. As "Jews by birth," they knew full well "that a man is not justified by observing the law, but by faith in Jesus Christ." A moralistic sermon on Leviticus 11 will therefore focus on the law. But a gospel sermon will point to Christ who fulfilled it on our behalf.

THE INDIVIDUAL CHRISTIAN

What can we say for the individual Christian? Through his atoning death on the cross, Christ has made us clean! He has removed the separation between us and God. Yet like the nation of Israel, the New Testament calls us to live distinct and holy lives that commend the character of God to unbelievers (cf. 1 Corinthians 10; 2 Corinthians 6). This means that every area of our lives counts—whether eating or drinking, or whatever we do, we should give glory to God.

THE CHURCH

What should be said for the church as a whole? The church is precisely what God means to use to grow us toward holiness. We should encourage and rebuke one another toward Christ-likeness. We should build into one another's lives. Just as we saw in the Old Testament, the New Testament does not have a category of "belonging before believing" (meaning that we should let non-Christians feel like they belong to our churches so that they would believe), as some church leaders say today. Holiness continues to have a corporate character (1 Peter 2). Therefore, the church is taught in the Scriptures to practice biblical membership and church discipline (Matthew 18 and 1 Corinthians 5). We must snatch one another from the fire (Jude 23).

THE SHEPHERD'S TAXONOMY

What are some of the concerns raised by the shepherd's taxonomy? Perhaps one of the most important is being sensitive to the fact that when dealing with law, some will be easily condemned, defeated, and discouraged by it, while others will just as easily ignore it or feel superior to or even justified by it. The complacent and the anxious will both need to be addressed. Also, since all of us are self-justifiers, the light of the text needs to shine on the inadequacy of our own holiness as well as the sufficiency of Christ's.

Joshua's Conquest of Canaan

THE POINT

God is faithful to judge by a man of his own appointing who (1) defeats his enemies and (2) delivers his people. Though the narrative often focuses on the actions of the tribes, and not just Joshua, the entire book is framed by God's faithfulness to Moses' successor, and through him to the entire nation. In the end, prophetically, Joshua is even held up in contrast to the nation as one who faithfully served the Lord.

THE BIBLE STORYLINE

Joshua 24 begins the process for us. There Joshua looks backward to God's promise of rest to Abraham, and how he has fulfilled that promise through the conquest. But even in his pronouncement, it's clear that he does not understand this to be the final fulfillment. Israel is warned of the disaster that will come when they forsake God. Clearly, a further deliverance and a further rest are needed. After looking backwards with Joshua, the preacher must then look forward to the New Testament, where we learn that the promise of the land is understood typologically and also escalated into a final fulfillment. Hebrews explains that the promise of rest given under Joshua was never intended to be the final rest for the people of God (Heb. 3:7–4:13). This means that we're not waiting for an earthly city but a heavenly one (Heb. 11:10, 14–16; 13:14), which has been won for us through the conquest of God's anointed Son—Christ. Therefore, the Christian has no justification for crusades or the establishment of earthly kingdoms.

NON-CHRISTIAN/WORLDVIEW

God intends his judgment of Canaan as a warning for an even greater judgment to come. What we see in the holy war of Joshua is what theologians call a proleptic (anticipatory) judgment. It's as if the final judgment day for that one corner of the world came early. As Peter assures us, history is not cyclical or meaningless. What happened before is meant as a warning for what is still to come (2 Pet. 3:3–7). History has an appointed end, and that end includes a final accounting before God, in which it will be seen that truth is not relative and that righteousness is not a matter of personal perspective.

SOCIETY

God can and does give a people or a nation over to its sin in judgment. This is part of Paul's point in Romans 1:24 when he declares that God "gave them over in the sinful desires of their hearts." Mercy has a time limit. However, while government has been entrusted with the sword for the punishment of law-breakers (Rom. 13:1–5), no earthly government has the authority to declare itself the agent of God's final judgment against another people and pursue a policy of genocide. The holy war of Joshua was unique to the nation of Israel. As we'll see below, the holy war that Christians are called to carry out is quite different, though no less radical.

CHRIST

Joshua is a type who points us to Jesus Christ, the final and true Judge of God's appointing (John 5:27) who came to defeat and destroy all rebellion against his Father in heaven and so deliver God's people. In his first coming, Jesus accomplished this ironically through the cross (Col. 2:13–15). In his second coming, he will accomplish it in glory from his throne (Rev. 14:14ff.).

THE INDIVIDUAL CHRISTIAN

The holy war of the New Testament occurs in our hearts. "Our struggle is not against flesh and blood . . . but against the powers of this dark world and against the spiritual forces of evil in the heavenly realms" (Eph. 6:12). "Put to death, therefore, whatever belongs to your earthly nature" (Col. 3:5). Like the Israelites of old, we are to make no treaties with and give no quarter to our sin. Rather we are to kill sin in our life, else it will kill us. In larger perspective, we are reminded that, though the victory has been won by Christ, this world and our individual lives remain a battlefield, not a playground.

THE CHURCH

How critical good leaders and faithful teaching of God's Word are in our churches, lest we be enticed by the gods of the surrounding culture and fall away as Old Testament Israel did (see the book of Judges). Furthermore, the spiritual battle that we are engaged in is not meant to be fought alone. There is a corporate dimension to the battle, just as there is a corporate dimension to the promised rest that still awaits us. We should see this in our local churches, as we spur one another on to love and good deeds (Heb. 10:24). And just as the various Israelite tribes partnered with each other in the conquest, so we should partner with other local evangelical churches for the advance of the gospel.

THE SHEPHERD'S TAXONOMY

Several issues immediately come to mind. First, the problem of genocide will have to be addressed, both because of the offense to the non-Christian and the tender consciences of many Christians. Second, the language and imagery of leadership and battle provide a real opportunity to speak powerfully to men in the congregation, in order to give them perspective on what the spiritual life is really all about. Third, there will be some in the congregation who have been badly wounded in the battle and are tempted to drop out. The importance of helping the weak, not least by reminding them of their hope in heaven, is paramount.

Psalms 1 and 2

THE POINT OF PSALM 1

There are two ways to live, and the way of faithfulness to God's Word is the way of blessing.

THE POINT OF PSALM 2

Despite the nations' arrogant rejection of God, God will establish his kingdom through his Son, who will in turn rescue God's people and judge his enemies.

TAKEN TOGETHER

The Psalter begins with the parallel statements that blessing comes through God's Word and through God's Son.

THE BIBLE STORYLINE

Looking backwards we see that from the beginning, God's son has been called to obey God's Word and so find blessing (Gen. 2:15–17). But again and again, the son has disobeyed and therefore has known God's judgment. We see this in Adam, Israel, David, and Solomon, just to name a few. Jesus is the true Son, who delights in God's Word, defeats God's enemies, and so is confirmed publicly as the Son who establishes God's kingdom and provides the Edenic blessings of a fruit-yielding tree (Matt. 3:13–17; 17:1–13). We are brought into that kingdom as the inheritance of the Son (Eph. 1:18; cf. Ps. 2:8). But we are also made sons ourselves, not finally through our own law-keeping, but through union with the Son, who not only rescues us from wrath, but fits us to walk in God's law and enjoy the tree of life (Gal. 3:26–4:7; 5:13–26; Rev. 22:14)

Non-Christian/Worldview

There is a universal application of God's law and God's reign through the Son. Therefore, there really are only two ways to live, regardless of how many variations one of those ways exhibits. These psalms together also point to the exclusivity of Christ as the sole way into the kingdom of God and the sole escape from the judgment to come.

Society

Any society is blessed to the extent that it reflects God's Word now. In that sense, much of the blessing the West knows in contrast to other parts of the world is derivative of an earlier, Christian heritage. Thus, there is no room for cultural pride. On the other hand, one day the nations will "become the kingdom of our Lord" (Rev. 11:15), as he subjects creation to final judgment. Therefore, governments should be encouraged to promote and defend religious liberty, and especially the liberty to convert and proselytize.

Christ

Jesus Christ is the one truly blessed man of Psalm 1, and the one and only true victory-declaring Son of Psalm 2. Psalm 2 also helps us to recognize the title "Son of God" in the Gospels as a title of kingship and necessarily a title of divinity.

The Individual Christian

The Christian is called to repentance and faith and a life that issues forth in walking in the truth. Ultimately, that truth is the truth of Jesus Christ, and not mere law-keeping. Recognizing therefore that Christ is the blessed man keeps us from preaching a merely moralistic sermon on Psalm 1.

THE CHURCH

The church is precisely the community of those who have found refuge in Christ, and who now walk in him. We recognize ourselves as the visible expression of his kingdom on earth, and our collective hope and energy is focused on giving witness in word and deed to that day when his kingdom comes in glory. This passage also speaks of the necessity of church discipline, which excludes the unrepentant from the assembly in anticipation of the last day. As Peter says, "it is time for judgment to begin with the family of God" (1 Pet. 4:17).

THE SHEPHERD'S TAXONOMY

Since Psalm 1 is talking about how to find blessing, there is a real opportunity to explore how we are all tempted to seek blessing through love of the world, rather than faithfulness to Christ. This psalm challenges us, therefore, in our definitions of the good life, prosperity, and approval. On the other hand, both psalms challenge us to examine, acknowledge, and repent of our mockery and scorn for God and his ways.

Mark 1:14–15

THE POINT

The message Jesus preached (and by implication would accomplish) is that the kingdom of God has begun for all who repent and believe his message. The kingdom of God here is therefore not a place (a realm), but a reign, in which the blessings of God in salvation are poured out on his people. It is quite literally the life of heaven breaking into this life on earth.

THE BIBLE STORYLINE

The kingdom of God—begun in Genesis 1 but frustrated by sin in Genesis 3, pictured in the nation of Israel and promised in the prophets—finds its inauguration in the preaching of Jesus and the response of all nations in repentance and faith. Today that kingdom is both hidden and spiritual. But one day the kingdom will be consummated in new heavens and a new earth. This text thus stands as a pivot, transitioning from the typological kingdom of Israel to the true spiritual kingdom of Christ.

NON-CHRISTIAN/WORLDVIEW

It's not in Paul that we find supposedly intolerant, unilateral claims about Christianity. Rather, the exclusivity of Christ finds its first articulation on the lips of Jesus. From another angle, Jesus' preaching of the kingdom of God challenges all human utopian efforts. He alone can and will establish paradise, and entry into it is through repentance and faith, not political or economic policy. Fundamentally, this text insists that we preach the imperative to repent and believe, just as Christ proclaimed it.

SOCIETY

According to Jesus, there is a sharp distinction between church and state, between the kingdoms of this world and the kingdom of God (Matt. 26:52–56; John 18:36). Does this mean Christians shouldn't care about what happens here, or that they can reject earthly politics? Not at all. In between the inauguration and consummation of the kingdom of God, earthly political authority is both legitimate and necessary for the common good (Romans 13). However, such authority is also both temporary and limited. We neither put our final hope in, nor give our final loyalty to, the political state (cf. Acts 4:19–20).

CHRIST

What is implicit in this first announcement, but which becomes clear after the crucifixion and resurrection, is that Jesus himself is the object of our repentance and faith. Ironically, the one who announces the kingdom is also the one who secures our inclusion in it through his death and who inaugurates it through his resurrection. This kingdom, as we've already observed, is less about a place than a rule, and inclusion in it is less about ethnicity than about submission to his rule.

THE INDIVIDUAL CHRISTIAN AND THE CHURCH

Having repented and believed, we have been entrusted with the same message of reconciliation with God through repentance and faith in Christ (2 Cor. 5:16–21). We also live in hope for the consummation of the kingdom. What is strikingly absent from the rest of the New Testament is any indication or mandate that we are supposed to build or bring the kingdom. We are to proclaim it and invite others to enter it through Christ. But it is Christ, not the church, who brings the kingdom of God. The New Testament speaks of the kingdom in some ways that indicate continuity with this existence (e.g., Rom. 8:20–21). But the majority of its references indicate radical discontinuity (e.g., 1 Corinthians 15; 2 Pet. 3:10–13). This underscores the radical nature of what God is doing, and will do, when Christ returns.

THE SHEPHERD'S TAXONOMY

Of course, the fundamental distinction to be aware of is the distinction between Christian and non-Christian. But even so, we must not miss the fact that part of the gospel as Jesus proclaimed it is our response, and that response includes both repentance and faith. In American culture, like many others, decades of decision-oriented, easy-believism evangelism has produced masses of nominal Christians who presume their home is heaven when in fact it may not be. This text provides an opportunity to explain what true repentance is and so bring clarity to what it means to be a genuine Christian.

Conclusion

I started this chapter by saying that biblical theology was like a tool that doesn't need a spot on the shelf, since you hardly ever put it down. As we've seen in our case studies, it is biblical theology that allows us to preach Christ from both the Levitical food laws and the Gospel of Mark. It allows us to recognize and preach the whole Bible for what it is, *Christian* Scripture. It prevents us from moralizing the Old Testament, while at the same time giving due weight to the meaning of every Old Testament text in its original context. It encourages us to constantly connect every passage we preach to what God has done in the past and what he has promised to do in the future. It provides us with a worldview, a storyline that challenges the reigning stories of our own culture. It prevents us from preaching narrowly on our own hobbyhorses. And most important, it focuses the main point of every passage within the grand storyline of Scripture, the story of God's actions to redeem a people for himself, through the judgment of his Son, to the praise of his glorious grace.

So if biblical theology doesn't belong on a shelf, where does it belong? It belongs on your work belt; it belongs in your heart; it belongs on your lips; it should surround your thoughts and color your vision. Every time you open your mouth to speak about Scripture, every time you sit at your keyboard to write about it, biblical theology should be the lens that focuses your thoughts and shapes your words. For biblical theology in this sense is nothing other than an understanding of the story of what God has done for us in Christ, applied to our lives today.

At this point, some of you may be feeling overwhelmed. You like what I'm saying, but you can't imagine doing it yourself. I'll talk about this more in the next chapter, but suffice it to say, the more you begin to think of the

Bible this way, the more natural it becomes. Set aside time each week to breathe the air of biblical theology. In your quiet times, don't just read the daily plan, or the text you're preparing to preach. Read widely in Scripture, and always with a view of how the passage you're reading fits into the whole, how it prepares us for Christ, how it's leading to the consummation of the kingdom of God.

It should be our ambition not to speak of Scripture unless we're speaking in these terms, for this is how Scripture understands itself. And in Scripture we have the words of life, the only words that will feed Christ's sheep and bring life to the dead.

CHAPTER TWELVE

Biblical Theology and the Local Church

In the previous chapter we considered how biblical theology impacted our approach to teaching and preaching specific texts of Scripture. We thought about how to get from a particular text to the larger biblical-theological threads that run through that text, so that when we preach the text we connect it to the rest of the Bible and apply it appropriately to our own context.

Yet while biblical theology is crucial for faithful preaching and teaching, that's not where its importance ends. I think it's fair to say that everything in the life and ministry of the local church is affected by a proper use of biblical theology.

Introduction: So What Else Does Biblical Theology Have to Do with the Church?

Let me give you some examples of where biblical theology has been helpful to me in practical ministry situations.

My first year in pastoral ministry, I attended a church member's funeral without my Bible, and unprepared to speak. That should have been okay, since the family had arranged for a different minister to conduct the service. However, at the last minute, the family asked me to speak as well. There were no Bibles, just the other minister's service book, which he graciously lent me. I found there the passage from John 14:2–3 that speaks of Jesus going to prepare a home for us. I had no time to prepare before I had to speak. But being able to put Jesus' words in the larger context of Scripture's narrative allowed me to preach a funeral sermon that afternoon. I was able to speak of the story of God's promise to bring his people to his place under his rule, and Jesus as the only one who can bring us there through the gospel. Instead of an American homeowner's gospel on steroids, I could quickly take an unusual image and make sense of it in a way that preached Christ.

I do a lot of weddings. Occasionally a couple asks if they can write their own vows. The argument usually runs something like, "We want vows that speak to our unique relationship and unique love. We don't want the vows that everyone else uses." I'm not a very sappy person, so my reflex is typically to say "No," but for no good reason, other than I don't like sappy wedding vows. But even so, something about these requests has always felt off-key.

As I started to reflect on the request and the meaning of marriage, biblical theology helped me understand why it was more than taste that was putting me off to these requests. While it's true that each marriage is unique and special, it's also true that what the Bible emphasizes about marriage is what's common to all marriages. All are held to the same standard, all are structured according to the same covenant. And so it's right that all essentially take the same vows.

Why the emphasis on what is common? Because as a biblical theology of marriage shows, marriage isn't finally about the unique love between one man and one woman; it's about the love affair between Christ and the church. Every marriage points to that ultimate marriage. And whether the couple realizes it or not, their marriage takes its meaning and significance from that other marriage. Now I'm not a curmudgeon. Sometimes I let a couple write their own vows. But I always ask that they also use the traditional vows, because what is finally important about their vows and the rest of their marriage isn't what makes it unique, but what makes it like every other. To give primary emphasis to what's unique, ironically, is to make Christ and the church secondary, suggesting that an idol *might* be hiding behind those personalized vows.

Here's one more example. Several years ago, as our church began to grow, people began to ask when we would move to multiple services. Of course these days, the question isn't multiple services. Everyone takes that for granted. The current question is multiple sites. But whether we're talking about services or sites, our church's answer was and is the same. No. We are a local church, and that means a single assembly. Multiple services/ sites mean multiple assemblies, which mean multiple churches. After all, the Greek word for church means "assembly," that is, those who assemble together in one place at one time.

Now is that just an argument based on a word? Yes and no.

Yes, it's an argument based on a word, at least in part. When Jesus and the apostles chose words under the inspiration of the Spirit to describe the local gathering of Christians, they chose a secular word that meant assembly. But there's more to it than that.

The idea of assembly makes its first appearance not in the New Testament, but in the Old. Israel was God's assembly, which he summoned at the foot of Mount Sinai and made his covenant with (Deut. 4:10). From then on, while the people may have gathered in their various villages to receive instruction from the Levites, the nation gathered only three times a year to worship God in sacred assembly at the tabernacle, and later the temple in Jerusalem. Looking forward then, the book of Hebrews calls the heavenly Jerusalem, Mount Zion, the "assembly of the firstborn" (Heb. 12:22–23, ESV). This is the final assembly of the New Covenant, and yet Scripture tells us that that our local assemblies are in fact participating in that heavenly assembly joined "together with all those everywhere who call on the name of our Lord Jesus Christ" (1 Cor. 1:2).

Surely then it's no coincidence that Jesus called his people the "assembly" and not the "synagogues." Just as there is one body, one bride, one loaf, one flock, and one vineyard, so there is only one assembly. As theologians have long noted, the local church is not the church entire, but she is the church complete. Everything the universal church is, the local church pictures in microcosm.[1]

The unity of this assembly works itself out in many practical ways. They are to bear with each other (Eph. 4:2). They are to wait on one another, and celebrate the Lord's Supper together (1 Cor. 11:33). They are to share with others of the assembly who are in need (Acts 4:32–35). They are contend together for the faith (Phil. 1:27).

Thus, when we construct a "biblical theology" of assembly, we learn much more than we learn from a basic word study of a Greek word. We learn, in fact, that a local church is meant by Christ to be a localized picture in real time of the church he bought with his blood, that single assembly that he will finally summon on the last day. If that's the case, then we're not going to have multiple sites or services. We must come up with another solution to the wonderful problem of growth.

Those are just a few brief examples of real questions that we've tried to answer at my church with the tools of biblical theology. What I want to do now is consider what biblical theology has to say to whole spheres of ministry. As we'll see, biblical theology sometimes helps guard us against error in

---

[1] For a brief but excellent discussion of the biblical idea of assembly, see Edmund Clowney, *The Church* (Downers Grove, IL: InterVarsity Press, 1995), 30–32.

our approach to ministry. In other cases, biblical theology helps set proper boundaries and goals for our life and work together as a church. So let's work through several examples. When I'm done I won't by any means have exhausted the application of biblical theology to the church. But hopefully I'll have demonstrated what I mean about the practicality and usefulness of biblical theology for ministry, and you'll be in a better position to apply it to the situations and opportunities you face in your church.

Case Studies

We're going to look at how biblical theology shapes our thinking in four different areas: counseling, missions, caring for the poor, and church/state relations.

Counseling

Whether we think about it or not, whether it's in our job title or not, all of us engage in counseling. A friend shares a problem with us and asks for advice. A younger Christian we're mentoring asks us for counsel on what he should do with his life. A married friend needs encouragement because of difficulties in her marriage. A church member confesses that he struggles with an addictive behavior. Your teenage daughter is concerned about being accepted at school. For better or worse, accurate or inaccurate, biblical or secular, what you say next is "counseling."

How do you decide what to say in situations like these and countless others? Well, if you want a longer answer, get hold of the excellent material put out by the Christian Counseling and Educational Foundation (CCEF).[2] But the short answer is: it basically depends on what you think human beings are, what their problem is, and how the Bible speaks to it.

In a lot of those situations, the temptation is to treat the person as the sum of either his thinking or his behavior. We then diagnose his problem as either wrong thinking or wrong behavior. For the cure, we turn to the Bible as an answer book to show them how to think rightly or act rightly. The result is a proof-texting approach to both diagnosis and prescription, and generally results in a sort of Christianized version of behavioral or cognitive therapy. The basic counsel here is, "You simply need to learn, by the power of the Spirit, to think or act differently."

But is that what a biblical theology of the human being and the human

---

[2]For example, Paul Tripp, *Instruments in the Redeemer's Hands: People in Need of Change Helping People in Need of Change* (Philipsburg, NJ: P&R, 2002) and Timothy Lane and Paul Tripp, *How People Change* (Greensboro, NC: New Growth Press, 2008).

problem leads us to? Absolutely not. A biblical anthropology begins with humans created in the image of God in order to worship God by reflecting back to him his glory through their lives (Gen. 1:26–28). Therefore, we are not finally defined by either our behavior or our thoughts. Rather, we are defined by who we worship. We are fundamentally worshipers, and our identity is defined by what or who we are reflecting.

That image was distorted and marred in the fall, so that now we freely and habitually worship the creature rather than the Creator, and our favorite creature to worship is ourselves (Romans 1). So our problem is not fundamentally behavioral, though it will show itself in our behavior. Our problem is not fundamentally mental, though it will show itself in our thinking. Our problem is fundamentally religious. Our problem is idolatry—disordered worship.

What's more, biblical theology helps us see that while Adam and all his progeny are created *imago Dei*, in the image of God, that act of creation was modeled on the uncreated image of God, Jesus Christ (Col. 1:15ff.). Luke refers to Adam as the son of God (Luke 3:37), but Jesus is the true Son of God, the true image of God in all its fullness. Thus, our goal isn't to be better adjusted in our thinking or our behavior. Our goal, and in fact the goal of all creation (cf. Rom. 8:19), is that we be conformed to the image of Christ, something accomplished only by the Spirit through the regenerating power of God in the gospel (Rom. 8:29; 2 Cor. 3:16–19). Through the gospel, the Spirit unites us to Christ, so that the life we live is his life (Rom. 8:9–11; Gal. 2:20; Phil. 1:21). One day, the Spirit's work of sanctifying us will be complete. On that day, when Christ returns or we go to be with him, we will be glorified. We will see him as he is, because finally we will be like him (1 John 3:2)! That, at least in broad strokes, is a biblical theology of the image of God in man. It doesn't say everything that a systematic theologian would say about theological anthropology, such as Adam's guilt problem. But it does give the trajectory of the story in light of Adam's corruption problem. It tells us where we've come from, where we are, and where we're heading, if we're in Christ. And it begins to lay down some parameters for what it means to be a human being.

So what does this mean for counseling? To begin with, counseling informed by biblical theology is not satisfied with merely fixing behavior or ideas. It's not satisfied because it knows this is neither the root problem, nor will it finally work. Rather, biblical counseling aims at the heart, the seat of worship. It knows that the mouth speaks from the overflow of the heart (Matt. 12:34). Such counseling is not content with a change of behavior that plasters over the real problem of a heart that worships idols. It also understands that lasting change of behavior and thinking will only come when we change the object of our worship.

How does a change of worship happen, which then causes a change in thinking, talking, and behaving? It doesn't come from therapy. It doesn't come from analysis. It only comes from above, as the Spirit regenerates and rejuvenates the heart (John 3). And the means the Spirit uses is the gospel, received through repentance and faith. Paul describes this change in the lives of the Thessalonians as a turning from idols and a turning to God, to serve God and wait for Jesus' return (1 Thess. 1:9–10).

- Their change involved turning, or repentance.
- It involved faith, as they received and trusted the message.
- It resulted in a change of loves, as they now served God.
- And it resulted in a reorientation of their hopes, as they waited for Christ to return and rescue them from the coming judgment of God.

According to Paul, and consistent with our understanding of human nature, real change happens through the gospel, through receiving and resting on what Christ accomplished on the cross, and then living in light of it. Real change involves moving from idolatry to the worship of the true God. Real change means repenting from sin and putting faith in the grace of God held out in Jesus Christ. And that applies as much to the Christian as the non-Christian. The Christian caught in sinful actions, destructive beliefs, or addictive behavior is someone who worships idols. Just as at the start of the Christian life, so in the middle, and to the very end of that life, the gospel calls us to turn away from our idolatry even as it holds out the hope of our becoming like Christ when he returns.

Sadly, much Christian counseling has become influenced by a therapeutic culture and treats the fundamental human need as wholeness or happiness. As a result, the gospel gets changed in order to meet these newly defined needs. B. B. Warfield, the nineteenth-century Princeton theologian, summed up this connection well when he said,

> The fact is, the views men take of the atonement are largely determined by their fundamental feelings of need—by what men most long to be saved from. And from the beginning three well-marked types of thought on this subject have been traceable, corresponding to three fundamental needs of human nature as it unfolds itself in this world of limitation. Men are oppressed by the ignorance, or by the misery, or by the sin in which they feel themselves sunk; and, looking to Christ to deliver them from the evil under

which they particularly labor, they are apt to conceive His work as consisting predominantly in revelation of divine knowledge, or in the inauguration of a reign of happiness, or in deliverance from the curse of sin.[3]

Biblical counseling refuses to hold out false and temporary goals, like an easier or more pleasant life now, or tricks and tips for better behavior. Rather it holds out the goal of sanctification and glorification, our transformation into the very image of Christ. Its method is therefore the gospel because Christ is the goal.

Missions

Lately there's been a lot of buzz about the need for the church to be missional. Being missional is not the same as being committed to missions, or being missions-minded. Being missional is a way of thinking about the church and how it relates to the world. A missional church understands that the church doesn't go on mission, or send people out to do missions. Rather, the church is the mission of God into the world, in order to heal the world and reconcile people to God. As a result, the church is not so much entrusted with a message, but is called to incarnate a person. We aren't primarily about proclaiming Jesus' work on the cross to the world. Rather we're about making the words, deeds, and life of Jesus visible in every corner of our city.[4]

Where have people come up with this understanding of the church and her calling in relation to the world? To be honest, it's arisen out of an attempt to think about mission and the church from the perspective of biblical theology.[5] What these missional theologians noticed is that God is a missional God. He moves into the neighborhood. He incarnates himself in our world. Why does he do this? He does it in order to redeem us, and in order to establish his kingdom. From afternoon walks in the garden of Eden, to the tabernacle in the midst of the Israelite camp, to the incarnation of Jesus Christ, to the final words of Revelation, God has consistently sought to be with his people, to be in their midst. It's a picture of intimacy, a picture of relationship, and it seems to be at the very heart of what heaven is all about (Rev. 21:3–4; 22:3–5). While sin has separated man from God, it has not discouraged God's missional character. In fact, as the history of redemption seems to show, human sin has made this missional orientation of God all the more imperative.

---

[3]B. B. Warfield, "Modern Theories of the Atonement," in *Works*, IX (Baker, 1932; repr. 2003), 283.

[4]For example, see Darrell L. Guder, ed., *Missional Church: A Vision for the Sending of the Church in North America* (Grand Rapids, MI: Eerdmans, 1998), 1–17.

[5]See especially Christopher J. H. Wright, *The Mission of God: Unlocking the Bible's Grand Narrative* (Downers Grove, IL: InterVarsity Press, 2006).

The church therefore is sent as God sent Christ—sent into the world to make his redeeming presence known (John 17:18). Here is the paradigm for the missional church. As Christ was sent, so we his body are likewise sent. As Christ incarnated the saving presence of God, so we incarnate the redeeming presence of Christ. We sacrifice ourselves through service, through engaging the culture around us with mercy and good deeds.

What do we make of the missional agenda? Should biblical theology lead us to scrap our missions program and set up tutoring centers and health clinics instead? Should we be more focused on "third spaces" like Starbucks or the local gym, where we can "go and be" Christians in the midst of the world, rather than building bigger buildings so that more people can "come and hear" the message of Christianity in the midst of church?

I think there's no question that we should go and be salt and light in the world (Matt. 5:13–16). I also think there's no question that God is a missionary God—he doesn't wait for us to find him (as if we could). Rather, he moves into the neighborhood and finds us. The language of John 1 is rich in biblical-theological connections, not least of which is the image of Christ coming and "tabernacling" in our midst (John 1:14). A huge component of the good news is that "this is love: not that we loved God, but that he loved us and sent his Son" (1 John 4:10). But the question of what the church should be and how it should think about mission is not quite the same as recognizing that the incarnation is the fulfillment of God's Old Testament missionary activity.

To begin with, a biblical theology of the church and its mission includes themes that the missional advocates leave out or downplay, themes like the church's call to be separate and distinct from the world in order to display the wisdom and the holiness of God. This is clearly seen in the calling out of Israel, as we saw in the last chapter with the Levitical laws, a call that is taken up and intensified in the life of the church. Paul (in 1–2 Corinthians), John (in 1 John 2), and Peter (in 1 Peter 1) are each at pains to define the church in terms of its holiness and distinctness from the world. It is emphatically not to conform to the world or its desires. Therefore, incarnational ministry, whatever it means positively, does not mean accommodating to the world.

Second, the church, like Israel, is given a corporate, even federal, identity. Israel is called God's son, and we are called Christ's body. But once again, that's not the whole story. The church is also given a specific mission by Christ its Head. It is to make disciples, it is to preach the gospel, and it is to teach disciples to obey everything Jesus has commanded us (Matt.

28:18–20). Again and again, Scripture emphasizes the message that the church must proclaim.

Far from being a point of disjunction between Christ and his body, a moment's further reflection shows that this is consistent with Jesus' own emphasis. Repeatedly, Jesus sought to keep his miraculous healings and exorcisms quiet. He charged people to tell no one what he had done. And when the crowds became too great, clamoring for his healing touch, he departed to go elsewhere. Why did Jesus do that? He had the power to heal everyone; why didn't he? Why did he leave just when the opportunity to demonstrate the healing power of God on a really large scale appeared? Jesus tells us why. In Mark 1:38, in response to similar questions from the disciples, he says, "Let us go somewhere else—to the nearby villages—so I can preach there also. That is why I have come."

Jesus didn't come primarily to do good deeds. He didn't come to heal and exorcise demons, or to demonstrate the redemptive life of the kingdom. No, Jesus came primarily to preach. That's what he says. Why preach? He came to preach because the work he had been given by God was to accomplish redemption through his atoning death on the cross. But that death was tragically mute—that saving work inaccessible to others—without the message of the gospel that he preached and entrusted to his disciples. This good news explained what his death had accomplished and how sinners like us could benefit from it through repentance and faith. Jesus came to die. But he did not only come to die. He came to preach first, so that we could understand and benefit from his death.

Part of the pattern that emerges therefore is that while Israel and the church point to, foreshadow, and even repeat and magnify some aspects of Christ's ministry, other aspects of his ministry remain unique to him. The church does not die for the sins of the world. It is not given for the healing of the nations. It does not usher in the kingdom of God. These are ministries uniquely given to the Son.

So what does the church do? It witnesses to the Son. It proclaims his message. It makes disciples. And it displays within itself the life of the kingdom. Like an outpost of heaven, it's a beacon and a display of the unique work that the Son is accomplishing within it.

Like Jesus, the church is sent into the world to proclaim this life-giving, kingdom-inaugurating message. So should we be missional? In one sense, yes. We should be salt and light in the world in word and deed. But does that mean we should stop sending out missionaries? Does that mean that we should stop focusing on the public proclamation of the good news in order to focus on incarnating the life of the kingdom of God in our communities? Absolutely not. That would mean not only disobeying the explicit command of Christ, who is the head of the body, but it would also mean erasing the distinction between the type and the antitype, the picture and the real thing.

What's more, to exchange "missions" for "missional" would be to miss another thread of the biblical story, the story in which the kingdoms of this world are not only blessed by the presence of the kingdom of God, but actually become the kingdom of our Lord and Christ. Because of sin, the nations were divided at Babel. In Christ, they have already been figuratively reunited at Pentecost, as the gospel goes out to all nations. But the end of the story isn't accomplished through the mercy ministry of the church. No, the end of the story is when the elect from all the nations are finally and forever made one in new heavens and a new earth. On that day, all nations on earth will be blessed through Abraham because a great multitude "from every nation, tribe, people and language" stands before the throne in robes washed white in the blood of the Lamb (Revelation 7). The church proclaims the kingdom-inaugurating message, but it will be the King himself who consummates it.

Furthermore, as this storyline makes clear, the purpose of God isn't finally mission, but worship. As Piper has pointed out, "missions exists because worship doesn't."[6] Therefore, the church is sent on mission, but the church exists to worship. To define the church by mission is ultimately to reorient God *away* from himself and *to* the world. In fact, it is just the opposite. God has come into the world because fundamentally he is committed to himself and the display of his glory. Bottom line: as a strategy for evangelism, the missional church has many helpful things to teach us. But as a critique of missions, and as a definition of the church, the missional concept is inadequate and misleading.

Caring for the Poor

Periodically in the history of the church, the cry has arisen that the gospel is better illustrated than proclaimed, or that it cannot be preached with integrity unless it is also demonstrated practically. Often this concern has focused on the poor, and the church's primary responsibility to alleviate that poverty.

In support of making care for the poor a primary responsibility of the

---

[6]John Piper, *Let the Nations be Glad! The Supremacy of God in Missions* (Grand Rapids, MI: Baker, 1993), 11.

local church, writers resort to key verses in the New Testament, the example of Old Testament Israel, and the Bible's vision of the New Creation. In the New Testament, we read Jesus' command to "let your light shine before men, that they may see your good deeds and praise your Father in heaven" (Matt. 5:16). In the larger context of the Sermon on the Mount, it's hard to deny that mercy to the poor was at least part of what Jesus had in mind when he referred to good deeds. The early Christians clearly practiced a radical generosity toward the poor (cf. Acts 4:32–37), and James seems to almost encourage a bias toward the poor, or at least condemns any bias against them (James 2:1–9).

In the Old Testament, we see God's people specifically commanded to show mercy toward the poor. This resulted in institutionalized and structural mechanisms for relieving poverty (for a few examples, compare the practice of gleaning, Lev. 19:9–10; the kinsmen-redeemer, Ruth 3; and levirate marriage, Deut. 25:5–10). The context of those institutions was their own history of being poor and oppressed in Egypt. Just as God loved them and rescued them from their poverty, so they were to treat the poor, the widow, the fatherless, and the alien with mercy and respect (Deut. 10:16–19; 24:18–22)

Looking forward, the prophets described the new creation as characterized by abundance and joy (Isaiah 65–66) and by the Messiah who would usher in this new age with good news for the poor (Isaiah 61).

Taken together, these passages seem to provide a biblical theology for the church as the outbreaking of the life of the new age and the fulfillment of God's promises to Israel, charged with demonstrating the coming of the kingdom through acts of mercy toward the poor in their communities.

This sounds compelling to many, but in fact I think biblical theology paints a slightly more complex picture.

To begin with, the question is not, "Should Christians care for the poor?" The answer to that question is clear, whether we think in terms of the grand story of Scripture or the specifics of how that story engages our individual lives. Christians should be people who display the love and mercy of God to all they come in contact with, and that includes the poor.

The question is, Does the church as a local institution have a special obligation to care for the poor?

On the one hand, a biblical theology of the church understands that there is continuity and discontinuity between the Old and New Testament people of God. Israel was a political nation, complete with internationally recognized borders, terms of citizenship, and therefore civic responsibilities to those citizens. The church, on the other hand, is scattered throughout the world as aliens and strangers, members of many nations, but whose citizenship is ultimately in heaven (Phil. 3:20). Israel's kingdom was earthly and political, but we have been brought into a kingdom that is spiritual and heavenly (John 18:36).

What's more, in the grand sweep of the storyline, we see that Israel was not meant to be a model for Christendom, a Christian political order. Rather, Israel's experience in the Promised Land is a type that points forward to heaven (Hebrews 4). And so it is in heaven that we see the perfect realization of Israel's laws, a realm in which there is no more crying or sorrow or pain, including that caused by material privation, because all such causes of sorrow have been removed (Rev. 21:1–4; cf. Matt. 26:11).

Recognizing this distinction between Israel, the local church, and heaven helps make sense of several things. First, we see why care for the poor inside the local church is commanded and modeled in the New Testament (Acts 4; 6; Rom. 15:25–27; 1 Corinthians 16; 2 Corinthians 8–9). As a colony of heaven, when people look inside the local church they are to see something different from the world around them. Second, we understand why the local church is never commanded to commit something like its budget to alleviate poverty in the world. Christians are so commanded, yes (e.g., Gal. 6:10). But insofar as a "church budget" exists, it exists principally to equip *the saints* for the work of the ministry, which, in turn, will involve them in personally caring for the poor. Third, we understand how the Great Commission, the call to proclaim the gospel, is in fact the primary mission that the local church has been given toward the poor. It is through the gospel, not a bank account, that the poor are truly rescued from their misery.

Can the church, institutionally considered, spend its budget on acts of social mercy? Yes, as an act of mercy and a prudential means of commending the gospel. Must it? No. What the church *must do* in order to be a church is to make disciples, baptize them, and teach them everything that Christ has commanded. What it must do is proclaim good news to the poor through the message of reconciliation with God through the death and resurrection of Jesus Christ. Insofar as caring for the poor *can*, in many circumstances, be used in making disciples and commending the gospel, the church may assess its various stewardships and responsibly choose to care for the poor outside the assembly. I say "choose" because a church that takes ownership of caring for the poor through its budget should be cautious. It neither wants to lose sight of its first priority, nor give its members an excuse to avoid the personal responsibility to love their neighbors. Other institutions in this world will feed the poor with bread and soup. But no other institution in this world will give the rich and poor alike the bread of life and living water that results in never hungering or thirsting again (John 4, 6).

Church-State Relations

There is no more vexing question in church history than the question of the relationship between the church and the state. From medieval Christendom and the union of church and state under a single crown, to the claims of medieval popes to exercise temporal and not just spiritual authority over Christians in every sphere of life, to today's culture wars with a politicized electorate divided in part along religious lines, to fears about Islam and its refusal to organize the state along secular lines, to fears that fundamentalist Christians might make a similar refusal should they ever come to power in America—the question of the relationship between political and spiritual authority continues to cause conflict and fear.

That such fears would attach to Christians is all the more amazing given Jesus' deft reply when the authorities presented him with a classic formulation of the problem: Should we pay taxes to Caesar? Holding up a Roman coin, stamped with the image of the emperor, Jesus replied, "Give to Caesar what is Caesar's and to God what is God's" (Matt. 22:21). Problem solved, right?

Well, what do we do about the example of Israel? Don't we see there a union of spiritual and civil authority? And what about Christianity's all-encompassing moral worldview, which declares not only the universal lordship of Christ, but the sacredness of human life and the moral character of the universe in which we live? Don't these truths argue for the obligation to pursue an explicitly Christian state?

The answer in some ways is related to the discussion we just had, and therefore will be briefer than the previous examples. We need to pay attention to the entire storyline, and not just the parts that appeal to our own agenda or predispositions. The kingdom of God is the goal of creation. Israel was not a prototype, however, but a type, a picture that pointed forward to the real thing. When the kingdom is inaugurated in truth, it is small, even invisible (Mark 4:30–32). In this way the antitype resembles the type, Israel, whom God noted was neither the largest nor the strongest nation when he chose her (Deut. 7:7). But there are important ways in which the kingdom is not like the type that prefigured it. The inaugurated kingdom of God is a spiritual kingdom, defined not by political borders, but rather by spiritual rule, the saving reign of God.

How does the church relate to this story of the kingdom? The church is called to be a witness to that saving reign, but she isn't identical to the kingdom itself, since there are many included in the kingdom that are not part of the church (e.g., Old Testament saints and elect angels). Rather the church looks in hope to the King's return, when he will establish his kingdom visibly and with power. In the meantime, our life in the kingdom is hidden, obscured and veiled, just as Christ the King's was in his incarnation. Earthly political authority is established by God, temporary and limited, but nonetheless legitimate (Romans 13). Separate spheres of authority and responsibility have been established by God until the return of the King. During this time between his comings, spiritual authority is vested in the preaching of the King's Word. But like Abraham, who had the promises but only looked ahead to the kingdom of Israel, so the church lives as aliens and strangers in this world. We have the promise, and we await the coming of the kingdom in its glory. But we will not be pilgrims forever. The Day will come when Christ returns, and all authority is submitted to Christ and he is publicly declared King and Lord (Revelation 11).

On the one hand, therefore, the church needs to resist the temptation to over-realize its eschatology. It is not up to us to decide when our pilgrimage as aliens is over, as if creating a Christian state would accomplish that anyway. On the other hand, the church is not to live as if this world does not matter. Our good deeds are to be evident to all. But our mission finally isn't the renewal of culture; it's the redemption of souls. Our war is not the culture war, but a war against spiritual forces of evil in the heavenly realms. And our hope is not in the political levers of power, but in the sovereign King of kings and Lord of lords, who even now reigns at the right hand of God. In the meantime, "we are looking for the city that is to come" (Heb. 13:14).

Conclusion

I've given a few examples of how biblical theology shapes our approach to whole categories of ministry. You may disagree with some of my conclusions and applications. What I hope you see, however, is that we can't even begin to approach topics like these, and many others, without biblical theology.

It's really up to you to take it from here. What does biblical theology have to say to your approach to children's ministry, and Christian education in general? How would it affect the way you think about music in the church? What does it mean for the way you teach about career and vocation? How will it impact your plans for renovating or expanding your building? If what I've said about biblical theology is true, and I'm convinced it is, then it has something helpful to say to all of these areas. Biblical theology is theology at work in the ministry of your church.

Epilogue

When you put this book down in a few moments, you're probably not going to rethink an entire sphere of ministry. Instead, you're probably going to walk into a meeting to talk about next year's budget or to plan next Sunday's service. Or you're going to have lunch with a new member who wants to get involved, or an old deacon who's concerned with some of the changes you've made recently. In that meeting, or at that lunch, you'll need to make concrete decisions and practical proposals. You'll need perspective and discernment. Most of all you'll need vision, a clear sense of where God is leading your church or ministry and how the issue at hand, big or small, fits in.

This is where biblical theology really pays off, but not in the way most practical tools do. It doesn't give you a method or a program. It doesn't outline the ten steps to building a bigger, better church. It doesn't tell you how to get the right people on the bus and the wrong people off it. Instead, it gives you something even better.

It gives you vision—theological vision, to be precise.

As we've seen, biblical theology, in both senses of the word, not only gives you the story of the Bible, but it places your story in the context of God's story. It immerses you in his storyline, which turns out to be more than a story about ancient and future history. It turns out to be a story of right now. As Richard Lints has said so well, when we understand biblical theology in this way, we discover that "the Scriptures are . . . the primary interpreters of the modern era."[1] Biblical theology in the ways we've discussed here produces theological vision for ministry today.

With such a vision in place, we are in a position to do the practical work of theology, the work of applying the truth of God's story to the details of our lives and the lives of those we minister to.

This includes people like my fellow elders' friend, whose story began this book. He had been wrongly taught that Deuteronomy 28 meant that God intended his best life now, defined as a life of material abundance, if

---

[1] Richard Lints, *The Fabric of Theology: A Prolegomenon to Evangelical Theology* (Grand Rapids, MI: Eerdmans, 1993), 312.

only he would have faith. Now that you've read this book, how would you respond to him? I hope you wouldn't just grab your Bible and quote 1 Peter 4:12 to him, as if dueling proof-texts will settle the matter.

Instead, I hope you see that what's happened isn't simply the misreading of a verse, but a misunderstanding of the whole story of the Bible, and therefore a misinterpretation of the story of his own life. Before he'll ever properly apply Deuteronomy 28 and 1 Peter 4, his worldview needs to be reordered and his theological vision reoriented. He needs to understand that the picture of Deuteronomy 28 was but a cartoon in comparison to what God has ultimately planned for his people in the new heavens and new earth. He needs to understand that God does intend his best life, but that in a fallen world, glory comes only through suffering and life comes only through death. He needs to know that the wealth that God intends to give him isn't finally the wealth of this world, but the wealth of uninterrupted fellowship with God himself through union with Christ. He needs to know that the worth of that inheritance is displayed through our faith in the midst of our current wanderings in the wilderness. This is the work of biblical theology and the systematic theology that arises out of it. And this in fact is what my fellow elder told him.

But he didn't just teach his friend to keep his eyes focused on Christ regardless of his circumstances. He kept his own eyes focused there as well. Because that elder's life is also being shaped by the biblical story, he understood that his real treasure, his final inheritance, and therefore his ultimate hope is in heaven, not on earth. And so, not tied to this world's lying story that wealth means security, he generously dug into his own earthly treasure to help his unemployed friend.

This is the vision we need for ministry, but we don't get it all at once, and it doesn't come from reading just one book. The vision I'm talking about arises out of the patient, repeated, observant reading of the whole Bible. It's going to mean making some changes in the way you read and study Scripture, in the time you set aside for meditation and reflection, and in the amount of time you set aside for sermon preparation. It's going to mean changing your habits of mind when faced with problems and challenges in ministry. Before looking for a pragmatic solution, you're going to insist on placing things in a theological context.

As we thought about earlier, biblical theology as a discipline is a way of reading the Bible, a hermeneutical strategy that refuses to turn God's story into life's little answer book, but rather recognizes it as the grand story that gives our stories meaning. This means that the vision we need comes not from brainstorming sessions or method-driven processes, but from a prayerful habit of mind that refuses to understand Today according to the terms of the cultural narratives at hand—the narratives of progress, ethnicity, and accumulation, to name a few. Instead, Today is defined in light of the biblical story. That story increasingly defines who we are, where we've come from, and where we're going. As a result, that story tells us what we should be doing and thinking and feeling Today.

The next time you walk into a planning meeting or discipling lunch, I hope you'll grab your Bible—not for an opening devotion or the perfect proof-text, but for the vision you need to orient yourself and your ministry to the work that God is doing in this world through Christ. Like I said, that vision doesn't come all at once. But by God's grace it does come, and it changes everything.

Biblical theology is really useful theology. Biblical theology is theology at work. So pick up your Bible, and let's get to work.

For Further Reading

In addition to the books recommended in the Introduction, the following will help you explore the themes of the selected chapters further.

Chapter 1

Beynon, Nigel, and Andrew Sach. *Dig Deeper: Tools to Unearth the Bible's Treasure*. Wheaton, IL: Crossway, 2010.

Carson, D. A., *Exegetical Fallacies*, 2nd ed. Grand Rapids: Baker, 1996.

He tells you many ways you can misread the text and gives some helpful hints at avoiding those mistakes.

Fee, Gordon D., and Douglas Stuart. *How to Read the Bible for All It's Worth*, 3rd ed. Grand Rapids, MI: Zondervan, 2003.

Though I strongly disagree with the egalitarian positions they take in this book, you won't find a better, more accessible introduction to exegesis of the Bible in English translation.

Chapter 2

Goldsworthy, Graeme. *According to Plan: The Unfolding Revelation of God in the Bible*. Downers Grove, IL: InterVarsity Press, 2002.

This book takes the approach of his *Gospel & Kingdom* and works it out across the entire canon.

Robertson, O. Palmer. *The Christ of the Covenants*. Phillipsburg, NJ: P&R, 1981.

Though I disagree with some of his paedobaptist conclusions, I know of no better introduction to the covenants overall.

Chapter 3

Baker, David. *Two Testaments, One Bible: a Study of the Theological Relationship between the Old and New Testaments*, rev ed. Downers Grove, IL: InterVarsity Press, 1991.

A thorough introduction.

Clowney, Edmund P. *The Unfolding Mystery: Discovering Christ in the Old Testament*. Philipsburg, NJ: P&R, 1991.

Provides clear, practical instruction for pastors and teachers.

Chapter 4

Lints, Richard. *The Fabric of Theology: A Prolegomenon to Evangelical Theology*. Grand Rapids, MI: Eerdmans, 1993.

Among other things, this book makes the case for a more explicit relationship between biblical and systematic theology.

Wells, David. *The Courage to Be Protestant. Truth-lovers, Marketers, and Emergents in the Postmodern World*. Grand Rapids, MI: Eerdmans, 2008.
Makes the case that doctrinal truth is essential to evangelical faithfulness.

Chapter 5
Frame, John. *Salvation Belongs to the Lord: An Introduction to Systematic Theology*. Phillipsburg, NJ: P&R, 2006.
Clearly delineates the various perspectives of doctrinal knowledge. Somewhat technical, but worth the effort.
Lints, Richard. *The Fabric of Theology: A Prolegomenon to Evangelical Theology*. Grand Rapids, MI: Eerdmans, 1993.
His exploration of the trajectory of theological reflection is worth the price of the book.

Chapters 6–10
Some other examples of biblical theology at both the pastoral and academic level:
Beale, G. K. *The Temple and the Church's Mission: A Biblical Theology of the Dwelling Place of God*. New Studies in Biblical Theology. Downers Grove, IL: InterVarsity Press, 2004.
Hamilton, James M. *The Center of Biblical Theology: The Glory of God in Salvation Through Judgment*. Wheaton, IL: Crossway, 2010.
Roberts, Vaughan. *Life's Big Questions: Six Major Themes Traced Through the Bible*. London: Inter-Varsity, 2004.

Chapter 11
Clowney, Edmund P. *The Unfolding Mystery: Discovering Christ in the Old Testament*. Philipsburg, NJ: P&R, 1991.
Goldsworthy, Graeme. *Preaching the Whole Bible as Christian Scripture*. Grand Rapids, MI: Eerdmans, 2000.
Covers some of the same ground as this book, but devotes the second half to the practical application of preaching from every genre.

Chapter 12
On Counseling:

Powlison, David. *Seeing with New Eyes. Counseling and the Human Condition Through the Lens of Scripture*. Resources for Changing Lives. Phillipsburg, NJ: P&R, 2003.
An excellent introduction to thinking about counseling in light of the Bible's framework.

On Missions:

Bavinck, J. H. *An Introduction to the Science of Missions*. Trans. David H. Freeman. Phillipsburg, NJ: P&R, 1992.
Brings together both the "come and see" and "go and tell" messages of the Bible through the lens of Pentecost.

Scripture Index

General Index

9Marks

Building Healthy Churches

9Marks exists to equip church leaders with a biblical vision and practical resources for displaying God's glory to the nations through healthy churches.

To that end, we want to see churches characterized by these nine marks of health:

1   Expositional Preaching
2   Biblical Theology
3   A Biblical Understanding of the Gospel
4   A Biblical Understanding of Conversion
5   A Biblical Understanding of Evangelism
6   Biblical Church Membership
7   Biblical Church Discipline
8   Biblical Discipleship
9   Biblical Church Leadership

Find all our Crossway titles
and other resources at
www.9Marks.org